A Kid's Guide to
LATINO HISTORY

More than 50 Activities

Valerie Petrillo

CHICAGO
REVIEW
PRESS

Library of Congress Cataloging-in-Publication Data

Petrillo, Valerie.

A kid's guide to Latino history : more than 50 activities / Valerie Petrillo.

p. cm.

Includes bibliographical references.

ISBN-13: 978-1-55652-771-5

ISBN-10: 1-55652-771-3

1. Hispanic Americans—History—Juvenile literature. 2. Hispanic Americans—History—Study and teaching—Activity programs—Juvenile literature. I. Title.

E184.S75P48 2009

973′.0468—dc22

2008040433

To Noelle:
A bright, shiny penny
Sparkling with promise, full of life
You forever delight and surprise

Interior design: Scott Rattray

Cover and interior illustrations: Gail Rattray

© 2009 by Valerie Petrillo
Published by Chicago Review Press, Incorporated

814 North Franklin Street

Chicago, Illinois 60610

ISBN: 978-1-55652-771-5

Printed in the United States of America

5 4 3 2 1

❖ Contents ❖

◈ **Acknowledgments** ◈

Special thanks to my editors, Michelle Schoob and Linda Gray, for the tremendous amount of time and attention they devoted to helping me mold this book; Scott Rattray, who put together a great overall design, and Gail Rattray for her engaging drawings; and Cynthia Sherry for sharing my interest in bringing this subject into book form.

I also want to thank my dear family: Hank, Mike, Nick, and Noelle, and the many members of our extended families for all the love, interest, and support they have given me in my writing projects over the years.

❖ Time Line ❖

1492 | Christopher Columbus lands on San Salvador

1494 | Columbus establishes La Isla Española on what is now called Hispaniola

1509 | Ponce de León founds the first Spanish colony in Puerto Rico

1513 | Juan Ponce de León discovers Florida

1526 | Explorer Lucas Vazquez de Ayllón establishes San Miguel de Gualdape

1528 | Alvar Nuñez Cabeza de Vaca embarks on a journey in the Southwest

1539 | Hernando de Soto leads an expedition through the southern United States

1540 | Francisco Vásquez de Coronado and his expedition explore the Southwest

1565 | St. Augustine established on the east coast of Florida

1598 | San Juan de los Caballeros established in New Mexico

1680 | The Pueblo Revolt

1690 | San Francisco de los Tejas established in Texas

1769 | Father Junipero Serra builds the first California Mission

1803 | The Louisiana Purchase

1821 | United States purchases Florida from Spain

1836 | Texas declares independence from Mexico

1846 | California declares independence from Mexico
        Mexican-American War begins

1848 | The Treaty of Guadalupe Hidalgo is signed between Mexico and the United States

1898 | The United States wins the Spanish-American War
Spain hands over Puerto Rico to the United States

1914 | Panama Canal opens

1942 | The Bracero program invites Mexican laborers to work in the United States

1948 | Operation Bootstrap in Puerto Rico

1952 | The Immigration and Nationality Act

1952 | Puerto Rico declares itself to be an "associated free state"

1960s | The first wave of South American immigrants comes to the United States

1962 | Cuban Missile Crisis

1962 | Cesar Chavez organizes the National Farm Workers Association

1965 | The Immigration Act of 1965

1968 | The Bilingual Education Act

1979 | Political turmoil and civil wars result in refugees from El Salvador, Guatemala, and Nicaragua

1980 | Mariel Boatlift

1986 | The Immigration Reform and Control Act

1990s | Thousands of *balseros* (rafters) are allowed to leave Cuba

1996 | Latino March on Washington

2006 | "A Day Without Immigrants" National Boycott

❖ Introduction ❖

id you know that the first immigrants to live in what is now the United States were not the English settlers who lived in Jamestown in 1607 or the Pilgrims who settled in Plymouth in 1620, but the Spanish? The descendents of these first Spanish settlers, as well as immigrants from Mexico and the Spanish-speaking countries of Central America, South America, and the Caribbean, are collectively known as Latinos.

Latinos are a diverse, multiracial group of people whose ancestors include not only the Spanish but also the Native Americans, Africans, Europeans, and Asians who have inhabited these lands throughout the centuries. Latinos have played an important role in the development of the United States, and their accomplishments, ideals, customs, foods, language, music, art, literature, and fashions continue to transform and enrich American life. Today Latinos make up almost 15 percent of the U.S. population—and, as their own population increases, Latinos' contributions, achievements, and influences are sure to have an even greater and more exciting impact in the United States—and in the world at large.

In *A Kid's Guide to Latino History* we'll explore the rich culture and remarkable history of Latinos in the United States through more than 50 hands-on activities. In chapter 1 we will discover how Christopher Columbus and the Spanish conquistadors forever changed the course of history in the Americas by enslaving the native people and plundering their land for gold and riches. We will learn how the "Columbian Exchange" brought food, animals, goods—and diseases—from the Old World to the New World and back; enjoy a steaming cup of *champurrado* (an ancient Aztec drink sweetened with sugar brought by the Spanish); and create a Columbian buffet of Old World and New World foods.

In chapter 2 we will walk in the shoes of the Spanish conquistadors, see the creation of the first Spanish settlements, witness the revolt of the Pueblo Indians in 1680, observe the establishment of the Catholic missions, and see how the Spanish helped the English colonists win a revolutionary war. We'll also experience this era by creating a Native American ring and pin game, stringing chili peppers like a Spanish colonist, and making a medicine man's rattle that resembles the one the natives gave the explorer Cabeza de Vaca, who was lost in the wilderness of the Southwest for eight years!

Chapter 3 discusses frontier life in the Mexican Southwest after Mexico's independence from Spain. We will travel the route of the Santa Fe Trail, observe the world of the Californio rancho, discover the legacies of the Mexican vaqueros, witness the battle of the Alamo in Texas, and learn how the Mexican-American War resulted in the Southwest becoming part of the United States. Try your hand at being a vaquero by throwing a lariat and designing your own cattle brand.

The immigration of Mexicans to the United States is discussed in chapter 4. We'll see how the first Mexican Americans worked on railroads, and at ranches, factories, and farms. We'll learn about the plight of migrant farm workers, labor reforms made by the civil rights leader Cesar Chavez, life in the Mexican barrio (neighborhood), and the Chicano movement. Come along and compose a Mexican *corrido* (ballad), play games that were played by migrant children, and make a skull figure for the holiday Día de los Muertos (Day of the Dead).

Chapter 5 covers Puerto Ricans and their status as U.S. citizens. We'll explore the long history between the United States and Puerto Rico, and we'll discover how Puerto Rican islanders have immigrated to the United States, especially New York, for a better standard of living. We will walk through the streets of New York's Spanish Harlem, join in a game of stickball or ring-a-levio, enjoy an icy *piragua* (snow cone), and create a scary *vejigante* mask for the National Puerto Rican Day Parade.

Cuban Americans are the focus of chapter 6. We find out how the Communist takeover of Cuba by dictator Fidel Castro resulted in thousands of Cubans fleeing to the United States as refugees. Contributions of the Cuban American community in Miami are explored, and we'll learn how to make a Cuban sandwich, start a conga line, and build Afro-Cuban bongos.

In chapter 7 we will study the turbulent history of Central America and the immigration of Salvadorans, Guatemalans, Hondurans, and Nicaraguans. Come and experience a bit of Central American culture: enjoy Salvadoran green mango slices, make Guatemalan worry dolls, play a Honduran game with seeds, and bake a Nicaraguan *tres leches* (three milks) cake.

Dominican Americans are discussed in chapter 8. Together we will find out about the Dominican dictator Rafael Trujillo, who ruled the Dominican Republic with an iron first for 30 years, and the economic chaos that shook that country after his death. The Dominican immigrant experience is explored as we look at life in Washington Heights, New York. We'll learn how to dance the merengue, put together a Dominican American "baseball hall of fame" exhibit, and stir up a delicious pot of *arroz con leche* (Latin rice pudding).

In chapter 9 we will learn about South American immigrants from Colombia, Ecuador, and Peru. We will try our hand at writing a short story that incorporates "magical realism," like the works of Colombian writer Gabriel García Márquez. We'll also mold Ecuadorian bread figurines and paint a maté (gourd) in the Peruvian style.

Chapter 10 discusses important issues within the U.S. Latino community, including undocumented immigration; activism; bilingual education; participation in the military; and family, religion, and other important aspects of Latino culture. We'll also take a look at the phenomenon of "Spanglish," the practice of celebrating Día de la Raza (Day of the Race) instead of Columbus Day, and new Latino celebrations such as Día, or El Día de los Niños/El Día de los Libros (Day of Children/Day of Books), and Hispanic Heritage Month. You are invited to celebrate a Día party and to create a meaningful poster for Hispanic Heritage Month.

Throughout the book, interesting facts about Latino history are provided in sidebars, such as the sidebar "From Sea to Shining Sea—in Spanish!" which honors the legacies of the Spanish in the names they gave to our cities, states, rivers, foods, and more. Each chapter contains biography sections that recognize the achievements of Latinos in the United States and around the world. The resource section includes recommendations for Latino books, movies, museums, and Web sites. The teacher's guide is a helpful resource for use in the classroom.

Enjoy this celebration of Latino history and culture and learn about the significant contributions Latinos have made in the creation and success of this nation.

◆ 1 ◆
Discovery of the New World

Christopher Columbus and the Spanish Explorers

In 1492 the Italian explorer Christopher Columbus was commissioned (hired) by the country of Spain to travel across the ocean in search of a western sea route from Europe to China. Hoisting the Spanish flag, Columbus set sail with a small fleet of three ships—the *Niña*, the *Pinta*, and the *Santa María*—and 90 men. He hoped to bring gold and spices from China back to the king and queen of Spain. Instead, on October 12, 1492, Columbus stumbled onto an island in what are now known as the Bahamas—and accidentally discovered a New World. At that time, no one could have predicted that one of the world's greatest civilizations, the United States of America, would be created on the shores of this strange "new" land.

The land may have been new to Columbus, but the island had been home to natives called the Taino (TAY-noh) for thousands of years. Columbus, who mistakenly believed he had landed in the spice islands of the Far East known as the Indies, named the native people Indians, and he named the island San Salvador, which means Holy Savior.

Eager to find gold, silver, and any other riches that he could bring back to Spain, Columbus explored the other islands in the area as well. On Christmas Day, the boat he was on—the *Santa María*—became shipwrecked on an island. Columbus named that island La Isla Española (it would later be renamed Hispaniola). He decided to use the wood from the wrecked ship to build a fort there, and he named the fort La Navidad (NAH-vee-dahd), which means Christmas. When Columbus left the island to return to Spain, he ordered some of his men to stay behind in order to build colonies and set up farms. Columbus would travel back and forth between the New World and Spain three more times in his lifetime.

At first the relationship between the Spanish who had "discovered" the new land and the natives who had lived there for centuries was friendly, but it soon turned hostile. The Spanish explorers enslaved the Indians and forced them to dig for gold and silver. The natives suffered from overwork, as well as from diseases they had never before encountered. The Spanish had unintentionally brought these diseases with them from Europe to the New World, and many natives died from them. Those who survived eventually turned against the Spanish explorers. All of the men who had been left behind by Columbus were killed, and the fort La Navidad was burned to the ground.

In 1494 Columbus returned to the islands and established the first permanent colony in the New World on what is now called Hispaniola. The colony, which was built near the place that La Navidad had been, was named Isabella in honor of Queen Isabella of Spain.

The Spanish were not the only people who sought gold, spices, and other riches in places far from their homeland. Explorers and adventurers from countries all over Europe, including Portugal, France, England, and others, soon followed Columbus's trail to try their luck in the New World. But it was the Spanish who led the way in exploring and conquering the land. In fact, the early Spanish explorers were called conquistadors (kon-KEE-sta-dohrs), which means conquerors. By 1513 the Spanish had established New World settlements in Cuba, Puerto Rico, Jamaica, and Hispaniola, and by the end of the 1500s Spain had claimed what is now Mexico, most of Central America, part of South America, and the Caribbean islands as its own.

The Catholic Missionaries

The natives of the New World had their own, deeply held religious beliefs and customs, and they worshipped many gods—most of which were rooted in nature. The Spanish, however,

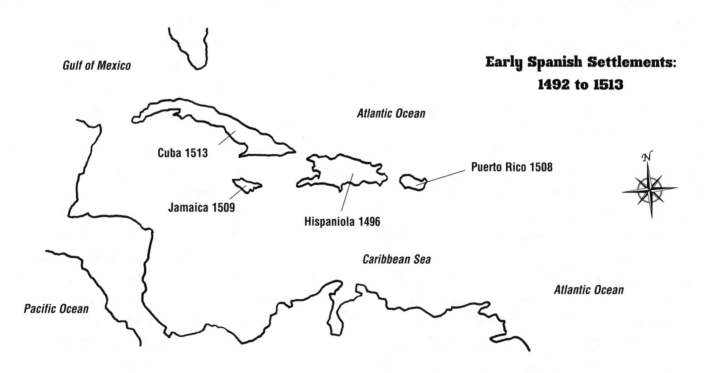

Gulf of Mexico

Early Spanish Settlements: 1492 to 1513

Atlantic Ocean

Cuba 1513

Puerto Rico 1508

Jamaica 1509

Hispaniola 1496

Caribbean Sea

Atlantic Ocean

Pacific Ocean

N

believed that it was their duty to spread their own religion of Catholicism to the Indians.

Spanish missionaries who accompanied the explorers and settlers set about persuading—and sometimes forcing—the natives to give up their own religious beliefs and become Christians. Although they usually continued to worship their own native gods, many Indians also embraced Christianity to some extent. The Spanish destroyed many of the native temples of worship, and the missionaries used the Indians as laborers to build Catholic churches near the places that the temples had been.

Hernán Cortés and the Conquest of the Aztecs

In 1521 the Spanish conquistador Hernán Cortés led a group of 500 men from Cuba (an island in the Caribbean) into what is now central Mexico. The area was ruled by a highly civilized society of natives known as the Aztecs, and their kingdom stretched out over 80,000 square miles (129,000 km) of land. The capital of their kingdom was a city called Tenochtitlán (teh-NOCK-tea-t'lan), and thousands of Aztecs lived there. In Tenochtitlán there were magnificent temples, pyramids, gardens, and—most important to the Spanish—gold and silver. Cortés and his men decided to take over the city. With the help of powerful firearms—the likes of which had never before been seen by the natives—the Spaniards defeated the Aztecs and set about ransacking and destroying Tenochtitlán. Three years later Cortés rebuilt the city and named it Mexico City. Mexico City is now the capital of the country of Mexico.

The defeat of the Aztecs by Cortés gave Spain control over the vast amount of land that had comprised the native king-dom, and the building of a Spanish city in the ruins of Tenochtitlán paved the way for other Spanish colonies to be established in the Americas.

In 1535, the King of Spain organized these colonies into territories called viceroyalties. One of the viceroyalties was called New Spain, and it included what is now the country of Mexico, most of present-day Central America, most of the present-day southwestern United States, California, Florida, and the Caribbean Islands.

New Spain in 1600

New Spain

New Spain

Atlantic Ocean

Pacific Ocean

N

Make *Champurrado*: A Hearty Spanish Beverage

The early Spanish colonists adapted an ancient Aztec beverage of water and masa harina (MAH-sah hah-REE-nah), or corn flour, by adding sugar, milk, and chocolate to the mixture to create what they called *champurrado* (chahm-poor-RAH-thoh). The Spanish settlers enjoyed *champurrado* both as a beverage and as breakfast because it is warm and filling, like hot cereal. The U.S. descendents of Spanish people still enjoy *champurrado*, especially during the celebration of Christmas.

4 servings

What You Need
Adult Supervision Required
¼ cup masa harina (corn flour, found in the
   baking section of grocery stores)
4 cups milk, divided
Blender
1 disk Mexican chocolate (found in the ethnic
   section of grocery stores or in Latino
   grocery stores)
½ cup packed dark brown sugar
1 cinnamon stick
Medium saucepan
Whisk
4 mugs

What You Do
1. Place masa harina and 1 cup milk in the blender. Put the lid on the blender and blend until smooth. Set aside.
2. Place remaining milk, chocolate disk, brown sugar, and cinnamon stick in the saucepan. Heat over medium heat, stirring constantly with a whisk, until the milk, chocolate, and brown sugar have melted together.
3. Add the mixture from the blender and stir constantly for several minutes, until the champurrado comes to a full boil.
4. Remove from heat, discard cinnamon stick, and pour into 4 mugs.

African Slaves in the Americas

The Spanish quickly set about colonizing New Spain, the vast expanse of land that had been seized when the Aztecs were defeated. But the conquistadors needed an enormous workforce to build and operate mines and plantations on their newly claimed land in the Americas. They first turned to the Indians who were living there, but they soon depleted the Indian population through overwork and disease. With insufficient numbers of Indians left to enslave, they then began to import slaves from Africa (just as the Portuguese, French, Dutch, and English would later do in their colonies as well).

Slaves that came to the Spanish colonies, especially to the Caribbean, were able to retain more of their language, religion, and cultural traditions than those that were sent to other European colonies. This was because there was a greater proportion of slaves (Africans) than Spaniards in the Spanish colonies. In addition, most of the Spaniards who came to the Americas to colonize New Spain were men who were either unmarried or had left their families behind in Spain, so marriages and children between the Spaniards and the African and Indian slaves were very common. Children of these unions were generally set free. In Cuba, slaves had the right to buy their own freedom. As a result Spanish slaves were able to pass down language, religions, and cultural traditions from all three origins: Africa, native America, and Spain.

In the English colonies, settlers came as families and in greater numbers than the Spanish. The English population outnumbered the African slaves, so marriage and children between them (and the Indians) was less common. In these colonies, English traditions were more apt to survive than African or Native American.

The Columbian Exchange

When Christopher Columbus and the other European explorers traveled to the New World, they brought to the Americas many of the foods, plants, animals, goods—and, unintentionally, diseases—of their homelands, as well as those of other places, such as Asia and Africa, that they had visited. When the explorers returned home, they carried back to Europe the new foods, animals, plants, goods, and diseases they'd encountered during their travels around the world. This exchange of items between the Old World and the New World would come to be known as the Columbian Exchange in honor of Christopher Columbus, the explorer who had started it all.

Did you know that when Columbus set foot in the New World there were no horses in the Americas? Horses had existed on the lands many thousands of years earlier, but they'd become extinct by the time the Spanish explorers arrived. Most people think of Native Americans on horseback greeting Columbus and the other explorers, when in fact it was those explorers who introduced the Native Americans to the horse! The European horse soon became an important part of Native American life.

Before the Spanish arrived, the only domesticated animals in the New World were guinea pigs, llamas, alpacas, and turkeys and a few other types of fowl. Pigs, sheep, goats, cattle, and chickens were all introduced to the Americas by the explorers. They also introduced many new plants, including sugarcane, tobacco, and coffee—three crops that would play a very important role in the economic success of the future colonies.

Thanks to the Columbian Exchange, Europe was introduced to a whole new world of things as well. The tomato, which is used in pizza, spaghetti sauce, and many other Italian dishes, did not exist in Europe until the Spanish explorers brought it back with them from the New World. Even potatoes, Ireland's favorite food crop, came from the Americas. Chocolate, one of the world's favorite treats, comes from the American cacao plant. And, if it weren't for the American chicle plant, there would never be chewing gum. The Spanish explorers had never seen corn, which was called maize, before they landed in the New World. They took that back to Europe, too. But the diseases that were exchanged between the Old World and the New World caused many people to become ill or even die. The Native Americans were the hardest hit. They had lived in isolation for thousands of years with exposure to very few diseases, and their bodies did not have the immunities needed to help protect them against the smallpox, malaria, yellow fever, and other germs and viruses that the explorers exposed them to. As a result, the Old World diseases caused the deaths of thousands of Native American peoples.

Plan Your Own "Columbian Exchange"

If you were moving to an island that had no plants or animals, what three plants would you bring to farm? Why? What three types of animals would you raise to eat or to work in your fields? Why?

Put Together a Columbian Buffet

A peanut butter and jelly sandwich is a product of the Columbian Exchange. Peanuts come from the Americas, while jelly (made from grapes) and bread (made from wheat) come from the Old World. If you have potato chips on your plate you can thank the Native American potato, but if you finish your lunch with a banana and a glass of milk you're eating Old World foods.

Have some fun putting together a buffet of Old and New World foods.

What You Need

5 or 6 plates of food (choose from lists at right)
Table

What You Do

1. Choose foods from the lists of New World and Old World Foods and serve a buffet of 5 or 6 plates to choose from. Invite friends or family members to guess which "world" is responsible for each food.

Old World Foods	New World Foods
chicken	corn
bacon	peppers
milk	tomatoes
eggs	pumpkins
bananas	chocolate
oranges	potatoes
cheese	peanuts
bread made from wheat	strawberries
onions	squash
peas	turkey
hamburgers	pineapple

From Sea to Shining Sea—in Spanish!

Among the delightful legacies of the Spanish are the musical names they gave to our cities, states, rivers, foods, and more. These names remind us of our country's Spanish heritage.

Here are some rivers in the United States that have Spanish names.

Sacramento River. The largest river in California was named *El Rio del Sacramento* ("Day of the Holy Sacrament") by Spanish explorers who found it on a holy day.

Colorado River. This river's reddish mud prompted the Spaniards to name it Colorado (the Spanish word for red).

Brazos River. This river, which flows through the middle of Texas, was named *Los Brazos de Dios*, which means "In the Arms of God."

Rio Grande. In Spanish this name means "Big River."

San Joaquin River. This river in California was named after Saint Joachim (the father of the Virgin Mary, according to the Catholic religion).

◆ 2 ◆
The Spanish North American Frontier

Until recently, many history books taught us that the English colonies of Jamestown and Plymouth were the first settlements in North America. In reality, the Spanish had established colonies in North America many years earlier. The first permanent North American settlement, St. Augustine, was established by Spanish explorers 42 years before the English began to build the colony of Jamestown in Virginia, and 55 years before the Pilgrims landed at Plymouth Rock!

These first settlers were Spanish and mestizo people who traveled overland from what is now Mexico to what is now the United States. The first Spanish colonies were in the Southeast, primarily in what is now Florida, an area historians call the eastern borderlands. The most developed of the Spanish land, however, was on the other side of the country, in present-day New Mexico, California, Arizona, and Texas, as well as in parts of what are now Utah and Nevada. From the 16th to the 19th century, this vast area was known as the western borderlands, the Spanish West, and—as it is still called today—the Southwest. The last section of North America that the Spanish claimed was a large expanse of land in the middle of what is now the United States. This land was called the Louisiana Territory.

Spanish Explorers in the North American Frontier

The explorers of the North American frontier were hoping to find rich reserves of silver and gold as had been found in Mexico. What they found was a vast wilderness populated by small groups of Native Americans.

Juan Ponce de León

The first Spanish conquistador to claim land (or even to set foot) on the North American frontier was Juan Ponce de León in

1513. He came upon what he thought was an island on Easter Day and named it Pascua Florida (PAHS-kwah floor-EEH-dah), which means "Feast of Flowers." Legend has it that Ponce de León was searching for the Fountain of Youth, a mythical water source that would make anyone who drank from it forever young. (There is no proof that the explorer really believed such a place existed, however.) In 1521 Ponce de León returned to Florida with 200 men to begin a settlement, but he was killed in a Native American attack before he could build his colony.

Alvar Nuñez Cabeza de Vaca

The story of Alvar Nuñez Cabeza de Vaca is as amazing as that of Robinson Crusoe. Instead of being stranded on a desert island like Crusoe was, de Vaca was lost in the wilderness of the Americas. He was originally part of an expedition of 300 soldiers and sailors who planned to search for treasure and start a new colony on the northwest coast of Florida.

The journey began from Spain in June of 1527 under Pánfilo de Narváez. On the way to Florida, they were forced to stop in Cuba because of a hurricane. The expedition left Cuba the following spring and successfully reached what is now Florida's Tampa Bay in 1528. De Vaca and the other soldiers went ahead on foot into the wilderness, while the sailors set off along the coast to look for a suitable harbor. The two groups were never reunited. After searching in vain for a harbor, and then for the soldiers, the sailors gave up and returned to Cuba, leaving the rest of the men behind.

The expedition was considered a disaster. No one in Cuba expected there to be any survivors, but the soldiers who had been stranded in Florida were not ready to give up. They decided to build their own ships to sail to Mexico. Using whatever tools they had, they cut down trees, made five rough barges, and began their ocean journey. The voyage was difficult, and many of the soldiers drowned or died of starvation or illness. Eventually the barge carrying de Vaca and about 80 other survivors washed up, badly damaged, on an island off the coast of what is now Texas.

Early on, Cabeza de Vaca became separated from his fellow Spaniards. Believing he had perished, they left to explore the coast without him. For eight years Alvar Nuñez Cabeza de Vaca survived in the American wilderness, living by his wits and the compassion of the Native Americans who helped him. De Vaca was at times enslaved by Native American tribes, but at other times—when he represented himself as a healer and a medicine man—the tribes he was with revered him. Eventually he became a successful merchant, trading with and selling goods to various tribes in the Southwest and what is now Texas.

In 1532 Cabeza de Vaca was reunited with three other survivors of the expedition who had been living with a Native American tribe called the Mariames. One of the three men was a Moorish (a person from North Africa) slave named Estevan. Thanks to his unlucky circumstances, Estevan had become the first African to explore the Southwest.

For four more years, Cabeza de Vaca and the three men traveled the Southwest together. At times they sold goods and traded with the native people; at other times, they worked as healers. Finally, in 1536, Spanish slave traders came across the four men and helped them return home to Mexico City. It is believed that, while they were stranded in North America, the men had walked about 5,000 miles.

Cabeza de Vaca wrote a book about his experience called *La Relación* in 1542. This was the first book about the Americas ever published.

Make a Medicine Man's "Gourd" Rattle

Cabeza de Vaca acted as a medicine man by mimicking the rites and ceremonies of the Indians and performing Catholic rituals, such as making the sign of the cross over an ill person. The Indians believed that he had powers and honored him by presenting him with a gourd rattle, which was traditionally given only to healers of the tribes. You can make your own "gourd" rattle using a plastic bottle.

What You Need

Adult Supervision Required

1 small bottle acrylic paint (choose an earth-colored shade of light brown, yellow, deep orange, or green)

Paper cup

Thick paintbrush or sponge

Empty 8-ounce water bottle with label and cap removed

Handful uncooked popcorn kernels, dried beans, or tiny stones, shells, or beads

Small funnel or index card (optional)

⅞-inch-wide, 7- to 9-inch-long dowel (if the dowel needs to be cut from a long piece, you must ask an adult to help you)

6 feet leather lacing (available at craft stores)

1 red feather

1 white feather

8 or more tiny bells (available at craft stores)

What You Do

1. Squirt paint into the paper cup. Using the paintbrush or sponge, paint the outside of the water bottle. Let dry. If necessary, paint again. Let dry.
2. Pour the popcorn kernels, beans, stones, shells, or beads into the bottle. (If you want to, use the funnel or the index card to help guide the items into the bottle.)
3. Push the dowel all the way into the bottle until it reaches the bottom of the bottle.
4. Measure 1 foot (30 cm) of lace from the end of the piece. Tie the lace around the neck of the bottle so that 1 foot (30 cm) of lace hangs on one side of the bottle and the remaining lace hangs on the other side.
5. Wrap the long piece of lace tightly around the neck of the bottle several times. Tie it to the shorter length of lace.
6. Tuck the feathers into the lacing.
7. Slide 4 bells onto each of the 2 pieces of lace hanging down. Tie a knot an inch or 2 from the bottom of each piece of lace to keep the bells from sliding off.

8. Shake the rattle and imagine what it must have been like to be Cabaza de Vaca, an accidental "healer" in the wilderness of early America.

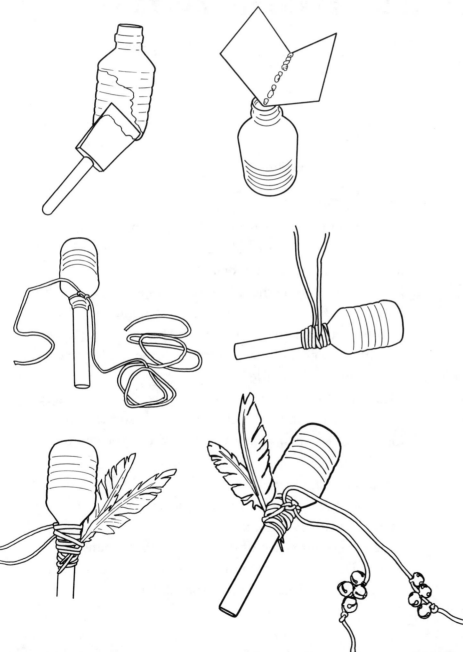

Francisco Vásquez de Coronado

When Cabeza de Vaca returned to Mexico, he told of his quest in crossing the North American Southwest. Although he never claimed to have found gold or riches, he did mention that he had heard rumors from the Native Americans about gold and turquoise that lay in the north. Many people believed that de Vaca had actually found the legendary Seven Cities of Cibola—mythical cities that were said to be made of gold and that were located somewhere in the "East."

The viceroy (head of the government) of New Spain, Antonio de Mendoza, was enthralled by the tales that de Vaca told of his adventures. Mendoza decided to send a trusted priest, Friar Marcos de Niza, and the African slave Estevan, who had traveled previously with de Vaca, to investigate possible sightings of the Seven Cities.

By the time they reached the Maya River, some speculate Friar Marcos was too weak and exhausted to continue. The two men devised a plan: If Estevan found something of interest, he was to send his Native American escorts and a small cross back to the friar (priest). If he found something spectacular, he was to send his escorts back with a large cross. After a few days passed, messengers returned to Friar Marcos—with a cross the size of a man! Friar Marcos interpreted this to mean that Estevan had found the Seven Cities of Cibola.

Estevan had actually found Hawikuh—the largest of the Zuni Indian pueblos, communities of dwellings, in what is now Arizona. It is thought that the slave might have mistaken the pueblo for a city of gold. The Zunis were not pleased to find Estevan (no one knows for sure, but it's thought that the Zunis might have believed they were in danger), and they killed him and many of the Indians who accompanied him.

The surviving members of Estevan's party returned to tell Friar Marcos what had happened. He ignored their warnings and said he wanted to see the cities of gold for himself. He wrote to Mendoza that he had indeed seen the golden city for himself. It was a lie. Historians believe he was probably miles away from the Zuni village where Estevan was killed. It is not clear why Friar Marcos lied. He might have been afraid that he would be punished for not completing the expedition, or he might have been looking for glory and recognition.

In 1540 Viceroy Mendoza, encouraged by Friar Marcos's lies, ordered an expedition to be sent to conquer this new frontier. The Spanish conquistador Francisco Vásquez de Coronado was chosen to be the leader. The expedition traveled for thousands of miles from Mexico to the American Southwest in search of the Seven Cities of Cibola.

Coronado and his men were near starvation when they reached Hawikuh. They stormed the village, and their powerful guns and horses quickly triumphed over the bows and arrows of the Zuni. They ransacked the pueblos, robbed the native people, and left the homes in ruins. When Coronado realized that Friar Marcos had lied about the cities of gold, Friar Marcos was sent back to Mexico in disgrace.

Although Coronado never found the Seven Cities of Gold, he was one of the first to explore the Southwest. His expedition saw the great plains of the Midwest, including herds of bison, and during the expedition his captain, García López de Cárdenas, became the first European to discover the Grand Canyon.

Hernando de Soto

In 1539 the Spanish explorer Hernando de Soto led an expedition of more than 500 men and horses through what is now Florida, Georgia, the Carolinas, Tennessee, Alabama, Mississippi, Arkansas, and Louisiana.

In a bizarre twist, the expedition came upon a member of Cabeza de Vaca's stranded expedition who had been living with local Native Americans for 12 years. De Soto's men were about to attack the Indians when the man, Juan Ortiz, spoke to them in perfect Spanish, explaining who he was and asking for mercy for the people who had protected him.

Juan Ortiz became the interpreter for de Soto's group, and he traveled with them until he died in the winter of 1541. The following spring—a year after he'd made his greatest discovery, the Mississippi River—de Soto died as well. His men continued through what is now Texas under a new leader and eventually returned to New Spain.

Spanish Settlements on the North American Frontier

Spanish settlements were built with two goals in mind: to secure Spanish claims on the land to prevent other European nations from colonizing, and to convert the natives to Catholicism.

San Miguel de Gualdape

In 1526 the explorer Lucas Vazquez de Ayllón established San Miguel de Gualdape, the first North American Spanish settlement, somewhere on the Southeast Atlantic coast, possibly in present-day South Carolina. The settlement was inhabited by Ayllón and the 500 settlers and African slaves that he had brought with him. The settlers were unprepared for the rigors of this new world, however. There were constant Native American attacks, fighting among the settlers, cold weather, and diseases such as smallpox and typhus, as well as malaria, which killed Ayllón in October 1526.

Within just a few weeks of its establishment, the settlement fell into chaos. The slaves revolted and fled to live among the Native Americans in the area, and the remaining settlers returned to Hispaniola.

St. Augustine

In 1565 King Philip II of Spain sent explorer Pedro Menéndez de Avilés, along with 300 soldiers and 500 Spanish colonists, to the New World to build a mission and colony. The French, who were also exploring the New World, had recently built a fort, which they named Fort Caroline, on Spanish-claimed land on the east coast of what is now Florida. King Philip gave Menéndez orders to expel the French and reclaim the land as Spanish territory.

Menéndez successfully set up a camp and set out to attack Fort Caroline. The Spanish soldiers surprised the French, overwhelming them with force and man power. The French returned to France in defeat. Menéndez built a fort and colony on his campsite, which he named St. Augustine. He also built two other Spanish forts, hoping to colonize the area, but in 1574 he died unexpectedly in Spain, and those two forts were abandoned.

Life in the colony of St. Augustine was hard. The settlers suffered from a lack of food and necessary supplies. They were also subjected to attacks by Native Americans, the English, and the French. In spite of their many difficulties, however, the colony of St. Augustine endured, and it is famous for being the oldest permanent European settlement in the United States.

San Juan de los Caballeros and San Gabriel

Although the conquistadors claimed their lands, the Native Americans did not consider themselves a conquered people.

They lived in their own communities, sometimes trading—but also frequently waging war—with the Spanish settlers.

In 1598 the Spanish government sent Don Juan de Oñate, a former soldier and member of a wealthy family from Zacatecas, New Spain, to be governor of the territory known as New Mexico. He brought with him a party of about 500 men, women, children, soldiers, and Franciscan friars who were to start a new settlement in New Mexico and spread Catholicism to the Native Americans. (De Oñate was also in charge of searching for a water route to the Pacific Ocean, but he never found one.) The group brought with them several thousand heads of livestock (horses, pigs, chickens, and cows), food, water, seeds, and supplies.

The territory of New Mexico was much bigger than today's state of New Mexico. It spanned all the way across what are now the states of New Mexico and Arizona, as well as parts of Colorado, Utah, and Nevada. It was a very remote area, and its dry desert climate allowed little to grow outside the river valleys. New Mexico was a lonely place compared to Mexico in New Spain, with its lively communities, outdoor bazaars, and gathering places. Even worse—it took six months to make the trip back to Mexico!

The pioneers left northern New Spain in January and walked 1,500 miles before reaching San Juan, in the Northern Rio Grande Valley, in July. They entered the Tewa village of Ohkay Owingeh and renamed it San Juan de los Caballeros. Instead of building their own settlement, they moved right into the pueblos with the native people. They allowed many of the Tewa to stay to provide labor for the Spanish, as well as food and clothing. The village soon became overcrowded. Six months later they moved to an area farther away from the Tewa village so that the settlement would have plenty of room

**New Mexico in 1598
(Route of Oñate)**

New Mexico

San Juan Pueblo

Santa Fe

New Spain

Present day
border of Mexico

(Present Day
Mexico)

Zacatecas

Gulf of Mexico

Pacific Ocean

Mexico City

N

to grow, and they named it San Gabriel. Again the Spanish moved into the native pueblos. They persuaded most of the natives to move to the old settlement of San Juan, so that the Spanish could take over their empty homes.

The settlement did not thrive. Instead of farming the land, building homes, and raising livestock, the settlers spent too much time searching in vain for gold and silver. Another problem was conflict with the Acoma Indians. When an exploration party led by de Oñate's nephew, Juan de Zaldívar, was attacked by the Acoma, Zaldívar and ten other Spanish settlers were killed. Juan de Oñate was merciless in his revenge for the death of his nephew and the other Spaniards. The Spanish soldiers attacked the Acoma village, and a fierce battled followed. Hundreds of Acoma were killed and the survivors were severely punished.

A lack of food and resources soon caused the settlement to fall apart. A few hardy settlers remained, but most of the colonists returned to Mexico. In 1607 Juan de Oñate was con-

victed on several charges in regard to the failed settlement, including his harsh treatment of the Acoma Indians. He was forced to resign as governor of New Mexico. Despite de Oñate's defeat, he was responsible for establishing the first colony in New Mexico and for making the capital of that territory San Juan Pueblo.

In 1609 New Spain declared that New Mexico would become a royal colony, which meant that the Spanish government would pay for the expenses involved in settling new lands. In 1610 the new governor of New Mexico, Don Pedro de Peralta, moved the colony of San Gabriel to the territory's new capital, Santa Fe (which means "Holy Faith"). Santa Fe is the oldest capital in the United States.

The *Carreta*

The *carreta* was a two-wheeled cart that the Spaniards brought from Mexico to carry items across the land. Because metal was so scarce, the *carreta* was made completely of wood—even its wheels were made of wood, and they made a tremendous screeching sound when they turned. From the time of de Oñate's first settlement in 1598 to the early 1800s, the *carreta* was the only vehicle that the Spanish settlers had to move goods.

Southwest Indians

"Pueblo Indians" was the term that the first Spanish explorers used to describe the Southwest natives who lived in large, apartment-like structures made of adobe, a mixture of straw and mud. These Native Americans had a long, rich history of their own traditions, religion, and culture. They were made up of many different nations or tribes including: the Zuni, from what is now New Mexico; the Hopi, from present-day Arizona; and the Jemez, Tigua, Tewa, and Keres, who lived along the Rio Grande.

Unlike some Native Americans who constantly traveled to hunt and gather food, the Pueblo Indians were farmers who settled and stayed in one location, and they built permanent communities, called pueblos, in which to live.

Pueblo homes were unique, multilevel structures. They were built with flat roofs and spouts that allowed rainwater to pour off the roofs. To help keep the pueblo home and its residents safe, doors were not built on the first floor. Instead, ladders were used to climb from the ground up to the second floor of the home, and a trap door inside the home was used to get down to the first level. If there were enemy tribes in the area, the residents pulled up the ladders so that no one could enter the pueblo homes.

The Spanish encountered other Native American tribes in the Southwest, such as the Navajo (or Diné, as they called themselves) and Apache, who were nomadic—instead of settling in one place, as the Pueblo Indians did, these tribes traveled constantly in search of food. The Spanish traded goods with these tribes; at other times, they fought with them.

The Navajo lived as hunters and gatherers, and they sometimes raided Pueblo Indian settlements when food was scarce. When the Spanish arrived, the Navajo plundered their

The Ancestral Pueblo Peoples

Some Indian tribes had existed—and mysteriously disappeared—long before the Spanish arrived in the Southwest. These include the Hohokam, who lived in what is now south and central Arizona, and the Mogollon, from what is now the southwest area of New Mexico, from 200 B.C.E. to C.E. 1400.

The most well-known extinct tribe is the Anasazi, or Ancestral Pueblo peoples, who lived in what is now New Mexico and Arizona from 100 B.C.E. to C.E. 1300. The Anasazi were the ancestors of the Pueblo Indians.

The Anasazi began as hunters and gatherers, but they eventually settled into farming life, growing maize, beans, and squash. Their first homes were hollowed-out caves on mesas (flat-top land formations, with steep sides), but the natives soon progressed to building multiple-room houses and apartments made of stone and adobe. Some of these structures contained hundreds of rooms! Toward the end of their existence, the Anasazi built homes in the sides of cliffs, possibly for protection. They wove baskets, created beautiful black and white pottery, and grew cotton.

By about 1300, the Anasazi disappeared, leaving their ruins but no written record as to what happened to them. There are many possible reasons for their disappearance: a long period of drought may have caused them to die off or to join other groups, or they may have been wiped out by warfare with other tribes.

dwellings for horses and sheep. Sheepherding eventually became an important part of Navajo life.

The Apache were also hunter-gatherers, primarily buffalo hunters, who traded animal meat and skins in exchange for corn, beans, squash, and pottery from the Pueblo Indians. After the Spanish arrived and began to trade with the Pueblo tribes, however, the trading relationship between the Pueblo Indians and the Apache ended. To survive, the Apache raided Pueblo and Spanish villages for horses and other provisions.

The Mission System

The Spanish had conquered vast amounts of land in the New World. In order to hold onto those lands, they needed settlers to protect it. But there were not enough settlers available to protect all the land, and the Spanish government was concerned that other European countries might invade and claim the unprotected areas.

The mission system was created to help solve the problem. A mission was a community in which Catholic priests, working as missionaries, instructed large communities of Native Americans in the teachings of the Catholic religion. Three orders (groups) of Catholic priests worked as missionaries: the Jesuits, the Franciscans, and the Dominicans. The Native Americans worked on the missions in return for their education. Along with religious instruction, the Native Americans were taught the Spanish language and Spanish traditions and customs. Spain hoped that, under the mission system, the thousands of Native Americans who were already living in the New World could be put to use to make up for the lack of Spanish settlers.

The Oldest Public Building in the United States

The oldest public building that still stands in the United States today is the Governor's Palace in Santa Fe. Settlers began construction on the Governor's Palace in the year 1610.

Missions were established in Florida, along the coasts of the Atlantic and the Gulf of Mexico, as early as 1563. Missions were also built in what are now Arizona, New Mexico, Texas, and California.

In the New Mexico territory, missions were built next to the pueblos in which the Native Americans were already living. Between 1598 and 1680, about 50 missions were built in New Mexico, mostly along the Rio Grande, an 1,800-mile river that originates in present-day Colorado and runs east to the Gulf of Mexico. It forms a natural border between the United States and Mexico. In Mexico today, the same river is called the Rio Bravo. Many of the missions that were built in this area closed almost as soon as they had begun operating, but others thrived. The mission system would continue to play a major role in the development of the New Frontier well into the next century.

Native Americans in the missions were forced to give up their traditional ways of life. Kivas (KEE-vuhs)—sacred underground rooms in the pueblos where native men went to pray to their gods—were destroyed, along with religious masks and prayer sticks. The songs and dances of native religions were banned. The Native Americans were overworked and mistreated, and many died after being exposed to European diseases. Although the missions were a great help to the Spanish, in many ways they destroyed Native American family and community life.

The Pueblo Revolt

Seventy years of Spanish oppression of the natives eventually erupted in 1680. There had been a drought in the New Mexican colony for several years, and the natives began to think that the Spanish God must not be very powerful if he could not cause it to rain. Unable to grow food, starvation set in. The Native Americans returned to worshipping their native gods and, under a leader named Popé, the Pueblo Indians finally revolted.

For the first time in history, the Pueblo tribes formed a unified front, which was brilliantly organized by Popé. For days, Santa Fe and the surrounding areas were under siege by the Native Americans. They carried not just bows and arrows, but also stolen Spanish guns and swords. After a brutal encounter, 21 missionaries and 400 Spanish settlers were dead. Thousands of settlers fled New Mexico in fear for their lives. Twelve years passed before the Spanish returned.

The Texan Frontier

Spanish settlers who had been chased out of New Mexico during the Pueblo Revolt sought refuge in Ysleta, a village near what is now El Paso, Texas. They established a mission and a small community there in 1682. "Tejas" (Texas) was the name that the Spanish gave to the area as well as to the native peoples. They chose the name based on a native word for "friend." Tejas (Texas) was much smaller and far less populated than the state of Texas today. It was claimed as a province of New Spain from 1690 to 1821.

The first permanent Spanish settlement in Texas, San Francisco de los Tejas, was established in 1690.

In 1691 the Spanish government appointed a Texan governor. Several other missions and forts were then built there. Among those was the mission of San Antonio de Valero; built in 1718, it would later be known as the Alamo.

Both the French and the Spanish claimed land in Texas, but neither country fully colonized the land.

Daily Life on the Spanish American Frontier

In 1693 Don Diego de Vargas, the governor of New Mexico, took the area back from the Pueblo Indians who had risen up against the Spanish settlers and re-conquered New Mexico. It was not an easy process but, eventually, the Pueblo Indians again adjusted to living under Spanish rule. This time the Spanish were more lenient in allowing the natives to retain traditional ways, and they did not interfere as much in the natives' daily lives.

The Spanish government encouraged settlers to live in New Mexico in order to protect the land. In return, settlers were given land grants (free land), seeds, livestock, and tools. Over the next 100 years New Mexico's inhabitants would become a population of people who had largely been born in New Mexico. They were the children and grandchildren of Spanish settlers and Native Americans.

The settlers made homes from adobe bricks that were held together with mud. These homes had flat roofs and small, high windows. As an additional safety measure, instead of having a back or a front yard, a settler's house was often built around an inner, open-air courtyard. This allowed the settler to enjoy being outside while still being protected within the walls of the home.

Most New Mexicans were subsistence farmers—they grew only enough food for their families to eat; they did not grow food to trade or sell to others. Common crops were wheat, corn, chilies, vegetables, beans, and fruits. They also grew cotton and raised sheep for wool, which they used to make clothing and bedding.

New Mexicans wore colorful layers of clothing. They used natural dyes to create blue, yellow, green, pink, and red items. Men wore straw hats, and shirts and pants made of cotton, wool, and even leather. The pants were open from the knee down and showed the men's white undergarments beneath. They wore leather boots and they braided their long hair. Often they had beards and mustaches as well. For warmth, they wore serapes (sah-RAH-pehs), shawls made from blankets. They have an opening that the head goes through so that the fabric falls over the shoulders. Women wore full skirts with loose, low-cut blouses. Over their heads and shoulders they wore lovely scarves called *rebozos* (reh-BOH-sohs). Like the Pueblo Indians, they wore rugged leather moccasins that were suited to the Southwest terrain.

Children worked alongside their mothers and fathers in the fields. They planted seeds, weeded the fields, and harvested the crops. They irrigated (watered) the fields by digging acequias (ah-SAY-kee-ahs), ditches that ran from a nearby river to the fields and funneled river water to the crops.

Metal and iron were scarce. As a result, the settlers had to make their own tools, kitchen utensils, carts, and farm equipment out of wood.

The Spanish settlers had frequent celebrations. They honored the saints of the Catholic religion with processions and fiestas (festivals), and everyone—old and young, rich and poor—participated in the popular community dance known as the fandango (fahn-DAHN-go).

The population of Spanish settlers eventually prospered and began to grow. By the end of the 1700s there were 10,000 or more Spanish settlers. One hundred years earlier, there had been fewer than 3,000.

Design a Straw Art Piece

Spanish settlers, or colonists, made beautifully intricate straw art pieces. It is thought that they were trying to imitate the gold leafing found on European religious items. In straw art pieces, straw is applied to crosses, chests, and boxes that have been painted in a black finish. Sometimes the object has a shallow design carved into it before the paint and straw are applied. Striking examples of straw art pieces can be seen at the Museum of Spanish Colonial Art in Santa Fe, New Mexico.

What You Need

Small unfinished (not painted, stained, or varnished)
    wood box (available at craft stores)
2-ounce bottle black high-gloss acrylic paint
Paper cup
Thick paintbrush or sponge
Mini bale straw (available at craft stores)
Glue
Tweezers (optional)
Toothpicks (optional)

What You Do

1. If the box has a lid, open or remove it so that, when you paint the box, the lid does not become "glued" to the box.

2. Squirt the paint into the paper cup. Using the paintbrush or the sponge, paint the box and, if there is one, the lid. (You may paint only the outside of the box and lid or you may paint the entire box and lid, inside and outside.) Let dry.

3. When the paint is dry, glue the straw to the outside of the box in any design pattern you choose. It is easier to dot the glue onto the box and drop the straw on it rather than to apply the glue to the straw. You may use your fingers or tweezers to pick up the straw, and you can use toothpicks to move the straw around until it is positioned just the way you want it. Let the glue dry.

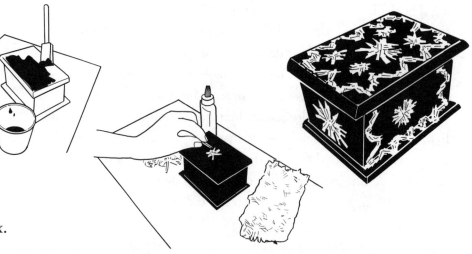

String Chili Peppers

Chile ristras (CHEEL-ay REE-strahs) are colorful strings of red chili peppers that are tied together and hung to dry. Brought to the Southwest from Mexico by the Spanish settlers, they are a special tradition in New Mexico. New Mexican colonists used the dried chilies to spice up their food throughout the winter. Nowadays *chile ristras* are used not only to flavor food, but also as a popular decoration to welcome guests. They are commonly seen hanging on front doors and porches and in kitchens throughout the Southwest.

This activity uses peppers that have already been dried.

What You Need

Several 12-inch lengths sturdy cotton string

12 ounces dried New Mexican chili peppers (Anaheim chilies) or other long, dried chili peppers (available in Latino grocery stores or in the ethnic section of large grocery stores)

1 foot ¼-inch sisal rope (available at hardware stores)

Natural raffia or raffia ribbon (available at craft stores)

What You Do

1. Using one length of string, tie 3 peppers together at the stems. You should have a few inches of string "laces" once the length of string is tied.
2. Tie the string laces to the bottom of the sisal rope so that the peppers cover the bottom of the rope.
3. Repeat steps 1 and 2, going up the sisal rope as you go, until you have used all of the peppers.
4. When you run out of peppers, fill in the top of the sisal rope by tying strings of raffia to it. Allow the raffia to fall over the peppers.

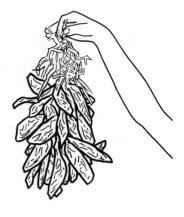

Craft a Corn Husk Doll

The Spanish colonists adopted the Indian tradition of making corn husk dolls. Children had easy access to corn stalks, which they dried and tied into simple dolls. Traditional corn husk dolls have no faces.

What You Need

7 dried corn husks (available at craft stores and in the ethnic section of some grocery stores)

Pan filled with warm water

Paper towels

5 8-inch lengths heavy twine

Scissors

What You Do

1. Soak the corn husks in the warm water for about 30 minutes. Remove the husks from the water and lay them out on paper towels to catch excess water.

2. Hold 6 husks together, pointed ends up. Using one length of twine, tie the husks together about 1 inch from their tops. Using the scissors, carefully trim the ends of the twine about ½ inch from the knot.

3. Turn the bunch of husks upside down. Pull husks, one at a time, over the twine, as if you were peeling a banana. (When you've finished doing this, the twine should be completely covered by husks.)

4. Tie a length of twine around the bunch of folded-over husks, about 1 inch (1.3 cm) down from the top (the place where all the husks begin to fold over) to make the doll's head. This length of twine must be tied very tightly. It helps to wet the twine first. Once the twine is tightly secured, use the scissors to carefully cut off the excess twine.

5. Pull a husk out of the left side of the doll's "body" to make an arm. Tie a length of twine about 1 inch (1.3 cm) from the bottom of the arm to make hands. Carefully cut off the excess twine. Repeat on the right side of the doll's body to make the right arm and hand.

6. Rip a 1-inch-length from the remaining husk to create the doll's waistband. Wrap the piece around the doll's waist, tie it to the doll with twine, and let the ends of the twine hang down in the back to look like apron strings.

The California Missions (1769–1848)

The Spanish used the natives to settle the empty lands of the California territory, just as they had in New Mexico and other territories. Gaspar de Portolá and Franciscan friar Junípero Serra led an expedition into California, where they constructed the first missions in what are now the cities of San Diego (in 1769) and Monterey (in 1770). The Spanish priests converted the Native Americans to Catholicism and then coerced them into working at the missions. They called them neophytes (NEE-oh-fites), a term that applies to people who have been newly converted to a belief. Once a Native American had agreed to convert to Christianity, he or she was not allowed to leave the mission without permission.

Indians built the mission structures, grew crops, tended livestock, prepared food, washed and tanned animal hides, made candles and soap, pressed olive oil, shaped iron tools, and more for the padres ("fathers," or Catholic priests) and for the Spanish soldiers along the California Coast. In all, more than 20,000 Indians worked on the missions—all under the control of fewer than 50 padres and the Spanish soldiers.

Native American children were also a part of mission life. They were responsible for picking olives for the mission's important industry of making olive oil. A common chore for the children was to chase birds from the fields so that they would not eat the growing food crops. Girls were taught to sew, weave, cook, and make pottery. Boys were trained to do blacksmithing, carpentry, and the washing and tanning of animal hides. They were also taught how to ring the mission bells, mill the olives for olive oil, and crush grapes to make wine. Today parts of California are famous for their wines, and it was at the missions that wine making in the area began. The first California winery was at Mission San Miguel, in the Central Coast area of California.

Most missions were set up in a similar way. The typical mission was built of adobe bricks. It was in the shape of a quadrangle, which is like a rectangle with long structures built into each of its four sides. Usually a church would be built into one corner that was much grander than the simple adobe mission building, and a bell tower. The other sides might include dormitories, storerooms, kitchens, and workshops. The quadrangle buildings had doors that opened into an outdoor space called a patio. In the center of the patio there was usually a garden and a fountain. Generally there were two kitchens in the mission. One was used for cooking meals, and the other was used for baking bread in clay ovens called *hornos* (OHR-nohs).

Each mission had two padres, each with his own living quarters. There were dormitories for the unmarried women who worked at the missions. Frequently Native American girls as young as eight years old were sent away from their families to live at the missions. They were under strict supervision. When they grew older and married, they moved into the village with their husbands. The villages where the workers went home each night to sleep lay right outside the mission walls, along with workshops to make metalwork, candles, soap, and other products.

Beyond the mission buildings there were fields of wheat and corn crops, orchards of fruit trees, olive groves, flocks of sheep and goats, herds of cattle, and horses. There were barracks for the soldiers who guarded the missions. The soldiers split their time between the presidios (forts built to guard against attacks) that were located nearby and keeping watch over the missions themselves. If there was trouble with the Indians working at the missions, the soldiers would administer whippings.

A total of 21 missions were built along the coast of California in a 600-mile stretch from San Diego to Sonoma. Their locations were carefully planned to be a day's horseback ride apart from each other. In addition, they were all built near the sea so that they could easily send and receive goods.

Although it was less restrictive than it had been before the Native American uprising, life on the missions continued to be very hard for the Native Americans. The European diseases that had killed so many natives continued to take their toll. The Native Americans continued to be overworked and underfed, and many were abused by the soldiers. Every day the mission bells rang out at different hours, indicating what was to be done at that time. Bells told the inhabitants when to wake up, when to go to work, when to pray, and more. Their ringing was a constant reminder to the Native Americans that they were not free.

Create a Ring and Pin Game

Mission children brought their traditional games to mission life. Among the more popular were ring and pin games, which are sometimes called toss and catch games.

The children made the equipment needed for these games themselves using whatever materials they could find—deer bones, fish bones, acorn caps, pumpkin rinds, squash stems, and other such "useless" items. You can use craft foam to create shapes that resemble the squash stems or other items the Indian children used in their ring and pin games.

What You Need

Circular objects to use for tracing: 1 4-inch diameter;
    1 1½-inch diameter; 1 3-inch diameter (you can use
    glasses that are the correct sizes or you can buy
    inexpensive wood or paper circles at craft stores)

1½ sheets 12-inch-by-18-inch craft foam, any color
    (available at craft stores; use oranges and browns
    if you want the rings to resemble squash stems)

Pen or pencil

Scissors

2-foot-long shoelace or cord

12-inch-long thin dowel

What You Do

Make the Game Pieces

1. Place the 4-inch-diameter circular object on the foam. Using the pen or pencil, draw around it to make a circle on the craft foam. Repeat 9 times so that you have 10 4-inch circles drawn onto the craft foam.
2. Using the 1½-inch-diameter circular object, draw a smaller circle (like a doughnut hole) in the middle of each 4-inch circle.
3. Cut out the 10 4-inch-diameter circles.
4. Fold each circle exactly in half and, starting at the fold, cut out the 1½-inch-diameter circle (be sure to cut through both layers of craft foam).
5. Tie the shoelace or cord about 2 inches from the bottom of the dowel. (It's OK if it slides along the dowel.)
6. Pull the rings over the cord.
7. Place the 3-inch-diameter circular object on the remaining craft foam and draw one circle on it. Cut it out. Using the scissors, poke a small hole in the middle of the circle. Tie the circle to the end of the cord that is not tied to the dowel. This is the "stopper"—it will prevent the rings from falling off the cord.

Play the Game

1. Start by holding the pin (dowel) crossways in front of you, allowing the cord to hang down straight. The "stopper" piece will be hanging on the bottom of the cord, and the remaining 10 rings will be stacked on top.
2. Pinch the cord that is knotted around the pin (dowel), between your thumb and pointer finger. Continuing to hold the knot, swing the cord and rings up into the air.
3. Catch the rings by putting the pin through the holes.
4. When all 10 rings are caught you win!

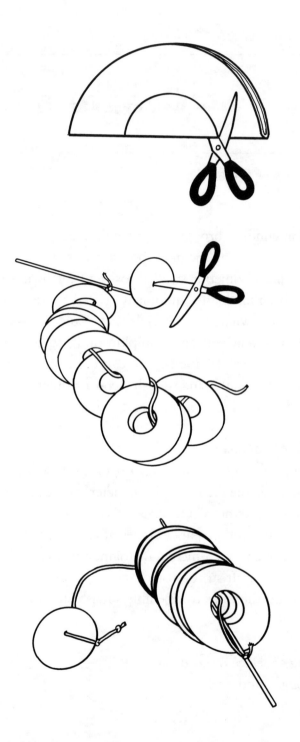

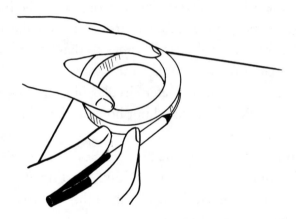

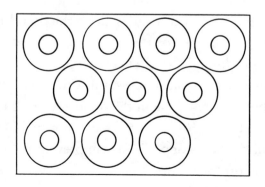

The Revolutionary War

By the mid-1700s the British had established 13 colonies of their own on the eastern side of the North American frontier. The English settlers grew tired of paying taxes to England, their home country, and they did not want to be ruled by a government where they had no representation, so they declared their independence from England and named themselves the United States of America. Great Britain did not believe the colonies had a right to claim independence, and in 1776 the British declared war on the colonies. This conflict would become known as the Revolutionary War.

Spain and France saw the war between the English settlers and Great Britain as an opportunity to get rid of their main competition for territory in the Americas: if the settlers won the war and their independence, England would no longer own any land in the New World. Spain and France both decided to help the colonists win the war, and they gave the English settlers food, guns, and supplies to fight the British. In 1779 Spain and France attacked England itself, forcing the British to fight two wars at the same time—one against the settlers in America and one in their own country in Europe. Great Britain soon realized that it did not have the strength or the number of soldiers needed to win both wars, and it decided to give up the colonies in the Americas to save its own country. In 1781 Great Britain surrendered the North American land it had claimed to the colonists who had settled it and fought to make it their own.

Now, in addition to the 13 colonies, the United States were the new owners of East and West Florida. Florida had previously been given to England in exchange for Havana, Cuba, in 1763. At that time they split it into two parts: East, which was present-day Florida, and West, which was parts of present-day Florida, Alabama, Louisiana, and Mississippi on the Gulf of Mexico. The new country of the United States decided to award East and West Florida back to Spain in gratitude for that country's help during the Revolutionary War.

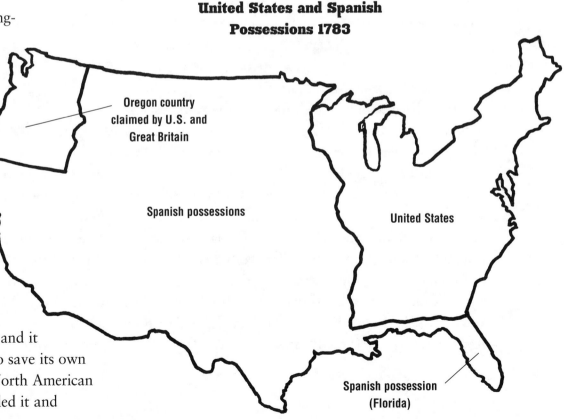

United States and Spanish Possessions 1783

Oregon country claimed by U.S. and Great Britain

Spanish possessions

United States

Spanish possession (Florida)

The Louisiana Purchase

In 1803 the new country made a purchase that would affect the lives of all the Spanish, Mexican, and Native American peoples living in North America, as well as the lives of the new citizens of the United States. It was called the "Louisiana Purchase."

The Louisiana Territory was a vast stretch of land in the middle of what is now the United States. It contained present-day Arkansas, Iowa, Oklahoma, Missouri, Nebraska, North Dakota, South Dakota, nearly all of Kansas, and parts of what are now Colorado, Louisiana, Montana, Minnesota, and Wyoming. It had originally been under Spanish rule, but the land was passed back and forth between Spain and France several times, and it was France that sold it to the United States. The leader of France, Napoleon Bonaparte, had promised the Spanish that he would never sell the territory to a third country, but France was desperately in need of money, and Bonaparte sold the parcel of land to the United States for 15 million dollars, a "bargain" price for more than 828,000 square miles of land that encompassed almost everything between the Mississippi River and the Rocky Mountains! The Louisiana Purchase doubled the size of the United States.

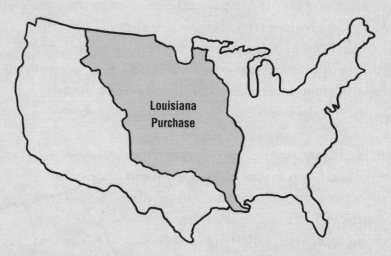

The United States was eager to find out more about the land it had purchased. In 1804 the government sent two officials, Meriwether Lewis and William Clark, to explore the vast area and come back to report on it. Lewis and Clark's expedition took two years to complete. It would be the first time that Anglo Americans (English-speaking people whose ancestors came from Great Britain or other parts of Europe) glimpsed the true wilderness of their new territory, and Lewis and Clark's journey would become known as one of the most important expeditions in U.S. history.

Zebulon Pike: The First Anglo-American to Document the Southwest

The second exploration of the Louisiana territory is less well known than Lewis and Clark's famous expedition, but it is also important. In July of 1806 a young military man named Lieutenant Zebulon Pike was sent to explore the Arkansas and Red Rivers and to report on the southern part of the new territory, which bordered the Spanish-owned lands (present-day Colorado and New Mexico). Some historians believe he might also have had orders to spy on the Spanish colonies.

In February of 1807, Pike and his men were arrested for trespassing on Spanish territory. They were taken through New Mexico to the Spanish governor in Mexico. Along the route, Pike and his men made secret observations and notes of the Spanish-owned lands and people.

By July of 1807, Pike and his men were escorted back to Louisiana by the Spanish, who did not want to cause ill will with the United States. Pike reported that they had been treated well by their captors as well as by the Spanish settlers. Although Pike is not remembered as a great explorer like Lewis and Clark, a Colorado mountain he discovered was later named "Pike's Peak" in his honor, and his diary about his expedition and his adventures, published in 1810, sparked great interest in the Southwest and the wonders and opportunities it offered.

From Sea to Shining Sea—in Spanish!

Here are some U.S. states and cities that have Spanish names, along with their meanings.

Arizona: dry or arid zone

Montana: mountain

Nevada: snow covered

Las Vegas: the meadows

Los Angeles: the angels

3

Frontier Life in the Mexican Southwest

Mexico Wins Independence from Spain

After Spain succeeded in helping the English colonists drive the British out of the Americas, it faced uprisings in its own North American territories. Spurred on by the victory of the 13 British colonies, the settlers in Spanish colonies began their own quests for independence.

On September 16, 1810, a leader emerged in Mexico. A priest named Miguel Hidalgo y Costilla, who wanted the colonies to break free from Spain, decided to put on a bold display to rally his followers. He climbed to the top of a church tower in the village of Dolores, rang the tower bell, and cried out to the villagers to fight for their freedom. The villagers yelled back, "Viva Mexico!" ("Long live Mexico!")

The priest's cry became famous throughout Mexico as El Grito de Dolores (the Cry of Dolores). It became the rallying call for the independence of what would soon be the new country of Mexico (the northern part of New Spain)—which, at that time, included all or part of what are now Mexico, Arizona, California, Colorado, Kansas, New Mexico, Nevada, Oklahoma, Texas, Utah, and Wyoming.

Hidalgo was shot by Spanish soldiers within a year, but the independence movement slowly continued without him for 11 years. Finally, in 1821, Mexico won its independence from Spain. To this day, Mexicans celebrate their Independence Day on September 16, the day of El Grito de Dolores.

The End of the Spanish Empire

By the early 1800s, Spain was no longer the wealthy, powerful force it had been in the early years of colonization. The empire was weakened by many years of war in Europe, as well as by its efforts to rule colonies that were a great distance away. One by one, Spain's colonies in Central and South America, as well as many of those in the Caribbean islands, broke free from Spanish rule and gained their independence.

**Mexico After
Independence, 1821**

Mexico

For more than 300 years, Spain had ruled a vast empire of territories and colonies in the New World—but, by the end of the 1820s, all that remained of that empire were Cuba and Puerto Rico, and those would be independent from Spain before the end of the century.

A Blending of Races

By this time the North American frontier contained a colorful mix of people. Criollo (cree-OH-yoh) was the name given to those who were of Spanish heritage and who were born in the Americas; mestizos (mes-TEE-sohs) had both European and Native American ancestors, and mulattoes (muh-LAH-tohs) claimed a mix of African and European heritage. This mix of heritages are what today comprise those that are collectively called Latinos.

The Santa Fe Trail

U.S. traders traveled from Independence, Missouri, to Santa Fe, New Mexico, to trade with the Mexican settlers. They took over old Native American trails and established the first route from the Midwest to the Southwest. The route, which ended in Santa Fe, was known as the Santa Fe Trail. The trip was a two-month-long, 780-mile journey that stretched across prairies, rocky mountains, and harsh deserts. Travelers always had to be on the lookout for hostile Native Americans and wild animals. The traders traveled in caravans of as many as 100 covered wagons drawn by mules or oxen.

Daily life on the trail was a battle against heat, dust, and mosquitoes. The day started at dawn and the first stop they took for a break was mid-morning. An attempt would be made to hunt game such as wild turkey. Kids and grown-ups would scurry to gather firewood or buffalo chips to light a cooking fire. A typical meal was meager portions of trail fare such as coffee, bread, bacon, beans, and maybe some dried fruit. Next it was time for wagon repairs, and then back on the road until nightfall.

The residents of New Mexico welcomed the traders who traveled to their area. After years of isolation, New Mexicans were hungry to exchange goods with the foreigners. The Santa Fe marketplace was a lively mix of settlers, Native Americans (especially Pueblo, Comanche, Ute, Navajo, and Apache), and traders and other travelers from the United States, including fur-trading mountain men from the East and North.

Traders from the United States brought wagons filled with goods that New Mexicans desired: bolts of cloth, medicine, clothes, hats, candlesticks, sewing needles, whale oil, knives, scissors, axes, and more. The traders returned to Missouri with gold and silver coins, furs, hides, and sheep's wool.

The Santa Fe Trail was seldom used after the Santa Fe Railroad was completed in 1880. Today, remnants of the trail have been preserved for visitors to see. In some places ruts from wagons are still visible.

The Californios

The first Spanish settlers in California were called Californios. They were mostly poor farmers and cattle ranchers who lived and worked in the towns and villages surrounding the missions. In 1833 the Mexican government dismantled the mission system and gave large land grants to a few favored families. These families set up huge cattle ranches, called ranchos (RAHN-chos), that were made up of several thousand acres. The owners of the ranchos were wealthy men called rancheros (rahn-CHEH-rohs).

The cattle that the Spanish had brought to the New World years before had multiplied and wandered all over the Southwest, and many of these cattle were rounded up and made property of the rancheros. Because of all the cattle, the crops that were grown, and the vast amount of land involved, the large ranches needed a very large labor force to keep them operating. The Native Americans who had worked at the missions did not leave when the mission system ended, but instead started a new life of servitude under the rancheros. The rancheros sold cattle hides and tallow (animal fat), which is used to make soap and candles, as well as fruit, wheat, and other crops they harvested. They traded these goods for products brought over the ocean by U.S. merchant ships.

A rancho usually had one big house for the owner's family, with housing attached for the servants and vaqueros. Several smaller buildings surrounded the large home, such as barns, houses for laborers, a granary, and stables. Ranchos were famous for their three-day fiestas, fandangos, and rodeos, where cowboys would show off their skills.

Vaqueros: The First Cowboys

The first cowboys were not U.S. citizens but mestizos and Native Americans who worked on cattle ranches in New Mexico, California, and Texas from the 16th to the 19th century. They were called vaqueros, which comes from the Spanish word *vaca* (cow). The term vaquero would later become, in the English language, buckaroo (buk-uh-ROO).

Texas Longhorns

Some of the cows that the vaqueros tended were long-horn cattle. The horns of the longhorn are typically five feet wide from tip to tip. An adult longhorn can weigh as much as 1,600 pounds! Longhorns are strong, and they can go for long periods without water, which made them ideal for long cattle drives in the Southwest.

Although about 10 million longhorns roamed the Southwest at the time of the Civil War (1861–1865), by the turn of the century they had become almost extinct. The invention of barbed wire fencing in the late 1800s allowed for controlled breeding, putting an end to the cattle's days on the open range. The meat of the long-horn is lean, but it tends to be tougher than that of some of the other cattle breeds. In search of both fat-tier, tastier meat and cows that would mature faster, owners crossbred the longhorn with Eastern cattle until there were few purebred longhorns left. The cattle most commonly found in the United States today are the Angus and Hereford breeds.

The Texas longhorns were saved from extinction in 1927 by the United States government when they were placed on a forest and game preserve in the Wichita Mountains of Oklahoma. In 1935 it was named the Wichita Mountains Wildlife Refuge and became part of the National Wildlife Refuge System. Today there are approximately 250,000 Texas longhorns. They have become a symbol of the Old West.

Vaqueros were daring, hardworking men who designed and developed the tools and techniques that American cowboys would use years later. They rode horses that they called *mesteños* (mes-TEH-nyos), which is where our word "mustang" comes from. During the mission era in California, the mission padres were among the first to employ vaqueros to run their cattle ranches. Cows that were on the mission grounds were used for their hides and fat. The meat of the cattle was eaten at the ranch but not exported because there was no way to refrigerate it.

The vaqueros were responsible for rounding up the cattle on the open ranges and for branding them with a special symbol to mark them as property. They were also responsible for busting broncos, which means to ride a wild horse until it stops bucking (knocking off) its rider. The vaqueros were skilled horsemen who taught the U.S. citizens who would become cowboys how to handle a horse with flair.

The vaquero wore clothing that was similar to the outfits American cowboys would eventually wear: a wide-brimmed sombrero (sohm-BREH-roh), or hat, to shield their eyes from the sun; a serape, which was used as clothing, as a blanket, and to steer cows in a roundup; *chaparreras* (chah-pahr-REH-ras), which in the United States are called chaps, to protect the legs; and bandanas around their necks so that they could shield their faces from flying dust. Vaqueros put their feet into leather foot covers called *tapaderas* (tah-pah-DEH-ras), a name that was eventually shortened to "taps," and they used rawhide ropes called reatas (reh-AH-tahs), which are now called lariats, to lasso the cows.

In the 1860s, after Texas had become part of the United States, the growing new country demanded meat in large quantities. Refrigerated rail cars made shipping meat to other parts of the country possible. Thousands of U.S. citizens, both white and black, rushed into the West to become cowboys. They learned everything about being a cowboy, from roping, steering, and horsemanship to dressing like a cowboy, from the men that started the profession—the Mexican vaqueros.

Throw a Lariat

No piece of equipment was more valuable to the vaquero than his lariat, or reata, which was a rawhide rope with a loop at one end. The loop was first thrown up in the air and then over a cow's neck, horns, or legs to capture it. As small boys, many Mexican vaqueros learned roping from throwing a reata around a fence post.

Vaqueros made their own reatas from rawhide, which is cowhide that has not been tanned. The cowboy soaked, dried, stretched, and oiled the rawhide until it was soft and pliable enough to use. Then he braided together strands of the rawhide to make a rope and fashioned a loop at one end. A typical reata was 60 feet long! The vaqueros were masters at rawhide braiding, and they made not only lariats, but also bridle reins, hobbles (used to keep the horse from running away), quirts (small whips), and more out of rawhide.

Try your hand at throwing your own lariat made of rope!

What You Need

Adult Supervision Required

30 feet ⅜-inch-thick manila rope (available at hardware stores)

Plenty of open space, such as a yard, a park, or a gymnasium, where there is no danger of accidentally hitting someone or something with the lariat

Object to rope, such as a fence post, a chair, a mailbox, or a stool (Warning: Never attempt to rope, or to put the lariat on, any part of a person or a live animal!)

What You Do

Make the lariat

1. First, tie a simple knot at each end of the rope.
2. Loosely tie the rope into a loop, as shown on the next page.
3. Push one end of the rope underneath the loop (see the arrow in the middle of the loop in the picture) and then over the top of the loop (see the arrow shown at the top).
4. Pull the knot tight, leaving a small loop.
5. Pull the other end of the rope (see arrow) inside the small loop. Continue to pull until the entire long piece of rope is pulled through the small loop. Tighten the knot.

6. Holding both ends of the rope and the knot, make a loop that is a few feet wide.

Try out your lariat
7. Stand a few feet away from the object you intend to rope. Hold both sides of the rope below the knot.
8. Throw the loop up and over the object, and then tighten it. It takes a few tries to get the hang of it!

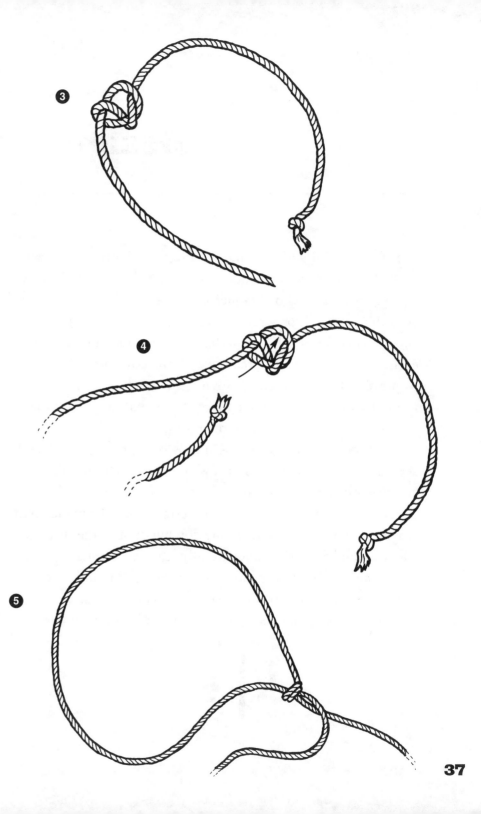

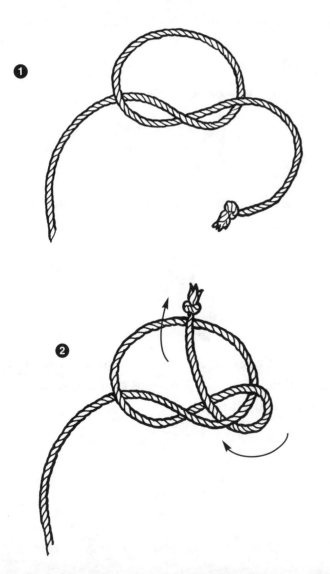

37

Design a Cattle Brand

Before barbed wire fencing was invented, North American cattle moved over the open range, mixing in with the cows of neighboring ranchos. Vaqueros marked the cattle of the ranchos they worked for with a special mark, called a "brand," to show ownership. Each rancho had its own unique brand, and each brand was officially recorded by the government in order to prevent disputes about the ownership of the cows. The brand was burned into the hide of the animal, usually in the hindquarters, with a hot branding iron.

A rancho's brand wasn't used only on its cattle. The brand served as a type of insignia or logo for the ranch. Brands were stamped on signs, fences, towels—even pie crusts!

A brand can be in any kind of design. It can be made up of letters, numbers, artwork, or any combination of the three. Mexican and Spanish brands usually featured artistic designs and symbols. One of the most famous Spanish brands is called the Holy Trinity (it's also known as the Three Christian Crosses), which belonged to the conquistador Hernán Cortés.

This is the brand of one of the biggest Mexican-owned ranchos, which was owned by Don Luis Terrazas. It is called the Terrazas brand.

Mission ranches also had brands. This is the brand for La Purisima Mission.

Most United States ranches past and present use letters, numbers, or pictures (or combinations of them) to create their brands. Here are just a few.

Stripes brand

Circle C brand

Flying T brand

Tumbling M brand

Lazy S brand

Rocking K brand

Diamond A brand

Horseshoe brand

A Down brand

Half Box B brand

Bar Y brand

Slash J brand

Here are some famous cattle brands:

Running W brand of the King Ranch, the largest ranch in the United States

Four Sixes brand of the Four Sixes Ranch (Legend has it that the ranch's owner, Samuel Burnett, won the money to buy the ranch in a poker game with a four-of-a-kind hand of four sixes!)

6666

Barbecue brand of the Campbell Cattle Company Ranch

Design your own brand by making either a Mexican- or Spanish-type design using symbols or art or by following the style used on most U.S. ranches—one that features letters, pictures, numbers, or a combination of those. When it's finished, you can use your brand to decorate all kinds of things—paper, bookmarks, giftwrap, book covers, and more!

What You Need
Paper
Pencil
Thick marker
5-inch-by-7-inch piece craft foam, any color
    (available at craft stores)
Scissors
Glue

What You Need (Cont.)

Foam tray used to package fruits and
    vegetables, washed and dried
Paintbrush
Acrylic paint

What You Do

1. Use the paper and pencil to experiment by drawing different designs or letters for your brand.
2. Once you have a design that you like, use the marker to draw it on the craft foam. Cut out the design. (Note: the pieces of the brand do not have to be connected.)
3. Glue the craft foam piece or pieces, front side down, onto the foam tray. (By gluing it front side down, the design will appear to be in reverse.) Let dry.
4. Using the paintbrush, paint the top of the brand.
5. Flip over the foam tray and press your design onto a sheet of paper. Let dry.

The Southwest Under Mexican Rule

One of the first changes that the new country of Mexico made after gaining independence from Spain was to abolish slavery. Even so, life for the Native Americans who worked at the missions and in the colonies did not change.

During the 300 years that it ruled the lands, Spain had kept outsiders from traveling to Spanish territories. In contrast, the new Mexican government welcomed foreigners, including those from the newly formed United States of America. The Mexicans wanted the Americans to help them "claim" the land of the southwest, especially Texas, so that other countries would not claim it. They needed the Americans just as the Spanish needed the mission Indians to claim their land.

Texas

Texas, or Tejas (TAY-hahs), as the Spanish called it, played a colorful and important role in Latino history in the United States. Since the late 1600s, when the Spanish claimed it as a province of New Spain, to the beginning of the 19th century, when it became part of a new state in Mexico, Coahuila y Tejas, this vast area of North American land, was a sparsely populated, dangerous place that attracted few settlers. The land was dotted with dense forests, and unpredictable Native American attacks occurred frequently. Although the first permanent mission there, San Francisco de los Tejas, was established in 1690, there were almost no other settlements in the vast area aside from the town of San Antonio and a few other missions.

Now that Texas was part of Mexico, the Mexican government came up with a plan to expand its own citizenship by actually encouraging U.S. settlers to move to Texas. They offered free land for farming or ranching, but in return the settlers had to become Mexican citizens and members of the Roman Catholic faith. They were also required to give up their slaves, as slavery was against the law in Mexico. Years before, a man from Connecticut named Moses Austin received permission from the Spanish government to be in charge of the Anglo American colonization of Texas. When he died, his son Stephen took over the job, but now it was under the Mexican government. Stephen built the town of San Felipe de Austin, which was later renamed Austin. Eventually Austin would become the capital of Texas.

Anglo American settlers, who called themselves Texians, soon outnumbered the Mexican settlers, who were called Tejanos (teh-HAH-nohs). They were drawn to the opportunities for farming cotton and corn, to the wild herds of cattle and horses, and to the Gulf of Mexico, which allowed for ships to travel to and from the land.

Anglo American settlers built ranches, farms, plantations, bridges, roads, and ferries. Although they were expected to speak Spanish and to join the Catholic religion, most settlers did neither, choosing to speak English and practice the faiths that they had been raised in. They also brought their slaves, which was against Mexican law. By 1836 there were 30,000 Anglo American settlers and their slaves in Texas, and only about 3,000 Tejanos.

Mexico began to realize, as Texas became more Anglo, that they would lose the area to the newcomers who had little interest in becoming Mexican. In 1830 they closed the border to new Anglo Americans settlers. They prohibited bringing in new slaves; placed duties (taxes) on any goods brought in from the United States, and built new forts to regain military control of the area.

Anglo Americans and Tejanos Join Forces

Anglo Americans and Tejanos formed a separate society from the rest of Mexico. They became increasingly unwilling to be controlled by the government of Mexico, which was 1,000 miles away and had little concern for their needs.

The large cotton farms owned by the Anglo Americans depended on the labor of slaves to succeed. They feared that Mexican laws prohibiting slavery would put an end to cotton farming. The Mexicans laws also provoked anger from the Tejanos who felt that they got little in return for the taxes they were forced to pay to the Mexican government.

When Antonio López de Santa Anna became the new president of Mexico, he declared in 1834 that the old Mexican constitution was no longer valid, and instead created his own constitution, which gave Texans even less rights. This was the final blow. Anglo American and Tejanos joined together to fight for Texas to become independent. War began on October 2, 1835, at the Battle of Gonzales, the first in a series of battles along the road to Texan independence.

Texans held a convention in the town of Washington, on the Brazos River, to put their goals of independence on paper for the world to see. On March 2, 1836, they listed their grievances against the Mexican government and declared their independence.

Battle of the Alamo

On February 23, 1836, the former mission of San Antonio de Valero became the site of the Battle of the Alamo. A small, ragtag group of about 184 Tejano and Texian settlers joined together for 13 days to fight somewhere between 2,000 and 6,000 soldiers (the exact amount of soldiers is unknown) of the Mexican army and claim Texas as their own. The president of Mexico, Antonio López de Santa Anna, led the troops to reclaim Texas for Mexico. The Mexican troops overpowered the small group of rebels, and all the Tejano and Texian soldiers were killed. Approximately 600 Mexican soldiers died as well.

Although the Texian and Tejano rebels lost that battle, the cry "Remember the Alamo!" became a rallying call in future American battles for liberty and freedom and in other heroic struggles against seemingly insurmountable odds.

The Tejanos and Texians may have been defeated at the Battle of the Alamo, but the war was not over. On April 21, 1836, more rebels, led by the newly named commander-in-chief of the Texas Army, former Tennessee governor Sam Houston, fought against the Mexican army at the San Jacinto River. The battle would become known as the Battle of San Jacinto. This time 850 rebels took the 1,250-man Mexican army by surprise and won the battle. The president of Mexico, Antonio López de Santa Anna, became Sam Houston's prisoner and was forced to sign a document called the Treaty of Velasco on May 14, 1836, which gave Texas full independence.

Free from Mexican rule, Texas was renamed the Republic of Texas and became known as the "Lone Star Republic." It was officially recognized as an independent country by the United States. Although Mexico did not try to reclaim Texas, it never acknowledged the republic's independence.

Texas Joins the United States

Texans wanted to become part of the United States in 1836, but were refused several times over a 10-year period. The United States was conflicted about adding another slave state to the union when more and more people wanted to end slavery. There were also concerns that accepting Texas as part of the United States would start a war with Mexico. Regardless, in 1845 the United States annexed Texas under President James Polk, who was in favor of it. Annexing meant that Texas had to pay all the debts (bills) that it had during its years as an independent republic. In 1845 Texas was proud to become the 28th state of the United States.

Manifest Destiny

Many early 19th-century Anglo Americans believed that it was their "manifest destiny" (a future event that is thought to be inevitable or already decided upon by God) to take over all the lands between the Atlantic and the Pacific Oceans, from Massachusetts to California. What they did not take into account was the fact that the Mexican descendents of the Spanish settlers, Native Americans, and Africans had been living, raising families, and farming in the West for more than 300 years. They had their own culture, language, and traditions that were just as valued to them as American culture was to Americans. Mexicans clearly had nothing to gain but everything to lose if the Americans followed their pursuit of "Manifest Destiny."

The Mexican-American War

From 1846 to 1848, the United States and Mexico were at war. Mexico had never recognized Texas as an independent country in the nine years since it declared itself free from Mexico, so it saw the United States' annexation (taking it as part of its own land) of Texas as being illegal. Mexico reacted to the annexation by breaking off diplomatic relations with the United States, and war soon followed.

In 1847, however, Mexico surrendered the war when the United States took over Mexico City. In 1848 the United States and Mexico signed the Treaty of Guadalupe Hidalgo. This allowed the United States to take over more than 500,000 square miles of territory that included what are now California, Utah, Nevada, and parts of New Mexico, Colorado, Arizona, and Wyoming. Five years later, in 1853, the Mexican government would sell 30,000 additional square miles of what are now New Mexico and Arizona to the United States. This was called the Gadsden Purchase.

Thanks to the Treaty of Guadalupe Hidalgo and the Gadsden Purchase, the United States grew in both size and strength. But this growth would prove very costly to the thousands of Mexicans who owned homes and land on what had suddenly become U.S. soil.

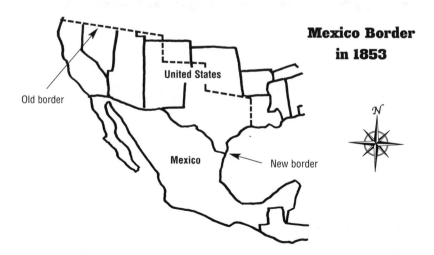

Mexico Border in 1853

United States

Old border

Mexico

New border

N

From Sea to Shining Sea—in Spanish!

Here are Spanish words that are related to horsemanship.

Rodeo: The word comes from the Spanish word *rodear* (roh-deh-AHR), which means "to surround." Now the word *rodeo* refers to an event at which horsemanship is displayed.

Corral: The word means "pen" (as in a place to hold livestock) in Spanish.

Stampede: This word comes from the Spanish word *estampida* (ehs-stam-PEE-dah), which means "uproar"; it's used to describe the mad rush of animals running together.

Mustang: This refers to the horses that were brought to the Americas by the Spanish. It comes from the Spanish word *mesteño*.

Lasso: A lasso is the loop at the end of the rope that is used to pull in an animal. It comes from the Spanish word *enlazar* (ehn-LAH-sahr), which means "to tie."

◇ 4 ◇
Mexican Americans

"We Never Crossed a Border; the Border Crossed Us!"

With the signing of the Treaty of Guadalupe Hidalgo in 1848, vast stretches of what had been Mexico suddenly became U.S. soil. Overnight, about 80,000 Mexican citizens who lived on these lands found themselves, their homes, and their property in a foreign country. The U.S. government gave them a choice: give up their land and homes and go to Mexico or stay and become U.S. citizens. Although some did go back to Mexico, most chose to stay and become citizens of the United States. They had been promised that, as U.S. citizens, they would have the same rights as Anglo Americans. But that promise was not kept. Mexican Americans were often denied many rights—including the right to keep the land and homes they had owned for many years.

Many Anglo Americans saw an opportunity to take land away from the Mexican Americans. They moved onto the Mexican Americans' property and became squatters (people who build homes and live on other people's land). Frequently the squatters then claimed the land as their own, and the Mexican Americans were forced to go to court in an effort to keep their own land. To prove ownership, they had to provide the U.S. government deeds and maps that showed well-defined property boundaries—but they had become owners of their property when it was still part of Mexico, a country in which land was usually passed down through families, from one generation to the next, with no formal papers that documented ownership. The U.S. courts ruled that, without formal proof of ownership, the Mexican Americans had no rights to their land. Even those that did have proof that they owned their property almost always ended up losing their land in U.S. courts.

Mexican Immigration

Now, for the first time in history people coming from Mexico to live in the Southwest of the United States were considered immigrants (people who have left their home country to live in another country). Mexicans moved to the United States to work as farmhands, miners, and vaqueros and to be cannery, construction, and railroad workers.

In January 1848, one month before the Treaty of Guadalupe Hidalgo was signed, an enormous vein of gold was discovered at Sutter's Mill near the Sacramento River in northern California. News of this incredible discovery spread quickly. By 1849 people from all over the world made their way to California to seek their fortunes mining for gold. This was the California Gold Rush, and the miners became known as '49ers. The discovery of gold, and the mad rush of miners to California, led to the development of the American West. In Mexico, silver, gold, and copper mining had been an industry for hundreds of years. Because many Mexicans were expert miners, you would think that they would have been successful during the gold rush. Unfortunately, just the opposite was true. Although they shared their knowledge of mining with the Anglo Americans and others who came to California, Mexicans and Mexican Americans were routinely robbed of their gold (as were Asians and other non-Anglos) and their claims (areas that miners claimed as their own and in which they dug for gold), and suffered violence at the hands of the Anglo miners. Many were chased off the land or forced to work the more difficult mines.

In 1850 a discriminatory tax called the Foreign Miners Tax was enacted to discourage mining by not only the Mexican miners, but also the Chinese, Central and South American, and European miners who had come to California to search for gold. The tax required any miner who was not a U.S. citizen to pay $20 per month (the equivalent of more than $400 per month today) in taxes—an enormous amount of money at that time. Almost no one could pay the tax and, facing resistance from foreign miners as well as from merchants, who lost a great deal of business because of the tax, the Foreign Miners Tax was repealed (done away with) in 1851.

Despite the prejudice and injustices they faced there, many Mexicans continued to seek jobs as laborers in the United States for many years. In the 1880s Mexicans found work on the railroads. The Southern Pacific and Santa Fe lines hired thousands of Mexicans to lay and maintain railroad track. Mexican railroad workers accounted for a large percentage of U.S. laborers through the first half of the 20th century as well.

In 1910 Mexico experienced what would become a 20-year battle as different groups fought for control of the Mexican government. This battle became known as the Mexican Revolution. It was a period of great turmoil in Mexico, and more than 700,000 Mexicans immigrated to the United States to escape the chaos, poverty, famine, lawlessness, and unemployment that were the result of the conflict.

Fortunately, the United States needed workers. By 1917 many U.S. men were being called to Europe to fight in World War I (an international war involving several countries), and many others left their jobs as laborers to make arms and ammunition for the war effort. These workers left job openings on railroads, ranches, factories, and farms.

Corridos: Mexican Ballads

Mexican immigrants often faced resentment from Americans who believed that the newcomers were "taking jobs away from Americans." Rumors spread that they were untrustworthy, even dangerous. These resentments often boiled over into confrontations between Anglos and Mexicans. Mexicans were called derogatory (insulting) names, such as "greasers" (referring to their dark hair) or "wetbacks" (referring to the fact that some immigrants crossed the Rio Grande to get to the United States), and some were even attacked by gangs. Mexican immigrants soon learned that they had to be cautious of situations where violence could break out.

To help protect themselves, Mexican immigrants developed a novel way to "secretly" pass along information to each other through *corridos* (kohr-REE-dohs), which are folk songs or ballads. *Corridos* were very popular around the turn of 20th century in the border towns between Mexico and the United States. The ballads told about the ordinary man overcoming adversity, problems in love relationships, horsemanship,

heroes and villains, gunfighters, and more. A *corrido* might tell an immigrant about a recent incident or warn of possible danger ahead. Here is an example of a *corrido*, which was inspired by a real event. On June 12, 1901, Gregorio Cortez Lira, a Mexican immigrant working as a ranch hand in Karnes County, Texas, and his brother Romaldo were accused of being horse thieves. The sheriffs and deputies interrogated Gregorio with the help of a deputy who translated the officers' questions and Gregorio's responses. But the deputy did not correctly translate Gregorio's answers. Because of the miscommunication, the sheriff believed not only that Gregorio and his brother were guilty, but also that they were threatening the officers. The sheriff shot and wounded Romaldo and tried to shoot Gregorio. In response, Gregorio shot and killed the sheriff and ran. Hundreds of Texan state police officers on horseback, known as the "Texas Rangers," joined the chase for Gregorio, who was eventually captured on June 21, 1901.

"El Corrido de Gregorio Cortez"

Translated by Américo Paredes

In the county of El Carmen
A great misfortune befell;
The Major Sheriff is dead;
Who killed him no one can tell.

At two in the afternoon,
In half an hour or less,
They knew that the man who
    killed him
Had been Gregorio Cortez.

They let loose the bloodhound
    dogs;
They followed him from afar.
But trying to catch Cortez
Was like following a star.

All the rangers of the county
Were flying, they rode so hard;
What they wanted was to get
The thousand-dollar reward.

And in the county of Kiansis
They cornered him after all;
Though they were more than three
    hundred
He leaped out of their corral.

Then the Major Sheriff said,
As if he was going to cry,
"Cortez, hand over your weapons;
We want to take you alive."

Then said Gregorio Cortez,
And his voice was like a bell,
"You will never get my weapons
Till you put me in a cell."

Then said Gregorio Cortez
With his pistol in his hand,
"Ah, so many mounted Rangers
Just to take one Mexican!"

From: *With His Pistol in His Hand: A Border Ballad and Its Hero* By Américo Paredes. Copyright © 1958, renewed 1986. By permission of the University of Texas Press.

Compose a *Corrido*: A Mexican Ballad

Corridos are still written and performed today, and although they now include modern issues such as drug trafficking and illegal border crossings, they still feature the traditional themes of courage, of rooting for the underdog, and of true love.

What You Need

Internet access or book of *corridos* (available
    at some bookstores and libraries)
Pencil
Paper
Colored markers
Poster board

What You Do

1. Listen to a few *corridos* over the Internet or read a few from a book to get the "feel" of the ballads. (You can listen to *corridos* over the Internet at the Smithsonian Institution's Web site Corridos sin Fronteras ["Ballads without Borders"]: www.corridos.org.)

2. Using the pencil and paper, write your own *corrido* about a person you admire. It can be about someone in your family, a friend, a teacher—even someone in history that you have never met. Write about a narrow portion of your chosen person's life that tells the listener a lot about who that person is. For example, if you wrote a *corrido* about Father Miguel Hidalgo y Costilla, you might write about the day he proclaimed El Grito de Dolores (the Cry of Dolores), calling for Mexicans to rebel from Spain.

Follow these guidelines to write your *corrido*:

- The *corrido* typically has 4-line stanzas, (a block of lines separated by a space, similar to a poem) with 8 syllables on each line.
- It usually has 36 lines (but it can have more or fewer).
- Typically it has no chorus, or repeated lines.
- It tells a story.
- It can include details about where the story takes place and the year.
- Often the first line tells the reason for the *corrido*.

- In most *corridos*, the last stanza or line is a farewell to the person or people it is written about.

3. When you are satisfied with your *corrido*, use the markers to copy it onto the poster board to create a broadside. A broadside is a large written piece that is meant to be sold, posted, or passed around in public. It can be illustrated, but the important part of a broadside is its clear, bold lettering. Before TV, radio, and the Internet, the broadside was a popular tool for spreading information and entertainment.
4. Display your *corrido* broadside for your friends, classmates, or family.
5. Try your hand at creating a tune for your *corrido* and singing it!

During the 1920s Mexicans and Mexican Americans began to move further north into the Midwestern states to fill jobs in the growing automobile, steel, tire, and meatpacking industries of Michigan, Ohio, Illinois, and Indiana.

In 1929, the United States experienced a severe economic collapse that resulted in many people losing their jobs, homes, and ways of life. Businesses and banks closed, citizens lost their life savings, and there was widespread unemployment. This was the Great Depression, and it lasted until the early 1940s. It affected all Americans, but Mexicans were particularly singled out. Employment was very difficult to find, and Americans feared that Mexicans would take the few jobs that were left. Because of this, thousands of Mexicans were deported, or sent back to Mexico. Some left voluntarily, but most were forced to leave by both their local governments and the federal government.

The Second Great Wave of Immigration

After the United States entered World War II (1941–1945), the country again needed foreign workers to do the work that U.S. citizens, who were now fighting in the war, had performed. And, once again, Mexicans entered the United States in large numbers to fill now-vacant positions in factories, farms, and ranches, as well as in manufacturing industries that supported the war effort. The United States government established a program in which Mexicans were invited to come pick the crops that were ripening in U.S. fields and needed to be harvested. This was called the Bracero (brah-SAY-roh) program, and it lasted from 1942 to 1964. The workers were supposed to stay in the United States temporarily until the work was done, but many Mexicans stayed permanently.

The Zoot Suit Riots

Like all teenagers, Mexican American teenagers in 1942 enjoyed dressing in the newest, most outrageous styles. One popular item of men's clothing was called the zoot suit. Considered fashionable attire for a night on the town, the zoot suit featured extremely wide pants and a long, oversized jacket, and it was very popular among young Mexican American men. In 1943 Los Angeles experienced a crime wave, and the police told the newspapers that the people responsible for the crimes were "Mexican American gang members wearing zoot suits."

On June 3, 1943, eleven white U.S. sailors, who were stationed at the Port of Los Angeles, got into a fight in a Mexican barrio (BAR-ee-oh), or neighborhood, in East Los Angeles. The following night more than 200 sailors went into the barrio and savagely beat *any* Mexican teen wearing a zoot suit. The riots went on for four days, with more and more American servicemen swarming the barrio. The violence spilled over to African Americans, Filipinos, and others. The police were unable to maintain order. Of those they arrested, only the non-Anglos were sent to jail. Finally the military intervened and forbade U.S. servicemen from entering the barrio.

Mexican American Soldiers in World War II

About 300,000 Mexican Americans proudly served their country, the United States, in all branches of the military during World War II. Thirteen Mexican Americans were each awarded the Congressional Medal of Honor, the country's highest award for bravery and valor in battle, for their heroic service.

After World War II ended and the servicemen returned home to resume their lives, the U.S. government decided that the country no longer needed as many foreign workers as it had during the war. Despite this, there was a constant stream of Mexicans crossing the border to work. To minimize the number of new immigrants coming to the United States, Congress passed into law the Immigration and Nationality Act of 1952. The law put strict limits on the number of immigrants that were allowed into the United States from Mexico and other countries. The government began an aggressive program to deport Mexicans who were in the United States illegally. It

was called "Operation Wetback" because many of the immigrants crossed the Rio Grande (getting their clothes wet) to enter the United States. During the 1950s nearly four million Mexican citizens were sent back to Mexico.

Migrant Farmworkers

Mexican farmworkers first started immigrating to America in the 1850s, when California farms needed help in the fields and many parts of the West needed vaqueros for cattle ranches. Migrant farmworkers earn money by traveling from farm to farm planting, weeding, and harvesting crops. Today Mexicans still come to the United States to work farms all over the country. They are traditionally among the lowest-paid workers in the United States.

Migrant farmworkers spend hours and hours each day picking crops of fruits, vegetables, cotton, and tobacco, packing the produce or goods in boxes, preparing fields for future planting, thinning crops, and more. Workers must stand on tall ladders or stoop and bend for hours in hot fields. They are often exposed to pesticides (chemicals that are used to kill bugs and that can be very harmful to humans), and frequently they are forced to use dirty and broken-down bathroom facilities and to work throughout the day with no clean water to drink. Few receive benefits such as health care or unemployment benefits. Over the years, migrant families have had no choice but to make do with whatever meager shelter was provided or available, from converted school buses to run-down shacks.

In the 1960s a Mexican American man named Cesar Chavez, whose own family had been migrant farmworkers, was concerned that migrant workers were being taken advantage of. He saw that they received low wages and had substandard housing; that sometimes they were forced to make their young children work as laborers in order to keep the families from poverty; that they did not receive good health care; and that migrant family children did not receive a formal education because the family had to relocate frequently to be able to pick the crops that ripened at different times, and in different places, throughout the year.

Chavez formed a labor union, which today is called the United Farm Workers of America. The union fought the farm owners tirelessly over the years to win rights for migrant workers through strikes, during which the workers refused to labor in the fields until good working conditions were agreed upon. They also organized marches and boycotts, in which they urged the public to stop purchasing certain crops, such as grapes or lettuce, until a fair working agreement between the growers and the migrant workers was established. Using only nonviolent tactics, Chavez and the United Farm Workers of America succeeded in helping to improve the lives of migrant farmworkers everywhere throughout the United States. Because of labor activists such as Chavez, there are now many more laws to protect migrant farmworkers. But problems still persist. Many migrant workers do not have the required permission and documentation to be in the United States at all, and they are often afraid to report problems or violations of laws for fear of losing work or of being deported. Agricultural labor continues to be one of the most dangerous types of work, for people of all ages, in the United States.

Play Games from the Fields

The children of migrant farmworkers (who were often farm-workers themselves) moved frequently and had few, if any, toys. Like children everywhere, though, they managed to have fun by playing games that required no equipment. One woman who grew up as a migrant child, Elva Treviño Hart, wrote about what her life was like and about the games she and the other migrant children played in the field, in her book, *Broken Heart: Stories of a Migrant Child.*

Play La Vieja Inez: Buyer of Colored Ribbons

What You Need
Several players
A large area to run in, such as a park or a gymnasium

What You Do
1. Select a "base," such as a tree or some steps, to run to.
2. Choose one person to play La Vieja Inez (lah vee-EH-ha ee-NEZ) which means "the old woman

Agnes." Choose another person to play the mother. The rest of the people play the mother's children.
3. All of the children stand close to the mother. La Vieja Inez stands far enough away so that the mother can whisper to the children without being overheard. The mother whispers the name of a different color to each of the children.
4. Once each of the children is given a color, La Vieja Inez comes over to the group, and the following dialogue takes place:

La Vieja Inez: "Knock, knock."

Mother: "Who is it?"

La Vieja Inez: "La Vieja Inez."

Mother: "What do you want?"

La Vieja Inez: "I want a [choose a color, such as blue or orange] ribbon."

5. The child whose color is called then races La Vieja Inez to get to the base. If the child gets to the base first, he or she is allowed to return to Mother and is given the name of a

new color. If La Vieja Inez reaches the base first, the child becomes her prisoner. After all the children have become prisoners, La Vieja Inez must catch the mother. Then the players change roles and play again.

Join in the Game of Ring

What You Need

Two or more players
Dirt or sand field (or hard surface such as a
  paved playground or driveway)
Rock or stick (chalk if using a hard surface)

What You Do

1. Select a "base," such as a tree, house, or school, to run around. Separate into 2 teams.
2. Using the rock or stick, draw a circle in the dirt or sand that is big enough for half of the players to stand in. (Use chalk for a hard surface.)

3. Half of the players stand inside the circle. The other half stand in various places outside the circle. The object of the game is for players to run out of the circle, go around a designated place (such as a house, school, or tree), and run back inside the circle without being touched by one of the players who is outside the ring.
4. If a player is tagged by an "outside the ring" kid, he or she must freeze in position. A player who has been frozen may become unfrozen only if a member of his or her team comes out of the ring and touches him or her. Once a player is unfrozen, he or she may return to the ring to try again.
5. The game continues until there is no one left to unfreeze people. Then the "outside the ring" kids switch places with the "inside the ring" kids and repeat the game.

Lowriders

Lowriders—cars that have low-riding bodies—have been a favorite of some Mexican American men and boys for generations. The custom of owning, driving, and modifying lowriders started in the urban barrios as an expression of pride and cultural identity. Today there are lowrider clubs, competitions—even museum exhibitions! Fellow lowriders often get together to share skills in areas such as mechanics, painting, upholstery fitting, and more.

The popular phrase "low and slow" describes the way in which these cars and trucks travel. In the 1940s, when the lowrider tradition began, people put bags of sand in the trunks of cars to weigh them down and make them ride low to the ground. These days, lowriders are created by mechanically altering the suspension systems of vehicles. Some lowriders even feature special hydraulic systems that allow the car to be raised or lowered at the push of a button.

Lowriders are frequently decorated with chrome, gold, and painted designs. Many have plush interiors and powerful stereo systems, and some are even outfitted with equipment that can produce a light show from inside the car or truck. Other lowrider features include "scrape plates," which drag along the ground and give off sparks when the vehicle is moving, and special exhaust systems that allow flames to shoot out!

Drivers sometimes form caravans to show off their amazing cars by cruising together, in a colorful procession, through the streets of their communities. Lowriders are considered an art form, and they are a great source of pride to their owners.

Life in the Barrio

As more and more Mexican Americans settled in United States cities, they began to congregate (come together) to live in neighborhoods of their own. The first Mexican American neighborhoods, which were called *colonias* (coh-LOH-nee-ahs), consisted of temporary dwellings for migrant workers. These dwellings were fashioned from abandoned boxcars or shacks. The *colonias* sprang up next to places where Mexicans worked, such as farms, mines, and railroads.

Mexican Americans who set down roots in a particular spot often lived in barrios, neighborhoods that had permanent housing and that were set off from other parts of a city where Anglos lived. Many times Mexicans were forced to live in the barrios because of discrimination in Anglo neighborhoods. Barrios were often in parts of the cities that were not well maintained. The rents were cheaper there than in other sections of town and, as a result, the landlords often allowed the buildings to fall into disrepair. Good plumbing, heating, water, and electricity were not always available in the barrios.

There were some good things about the barrios, though. In most barrios, residents had a sense of living in a Mexican village. Neighbors watched out for each other and helped each other out. They tended to the sick and took up collections to pay for funerals and to help neighbors who were out of work. This spirit of community eventually became formalized in organizations called *mutualistas* (moo-twa-LEES-tuhs), or mutual aid societies. The *mutualistas* offered their communities services such as monetary loans and help in finding employment. They also sponsored dances and fiestas for the barrio.

People in the barrio usually lived with an extended family of parents, grandparents, cousins, aunts, and uncles. In addition, they usually had a close, lifelong relationship with their godparents, who probably also lived in the barrio. Instead of seeing an Anglo doctor, many barrio residents sought help from the neighborhood *curandero* (koo-ran-DEH-roh), or folk healer. Religion was very much a part of barrio life, and most residents prayed to their patron saints for assistance in daily life.

If you walk through a barrio today you can hear people speaking Spanish, peek into small shops called botanicas (boh-TAH-nee-kahs), which sell herbs and religious items, and smell fresh tortillas being made in stores called *tortillerias* (tor-tee-ah-REE-ahs). You can buy Mexican food items that might not be available in other neighborhoods. Take a stroll through a *carniceria* (cahr-nee-ceh-REE-ah), or meat market, and you might find any of the following: *cabeza de res* (cah-BAY-sah deh rehs), or a whole cow's head; tripe (the lining of a cow's stomach); chorizo (cho-REE-zoh), a seasoned sausage; and pig's feet! Mexican American grocery stores in the barrios (and elsewhere) sell ingredients such as plantains, masa harina, jalapeños (hah-lah-PEHN-yos), and yucca roots. Grocery stores also offer the service of wiring money home to Mexico, and other countries.

In the barrios you can listen to Latino music, see unusual cars called lowriders, play dominoes outdoors, and read Spanish-language newspapers. Signs are written in both Spanish and English, colorful murals cover outside walls, and holidays such as Mexican Independence Day, Cinco de Mayo (SIN-coh day MY-oh) and the Feast of the Virgin Guadalupe are celebrated.

Thanks, in part, to their proximity (closeness) to their homeland, Mexican Americans have been able to retain many aspects of their Mexican culture—from their native language, foods, and music to celebrations and customs—in their new country.

Mexican American Murals and the Chicano Movement

Like African Americans, Mexican Americans frequently faced prejudice, violence, and injustice in this country. During the 1960s, after years of mistreatment and discrimination, Mexican Americans fought for their civil rights in a struggle that would become known as the "Chicano movement." The movement, which occurred from the 1960s to the 1980s, resulted in a number of achievements for Mexican Americans, and it was instrumental in making non-Latino citizens aware of the hardships faced by Spanish-speaking children in English-speaking schools. Thanks to the Chicano movement, the United States established the Bilingual Education Act of 1968, which funded programs that allowed schools across the country to teach Spanish-speaking children in their native language. Today Mexican Americans are still often referred to as Chicanos (chee-CAH-nohs).

Music, art, and theater played important roles in the Chicano movement. In the 1930s, more than 30 years before the Chicano movement began, a Mexican artist named Diego Rivera had created huge, magnificent, colorful murals in Mexico and in the United States. Rivera's murals portrayed the dignity and beauty of Mexicans' heritage.

During the Chicano movement, artists were encouraged to decorate city walls with new murals that reflected the style of Diego Rivera's works of art. These new murals not only provided beauty; they also served to remind citizens that the United States was made up of many diverse cultures and peoples.

One of the largest murals ever created is in Los Angeles. It is called *The Great Wall of Los Angeles* and stretches a half mile long! Judith Baca, a Mexican American painter, and 400 teenagers from the area painted the mural over the course of seven summers in the 1970s. It shows the history of California, and it emphasizes the roles Native Americans and minorities played in shaping that history.

Diego Rivera's *Open Air School*, from the murals at the Ministry of Public Education in Mexico City.

Play *Loteria*: Mexican Bingo

If you know how to play bingo, you can play *loteria* (loh-teh-REE-ah)! This is a traditional Mexican game that is popular in the United States as well as in Mexico. In *loteria*, a deck of 54 cards—each with a unique illustration—is used instead of the numbered balls that are used in bingo. Players each play at least one tablet that contains a grid of 16 of those illustrations. As a card is drawn by the *loteria* caller, everyone who has the corresponding illustration on his or her tablet marks that spot with a pinto bean or other marker. The first player to cover an entire straight or diagonal line of illustrations wins!

In this activity we will make the pieces of a *loteria* game using just 16 of the 54 illustrations.

What You Need

Access to a photocopy machine
This book
13 sheets paper to use in photocopy machine
Scissors
Glue stick
16 blank index cards
Crayons, colored pencils, or markers to color
   pictures (optional)

6 clear plastic page-holder sleeves to protect
   game boards (optional)
3 to 7 people
Bag of dried pinto beans

What You Do

Make the Game Pieces

1. On page 61 is a drawing of a blank game board. Make 6 copies of that page.
2. On page 62 is a grid of 16 *loteria* illustrations. Make 7 copies of that page.

Here are the Spanish and English names of the pictures that appear on the grid.

 El Gallo (ell GAH-yo): the Rooster

 El Diablito (ell dee-ah-BLEE-toh):
the Little Devil

 La Dama (lah DAH-mah):
the Lady

El Catrin (ell cah-TREEN): the Dandy (a man who wears fancy clothes)

 El Paraguas (ell pah-RAH-gwas): the Umbrella

 La Sirena (lah see-REH-nah): the Mermaid

 La Escalera (lah ehs-kah-LEH-rah): the Ladder

 La Botella (lah boh-TEH-yah): the Bottle

 El Barril (ell bah-REEL): the Barrel

 El Arbol (ell AHR-bol): the Tree

 El Melon (ell may-LOHN): the Melon

El Valiente (ell vah-lee-EHN-tay): the Brave One

 El Gorrito (ell gohr-REE-toh): the Bonnet (a lady's cap that ties under the chin)

 La Muerte (lah MWER-teh): the Death (represented by a skeleton)

 La Pera (la PAY-rah): the Pear

 La Bandera (lah bahn-DER-ah): the Flag (represented by the green, white, and red Mexican Flag; in the center of the flag is the image of an eagle sitting on a cactus and holding a snake in its mouth)

3. Use the scissors to cut out each of the 16 squares of pictures from one of the photocopies. Use the glue stick to glue each picture to a square on a photocopy of the blank game board. (Don't arrange the pictures in order; mix them up on the game board.)

4. Repeat with another photocopy of illustrations and another photocopy of a blank game board (making sure that the various pictures are placed in different locations on each game board) 5 times, until you have 6 completed game boards.

5. Cut the last photocopy of loteria pictures into 16 squares. Glue each square onto an index card, so that you have a "deck" of 16 cards, each with an illustration on it.

6. If you want to, you can use crayons, colored pencils, or markers to color each illustration in your deck of cards and on the game boards. You can also slip each game board into a page-holder sleeve to protect it.

Play the Game

1. Gather 3 to 7 people; 1 to be the "caller" and the rest to play the game.

2. Pass out one loteria game board to each player.

3. Pass out a handful of pinto beans to each player.

4. The caller shuffles the index cards and draws the top card to "call." Instead of just calling out the name of the picture, though, he or she makes up a question about the object that is easy to answer, and the players guess which object the caller is talking about. For example, the caller might say, "This animal wakes you up when you want to sleep." The players would yell out, "El Gallo" ("the Rooster"). Then they would each put a pinto bean over the picture of El Gallo on their game board.

5. The first player to cover a whole vertical, horizontal, or diagonal line of 4 pictures yells, "Loteria!" and is the winner.

El Gallo

El Diablo

La Dama

El Catrin

El Paraguas

La Sirena

La Escalera

La Botella

El Barril

El Arbol

El Melon

El Valiente

El Gorrito

La Muerte

La Pera

La Bandera

Holidays and Celebrations

Celebrating special occasions for Mexican Americans is a mix of the old and the new. Thanksgiving is celebrated with a turkey like most Americans, but there might also be tamales on the table. Other celebrations like Day of the Dead are uniquely Mexican or Latino, but at the center of every holiday is family.

Easter Sunday (Domingo de Pascua) and Holy Week (Semana Santa)

Easter in Mexico is the most important religious holiday of the year. During Holy Week, which are the days that lead up to Easter Sunday, there are processions and re-enactments (plays) of Christ's final days. Here are some Mexican Easter traditions that have continued in the United States.

Prepare *Capirotada*: Mexican Bread Pudding

Capirotada (CAH-pee-roh-tah-dah) is a comforting Mexican bread pudding. In many Mexican households, it's tradition to enjoy this dessert during Lent (the 40 days before Easter Sunday). Every family has its own "special" recipe that uses slightly different ingredients. Here is one delicious version.

6 servings

What You Need

Adult Supervision Required
1 tablespoon butter
Paper towel
1½ quart baking dish
Knife
Cutting board
½ cup cubed very dry bread (any type)
½ cup peeled, diced apple
½ cup dark raisins

½ cup shredded Monterey Jack cheese
Fork
Large bowl
2 eggs
1 cup milk
½ cup packed dark brown sugar
½ teaspoon ground cinnamon

What You Do

1. Preheat the oven to 350° F.
2. Place the butter on the paper towel and grease the inside of the baking dish.
3. Place the bread, apple, raisins, and cheese in the baking dish. Using the fork, stir until mixed.
4. Crack the eggs into the large bowl. Using the fork, lightly beat them.
5. Add the milk, sugar, and cinnamon to the eggs. Using the fork, stir to mix well.
6. Pour egg mixture over bread mixture.
7. Bake, uncovered, for 45 minutes. Serve warm.

Make *Cascarones*: Confetti-Filled Eggshells

Like many U.S. citizens, Mexican American families celebrate Easter by attending church, having a special holiday meal, and enjoying an Easter egg hunt.

Mexican Americans also enjoy making (and breaking!) special Easter eggs called *cascarones* (kahs-kuh-ROH-nays). A *cascarone* is created by making a small hole in a raw egg, and draining out the egg yolk and white. The empty shell is then dyed a bright color and filled with confetti, and the small hole is sealed. On Easter Day, kids run after each other and break the *cascarones* over each other's heads! The shells break easily, and the activity makes for a fun, colorful mess—one that is best done outside.

What You Need
Pushpin
6 or more raw eggs (white eggs take color best, but
   brown eggs may be used instead)
Bowl
Paper towels
6 tablespoons white vinegar
3 large coffee mugs
1½ cups hot water

3 different colors food coloring (an Easter egg
   coloring kit may be used instead)
3 spoons
Tongs
Empty egg carton
Scissors
3 sheets of paper (various colors) to cut up for confetti
Index card or sturdy piece of paper
1 sheet tissue paper
Glue

What You Do
1. Gently use the point of the pushpin to create a hole on the "fat end" of the egg. Chip away at it, until it is about the size of a dime. Don't worry if the hole ends up crooked or jagged; it will still work.
2. Hold the egg over the bowl and gently shake it, letting its egg yolk and white drain out. (An adult can use the egg yolks and whites to make scrambled eggs.)
3. Gently wash out the inside of the shell by holding it under a slowly dripping faucet until it is about half full of water.

Swirl the water around inside the shell, then gently shake the shell to drain the water. Gently wash the outside of the shell, then place it on a paper towel and let it dry for a few minutes.

4. Repeat with the remaining 5 eggs.

5. Pour 2 tablespoons vinegar into each coffee mug.

6. Pour ½ cup hot water into each mug.

7. Add drops of food coloring to each mug (a different color for each mug) until you see vivid color (about 15 drops per mug). Be careful not to spill the food coloring on your clothes.

8. Place 1 eggshell on a spoon and slowly lower the spoon into one of the mugs. Repeat with 2 other eggshells, using a clean spoon each time, until each mug has an eggshell in it. Using that mug's spoon, gently push the eggshells around in the mixture so that the eggshells are colored evenly. Let each eggshell soak in the mixture about 5 minutes, or until they are the color you want. (If necessary, add more drops of food coloring.)

9. Using tongs, gently remove the eggshells from the cups. Tip each eggshell, hole down, over its cup to let the dye run out of the eggshell. Gently place each dyed eggshell, hole down, in the empty egg carton. Let dry.

10. Repeat with the remaining eggshells.

11. While the eggshells are drying, cut the colored paper into tiny pieces to make confetti.

12. When the eggshells are completely dry, gently pour the confetti into each one until it is almost full (leave a bit of space at the top). If desired, use an index card or a sturdy piece of paper to help guide the confetti into the small hole in the eggshell.

13. Cut or rip off a small piece of tissue paper and glue it over the hole. Repeat with the remaining filled eggshells.

14. Place the eggshells, tissue-end up, in the egg carton to dry. The *cascarones* may be stored in the egg carton at room temperature for several days.

15. Have a *cascarone* party outdoors. It's tradition for kids to chase each other and break (gently!) the *cascarones* on each other's heads. You can also use them to have an egg toss.

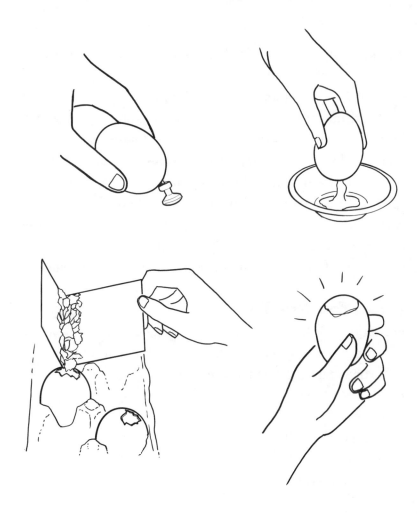

Feast of the Virgin of Guadalupe (La Fiesta de Nuestra Señora de Guadalupe)

The Virgin of Guadalupe, or the Virgin Mary (the mother of Jesus Christ), is the patron saint of Mexico. In 1531 an Aztec convert to Catholicism named Juan Diego claimed he saw a vision of the Virgin Mary, who the Mexicans call "Our Lady of Guadalupe," as he was walking to mass (Catholic church service). She told Diego to go to the Spanish bishop and ask that a church be built where she had appeared.

The bishop did not believe the man's story and demanded that Diego show him proof that he had seen the Virgin Mary. Diego returned to the site of his apparition, and the Virgin once again appeared to him. The Lady of Guadalupe carefully arranged a bouquet of roses in Juan Diego's cloak and told him to show them to the bishop.

Diego returned to the bishop. When he opened his cloak the roses fell to the ground, and the cloak became illuminated with a life-sized apparition of the Lady of Guadalupe. The bishop fell to his knees in amazement and worship. The church was built, and the cloak hung inside it for all to see.

Today the cloak hangs in the Basilica de Guadalupe, which is located on the outskirts of Mexico City, and is visited by approximately 10 million people a year.

The miracle that Juan Diego experienced is celebrated every December 12 with the Feast of the Virgin Guadalupe, a major holiday in Mexico. In the United States, Mexican Americans observe the holiday by attending Mass. A common custom is to bring roses to the Mass, which often features mariachi music. The holiday is also celebrated with the Matachines (mah-tah-CHEE-nehs) dance, a traditional Spanish Indian dance.

Christmas (Navidad)

Mexican Americans generally consider December 12, the day of the Feast of the Virgin of Guadalupe, the beginning of the Christmas season. But it's on Christmas Eve, which is called Noche Buena (NOH-cheh BWEH-nah), that the main celebration of the holiday takes place.

One well-loved Mexican American Christmas tradition involves family members gathering together to celebrate and to make tamales (tah-MAHL-ays) on Christmas Eve. Tamales are pieces of cornmeal dough that are stuffed with meat, cheese, or vegetables, wrapped in corn husks (or banana leaves), and steamed. Families spend the whole day (and sometimes more than one day) talking, laughing, and enjoying each other's company as they prepare these delicious holiday treats.

On Christmas Eve night, families attend a midnight mass at the church. Afterward, they share a big dinner and exchange gifts. The Christmas Eve dinner traditionally includes tamales; sweet fried pastries called *boñuelos* (boh-NWEH-lohs); *champurrado*; *posole* (poh-SOH-leh), a hearty stew made with pork, chili peppers, and dried hominy corn; *menudo* (meh-NOO-doh), a soup made of tripe and hominy; and popular, anise-flavored cookies called *biscochitos* (bees-koh-CHEE-tohs). Although most Mexican American families have a Christmas tree, they consider the Nativity scene, or *nacimiento* (nah-see-mee-EN-toh), which shows the baby Jesus in a manger, their most important symbol of Christmas.

Las Posadas: The Christmas Play

Las Posadas (LAHS poh-SAH-dahs) is a nine-day-long series of processions that begins on December 16 and continues until Christmas Day. Many Mexican American neighborhoods, especially those in the Southwest, hold their own Las Posadas plays, which reenact the sojourn of Mary and Joseph seeking shelter the night Jesus was born. Adults and children play the roles of Mary, Joseph, the Three Kings, and an assortment of angels, shepherds, and animals. In the processions, they hold lit candles and travel from house to house. To observe Mary and Joseph's hardship in finding a place to lay their heads, it is tradition that, at each house, the people in the procession are refused entrance a number of times before they are finally let in to kneel and pray at the house's *nacimiento*. Afterward there is a party, in which a piñata is broken. On the final night of Las Posadas, the procession leads to the church, where everyone celebrates Christmas Eve Mass.

Light Christmas Eve *Farolitos*: Candles in Paper Bags

In the 1800s people in the Southwest lit bonfires, called luminarias (loo-min-AHR-ee-ahs) to commemorate Christ's birth and to guide people to the Christmas Eve Mass. Over time the tradition changed, and instead of lighting bonfires, people carried small, sand-filled paper bags that cradled a lit candle. These are called *farolitos* (fahr-oh-LEE-tohs). Today *farolitos* (which are also known as luminarias) are still used as part of Las Posadas processions, and many homes in Santa Fe, New Mexico, and other parts of the Southwest decorate their yards, rooftops, porches, and more with rows of the glowing bags during the Christmas season.

What You Need

Paper lunch bag

About 2 cups sand

3 flameless (battery-operated) tea light candles or 1 large flameless (battery operated) candle (available at some craft stores, hardware stores, and novelty stores)

What You Do

1. Open the bag. Fold or roll the top edge of the bag over to form a 1-inch-high "cuff."
2. Pour enough sand into the bag to make a 1- to 2-inch layer at the bottom.
3. Turn on the flameless tea lights. Place them in the bag on top of the sand.
4. Use your *farolito* outside as a festive nighttime decoration. You can make several *farolitos* and use them to line your sidewalk, porch, or yard.

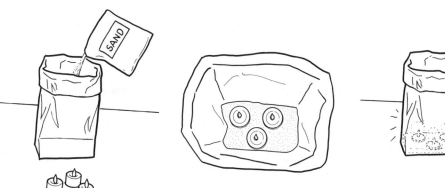

Three Kings Day (El Día de los Tres Reyes)

For many Mexican Americans, Three Kings Day, which is also called the Epiphany, marks the end of the Christmas season. Held on January 6, this is the day that celebrates the arrival of the Three Kings to Bethlehem to see the baby Jesus. The night before Three Kings Day, each child leaves a shoe next to the family's nativity scene or under his or her bed. When the children wake up, they find their shoes filled with small presents from the Three Kings.

Some Mexican American families also celebrate Three Kings Day with a special bread called Rosca de Reyes (ROHS-kah day REH-yehs), which means "King's Cake." Hidden inside the sweet, ring-shaped loaf is a tiny plastic doll. In earlier times, tradition held that the person who got the piece of bread that held the doll was expected to host a party called Candlemas, which celebrates Jesus' first trip to the temple, on February 2. Today, although families may still enjoy a Rosca de Reyes, the Candlemas celebration does not happen as frequently as it used to.

Cinco de Mayo

Cinco de Mayo means "Fifth of May." Although this holiday was created to celebrate the Mexican Army's victory over the French in 1862, Cinco de Mayo is more widely celebrated in the United States than in Mexico! It is a day for Mexicans and Americans to celebrate the friendship between the two countries and for Mexican Americans to celebrate their her-itage. But Mexican Americans aren't the only U.S. citizens who celebrate the holiday. Like the Irish holiday Saint Patrick's Day, Cinco de Mayo has become a very popular holiday among U.S. citizens of all nationalities.

Cinco de Mayo parties often feature mariachi music, dancing, Mexican food, piñatas, Mexican flags, brightly colored paper flowers, and more.

Mariachi Music

Mariachi (mah-ree-AH-chee) music is a type of folk music that is very popular in both Mexico and the United States. It is lively, animated music that makes you want to dance!

A mariachi band features several musicians and instruments that include violins, trumpets, a Spanish guitar, a *guitarron* (guee-tah-ROHN)—which resembles an oversized guitar, has a large body and a short neck, and produces a low sound—and a *vihuela* (vee-HWAY-lah), a small, guitar-like instrument that has five strings (instead of a guitar's six strings) and that makes high-pitched sounds.

Members of a mariachi band dress in flamboyant *charro* (CHAR-roh) suits that resemble the outfits worn by old Mexico's *charros*, wealthy landowners and horsemen who did not perform the daily duties of the vaquero. The outfit includes studded pants and a decorative sombrero. Mariachi bands play at many Mexican American weddings, festivals, holidays (such as Cinco de Mayo), and *quinceañeras* (KEEN-say-ahn-YARE-ahs), which are special celebrations held for girls when they become 15 years old.

Join in the Mexican Hat Dance

La Raspa (lah RAHS-pah) is sometimes called the national dance of Mexico. Although there are various forms of the dance, the basic movements are the same. The traditional costume for the female performer to wear is a colorful, ruffled blouse and full skirt and for the male, a charro suit and sombrero.

What You Need

Any even number of dancers in groups of 2 (the more, the merrier!)

Music: "La Raspa," or "Mexican Hat Dance" (Look for these traditional songs on dance music CDs sold at music stores or borrowed from the library)

What You Do

In step #1 you dance alone; in step #2 you dance with your partner.

1. Face your partner and put your hands on your hips.

   When the music begins, cross your arms in front of your chest.

   Heel touch on your RIGHT foot. Hop on your LEFT.

   Heel touch on your LEFT foot. Hop on your RIGHT.

   Heel touch on your RIGHT foot. Hop on your LEFT.

   Clap twice.

   Heel touch on your LEFT foot. Hop on your RIGHT.

   Heel touch on your RIGHT foot. Hop on your LEFT.

   Heel touch on your LEFT foot. Hop on your RIGHT.

   Clap twice.

   Heel touch on your RIGHT foot. Hop on your LEFT.

   Heel touch on your LEFT foot. Hop on your RIGHT.

   Heel touch on your RIGHT foot. Hop on your LEFT.

   Clap twice.

   Heel touch on your LEFT foot. Hop on your RIGHT.

   Heel touch on your RIGHT foot. Hop on your LEFT.

   Heel touch on your LEFT foot. Hop on your RIGHT.

   Clap twice.

2. Link arms with your partner (facing opposite directions)
   Put your free arm up into the air.
   Dance around in a circle to the right.
   Face each other.
   Dance around in a circle to the left.
   Face each other.
3. Repeat the dance from the beginning.

The Poinsettia: A Gift from Mexico

The lovely poinsettia plant that we see everywhere at Christmas originally came from Mexico. It was introduced to the United States in the 1820s by a man named Joel Poinsett, who was serving as the U.S. ambassador to Mexico. Poinsettias are now the most popular indoor flowering plant in the United States. Although the most popular poinsettias are deep red, poinsettias also come in other colors, such as pink and white.

Day of the Dead (Día de los Muertos)

Mexican Americans celebrate Día de los Muertos (DEE-ah day lohs MWER-tohs), or Day of the Dead, on November 1 and 2. It is a festive and happy holiday.

Mexican Americans feel that life and death are connected and that, by celebrating and even poking fun at death, you show appreciation for life. The holiday evolved from a combination of Aztec and Catholic beliefs. In Mexico, families celebrate Día de los Muertos by visiting the graves of loved ones at night and decorating them with offerings of flowers, candles, and food.

Many Mexican Americans create *ofrendas* (oh-FREN-dahs), or altars, in their homes or communities. On the *ofrendas*, they display pictures of loved ones who have passed away, symbols of those people's favorite things (such as a baseball for someone who loved sports, or a needle and thread for someone who enjoyed sewing), and their favorite foods. *Ofrendas* are not used to worship the dead; they are heartfelt works of art that are meant to honor relatives and other people who have died and to serve as a reminder of them in this world.

Día de los Muertos celebrations usually feature plenty of marigolds (the traditional flower of Day of the Dead), candles, and special foods, such as *pan de muertos* (PAHN day MWER-tohs), or "bread of the dead." Prayers are offered at home as well as at the gravesites.

Skulls and skeletons play a big role in Día de los Muertos celebrations. People paint their faces to look like skulls, give colorfully decorated, skull-shaped candies and cookies as gifts, and display little figurines of skeletons that are dressed in elaborate costumes and that depict people engaging in everyday activities. The skulls and skeletons are not meant to be scary—they are intended to remind people, in a lighthearted way, that death is simply a part of life.

Mold a Day of the Dead Skull

Mexican Americans traditionally enjoy making or purchasing "sugar skulls" for the Day of the Dead. They are frequently given as gifts, and they are also used to decorate *ofrendas*. In Latino bakeries in the Southwest and Mexico, store shelves come alive with three-dimensional sugar skulls decorated in bright, festive icing. In this activity, we will make a simple, flat figure of a skull out of clay instead of sugar.

What You Need

Adult Supervision Required

Polymer molding clay (available at craft stores):
   2 ounces white; 1 ounce each of a variety of
   colors (red, green, yellow, pink, or others)
Aluminum foil
Empty jar
Plastic or craft knife
Eraser-tipped pencil
Cookie sheet

What You Do

1. Preheat the oven to 275° F.
2. Knead the white clay until it is soft enough to mold.
3. Roll the white clay into a ball and place it on the aluminum foil. Using the empty jar on its side as a roller, roll out the clay until it is flat and ¼-inch thick.
4. Using the knife, carefully cut a skull shape into the clay. (If you accidentally cut the aluminum foil as well, simply place the clay on a new sheet of aluminum foil.) Trim off and discard the excess white clay. Set aside.
5. Knead each piece of colored clay until it is soft. Use various colored clays to make the features shown in the drawing. You can add other features, such as earrings, flowers, hair, bow ties, glasses, swirled designs, hats, and more, and you can use the eraser on the pencil to make indentations, such as for eyes or teeth, in your skull. Place each shape firmly onto the skull shape in the design that you want.
6. Line the cookie sheet with a clean sheet of aluminum foil. Place the decorated skull on the aluminum foil.
7. Bake for about 30 minutes (approximately 15 minutes for each ¼ inch).
8. Remove from the oven and let cool.
9. Use your new skulls to decorate an *ofrenda* for Día de los Muertos!

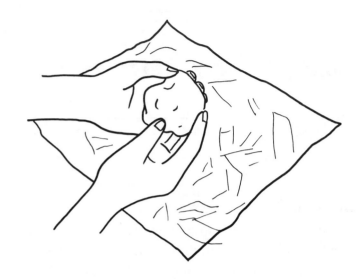

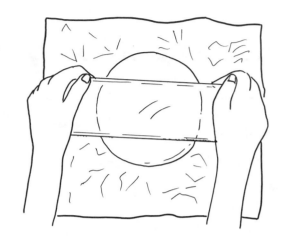

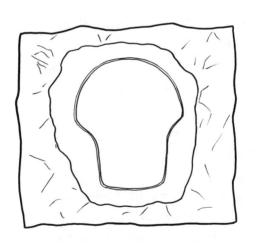

Make *Pan de Muertos*: Bread of the Dead

What You Need

Adult Supervision Required

Large bowl

Cooking spray

1 1-pound loaf frozen bread
  dough

Plastic wrap

Cutting board

½ cup flour

Knife

Cookie sheet

Pastry brush

1 egg white, placed in a small
  bowl

1 teaspoon anise seed

2 oven mitts or pot holders

2 tablespoons butter

1 small microwave-safe bowl

2 teaspoons sugar

½ teaspoon
  cinnamon

Wire rack

What You Do

1. Spray the inside of a large bowl with cooking spray. Place the frozen bread dough in the bowl. Tightly cover the bowl with plastic wrap and let sit in a warm place (such as an oven or microwave oven that is not turned on) for 4 to 6 hours, or until the bread dough has doubled in size.

2. Dust a cutting board with flour. Place the dough on the center of the cutting board and press or punch it down to let the air out. Cut 4 slices of the dough, each about an inch wide, and set them aside.

3. Gently flatten the rest of the dough with the palm of your hand, into an 8-inch-wide circle about ¾ of an inch thick. Place the dough in the middle of the cookie sheet.

4. Tear apart the slices of dough that were set aside to form 8 bone shapes (each about 4 inches long) and one skull shape (about 3 inches long). Press the skull shape into the middle of the large circle of dough. Press the bone shapes all around the skull, like bicycle spokes that stretch to the end of the circle. Don't be afraid to roll, twist, or squeeze the dough. This is the fun part!

5. Drape a piece of plastic wrap loosely over the dough. Set aside in a warm place until it has doubled in size (about 1 hour).

6. Preheat the oven to 350° F.

7. Using the pastry brush, brush the egg white onto the dough. Sprinkle with anise seed.

8. Bake the dough for 30 minutes, or until the bread is golden. While the bread is baking, clean and dry the pastry brush.

9. Using oven mitts or pot holders to protect your hands, remove the bread from the oven.

10. Place the butter in the small microwave-safe bowl and cook in the microwave until butter is melted (5 to 15 seconds). Using the clean pastry brush, brush the melted butter lightly onto the bread. Sprinkle with the sugar and the cinnamon.

11. Transfer the bread to a wire rack and let cool. Enjoy!

Mexican Independence Day (Diez y seis de Septiembre)

Mexican Americans celebrate the anniversary of Mexico's independence from Spain on September 16 each year. The holiday is called Diez y seis de Septiembre (dee-AYS ee SAYS day sehp-tee-EHM-breh), which means "the 16th of September." In Mexico the holiday is celebrated at midnight on September 15, but in the United States it is usually celebrated during the day and into the evening of September 16.

Diez y seis de Septiembre is often celebrated in community-sponsored events throughout the Southwest. These fiestas usually start with the ringing of bells to symbolically re-create *El Grito de Dolores* (the Cry of Dolores), Father Miguel Hidalgo y Costilla's cry for Mexicans to rebel from Spain. Festivities include parades, Mexican flag flying, mariachi music, traditional Mexican folk dancing called *ballet folklórico* (bah-LEH fohlk-LOHR-ee-koh), and fireworks.

Special treats enjoyed on this day include fried pork rinds, called *chicharrones* (chee-cha-RHON-ehs), tacos, tamales, and *chiles en nogada* (CHEE-lays ehn noh-GAH-dah), a delicious dish of stuffed chilies. *Chiles en nogada* is actually the traditional dish of Mexican Independence Day because, like the Mexican flag, it features the colors red (pomegranate seeds), green (chilies), and white (a creamy walnut sauce).

Quinceañera

The Mexican religious tradition known as *quinceañera* marks the entrance of a young woman to adulthood. It is sometimes called the "Sweet Fifteen" celebration because it occurs on a girl's 15th birthday. A girl who is celebrating her *quinceañera* is referred to as "la Quinceañera."

A girl's *quinceañera* can be simple or elaborate, but it is always important to both her and her family. A typical *quinceañera* in the United States starts with a ceremony in the church. The Quinceañera's "court" of 14 female attendants and their male escorts walk down the aisle. They are followed by the Quinceañera's parents, then by the Quinceañera and her escort (who is usually a brother, cousin, or friend). The Quinceañera wears a beautiful ball gown, and her attendants wear gowns and tuxedos.

It is customary for the Quinceañera to be given symbolic gifts for her use during the ceremony. These items may include a tiara, to indicate that she is a princess before God; a ring or bracelet, which symbolizes the circle of life and the girl's commitment to be a part of the community; and a religious medal or Bible, as a reminder to keep God in her life.

After the ceremony there is a great celebration, complete with a mariachi band or a DJ, dancing, and an abundance of food. Some *quinceañera* traditions include the girl's mother or father replacing her flat shoes with high-heeled shoes as a symbol of her passage into womanhood; a special dance with her father; and the display of a *quinceañera* doll that symbolizes the girl's childhood. In some Latino cultures, ribbons commemorating the celebration are pinned to the doll, and, as the Quinceañera thanks her guests for coming to the celebration, she presents each with one of the ribbons.

Mexican American Food

The traditional foods of Mexico are a combination of native American foods, such as corn, tomatoes, peppers, avocados, squash, and beans, and foods that are prevalent in Spain, such as wheat, beef, pork, chicken, and cheese. In the United States, Mexican food often takes on additional influences, resulting in what is sometimes known as Mexican American or "Tex-Mex" cuisine.

In a traditional Mexican American home the staple food is the corn tortilla, a thin, flat, circle of bread made of corn.

Tortillas are either made at home or bought fresh at a *tortillería* (tortilla store). They may be eaten plain, as bread, or they may be stuffed with a variety of fillings. *Empanadas* (ehm-pah-NAH-dahs) are turnovers that are filled with meat or seafood. Soups and thick stews of meat, corn, and chili peppers are commonly found on the Mexican American family table. Sauces, especially tomato-based sauces, are very popular as well. One of the most traditional Mexican sauces that is still enjoyed in Mexican American households is mole (MOH-lay). This delectable, spicy sauce contains 28 ingredients, including anise seed, choco-late, and chili peppers. The sauce is served over chicken or turkey. Other commonly enjoyed foods include guacamole (a mixture of mashed avocados, tomatoes, onions, and other ingre-dients), salsa (a sauce-like mixture of tomatoes, onions, and chili peppers), and *nopales* (noh-PAH-lays), which are prickly pear cactus pieces that are boiled or grilled.

Notable Mexican Americans

Mexican Americans have contributed to the culture of the United States in many ways. There are Mexican Americans at every level of society and in every profession. Here are just some of the noteworthy Mexican Americans who have helped to shape the United States.

Athletes

Nancy Lopez (1957–)   A championship golfer

Pancho Gonzales (1928–1995)   A championship tennis player who was ranked number one in the world for several years

Oscar De La Hoya (1973–)   A professional boxer and an Olympic Gold medal winner

Entertainers

Joan Baez (1941–)   A folk singer and a political activist

Salma Hayek (1966–)   An actress and the creator and executive producer of the TV show *Ugly Betty*

Edward James Olmos (1947–)   An actor who has appeared in films, including *Stand and Deliver*, and television shows, including *Battlestar Galactica*

Selena Quintanilla Pérez (1971–1995)   A very popular young singer who was called "the queen of Tejano music"

Linda Ronstadt (1946–)   A singer whose hits include the popular song "You're No Good"

Carlos Santana (1947–)   A guitarist and a member of the popular group Santana

Authors

Rudolfo A. Anaya (1937–)   The author of *Bless Me, Ultima* and other books

Sandra Cisneros (1954–)   The author of *House on Mango Street* and other books

Gary Soto (1952–)   The author of several uplifting books about the Mexican American experience

Michael Anthony Muñoz (1958–)   An NFL football player and a member of the Pro Football Hall of Fame

Other Notable Mexican Americans

Mario J. Molina (1943–)   A scientist who won the 1995 Nobel Prize in chemistry

Ellen Ochoa (1958–)   The first Latina astronaut

Politicians

Lucille Roybal-Allard (1941–)   The first Mexican American woman elected to the U.S. Congress

Bill Richardson (1947–)   Governor of New Mexico

Joseph Montoya (1915–1978)   A U.S. senator who fought for Latino civil rights

Henry Gonzalez (1916–2000)   A U.S. congressman who worked to protect migrant farmworkers

Alberto Gonzalez (1955–)   The first Latino attorney general of the United States

Henry Cisneros (1947–)   The first Latino mayor of a major U.S. city (San Antonio, Texas)

Romana Bañuelos (1925–)   The first Latina (Latino woman) to become treasurer of the United States

Labor Organizers

Cesar Chavez (1927–1993)   The cofounder of the United Farm Workers of America

Linda Chavez-Thompson (1944–)   Served as the executive vice president of the AFL-CIO, the largest federation of unions in the United States

Dolores Huerta (1930–)   The cofounder of the United Farm Workers of America

Ritchie Valens (1941–1955)   A pioneer in rock 'n' roll whose hits include the popular song "La Bamba"

From Sea to Shining Sea—in Spanish!

Here are the Spanish names of some of the mountains in the United States and what they mean.

Sierra Nevada Mountains (California): This translates to "Snowy Mountains."

San Juan Mountains (Colorado): This means "Saint John Mountains."

Sangre de Cristo Mountains (Colorado and New Mexico): The English translation of Sangre de Cristo is "blood of Christ"; the mountains were named that because of the red glow that the setting sun casts over them.

Sierra Estrella Mountains (Arizona): This means "Star Mountains."

Sierra Blanca Mountains (New Mexico): This means "White Mountains."

Tex-Mex Cuisine

Here are some popular Mexican American or "Tex-Mex" foods that are available almost everywhere in the United States.

- Tacos. While authentic Mexican tacos are usually made with soft flour tortillas, Mexican American tacos are usually made with corn tortillas that have been deep-fried or baked into a hard shell. These shells are filled with ground beef, chicken, or beans, as well as lettuce, tomatoes, and cheese.

- Fajitas. Sizzling plates of grilled beef or chicken and grilled vegetables, such as onions and bell peppers, are brought to the table. They are served with soft flour tortillas and a variety of additional items such as guacamole (gwah-kah-MOH-lay), salsa, and sour cream. Individuals make their own fajitas by placing ingredients in the tortillas, wrapping them up, and eating them.

- Enchiladas. Soft corn or flour tortillas are filled with meat or cheese, topped with a tomato-based sauce (or, sometimes, a cream-based sauce) and more cheese, and baked.

- Nachos. Nachos are very popular in the United States but, in terms of being a Mexican American food, they are much more "American" than they are "Mexican." To make nachos, corn tortilla chips are simply topped with cheese (and sometimes beans, ground beef, or chicken) and baked. Nachos are usually served with jalapeños, pico de gallo (a relish made of tomato, onion, and chilies), gua-camole, and sour cream.

- Chile con carne (CHEE-leh kohn KAR-neh). This is a spicy, stew-like dish that is made of beans, chilies, meat, and sauce.

- Chimichangas (chee-mee-CHAHN-gahs). These are burritos (bur-REE-tohs)—soft tortillas filled with meat, cheese, or beans—that are deep-fried.

❖ 5 ❖

Puerto Ricans on the Mainland

Because Puerto Rico is a commonwealth of the United States, Puerto Ricans—whether they live in their home country or "on the mainland" in the United States—are U.S. citizens. Those who move from Puerto Rico to the United States are not immigrants; they are migrants who moved to a different part of what is considered the same country.

Beginnings

Christopher Columbus discovered Puerto Rico, an island in the Caribbean, in 1493, during his second trip to the Americas. At that time the island was inhabited by Taino Indians, who had a distinct culture and lifestyle based on fishing, hunting, and farming. They called their island Borikén (bo-ree-KEN), which means "the land of the brave lord." Columbus claimed the island for Spain and renamed it San Juan Bautista, which means "Saint John the Baptist."

In 1509 the explorer Ponce de León renamed the island yet again. He called it Puerto Rico, which means "rich port," and it was there that he founded the first Spanish colony. The Spanish instructed the natives in Catholicism and in Spanish culture, and Ponce de León became Puerto Rico's first governor. Spain would rule the island for the next 400 years.

Under the Spanish, the Taino were enslaved and forced to work in gold mines and on Spanish-owned farms. Thousands of Taino died of overwork, mistreatment (6,000 Taino were shot after an uprising in 1511), and European diseases. In 1513 the Spanish started importing African slaves to replace the Taino workforce. After the gold was depleted Ponce de León introduced sugarcane to the island—it would eventually become the most important crop in Puerto Rico. The African slaves and the remaining Taino were forced to work on the large sugarcane plantations. The Spanish neglected the island for a number of years until they realized its potential as a military port for protecting the Spanish Empire. In the late 1500s they built great fortresses and a 25-foot-high wall around the city of San Juan.

Spain began a rigorous campaign to promote trade between itself and Puerto Rico in the 1700s. Puerto Rico grew large amounts of coffee and sugarcane for export, and imported thousands of additional African slaves to work on the farms. During the 1700s and 1800s, there was a large immigration movement from Europe and other Spanish colonies, and several new towns were built along the coast.

The 19th century saw the beginning of several movements by Puerto Rico's inhabitants to gain their independence and free the island from the shackles of Spain. In 1873, slavery was outlawed. But it was the 1898 Spanish-American War, in which Spain and the United States battled over the island of Cuba, that changed the fate of Puerto Rico's residents. The United States won the war in a short period of time, and Spain was forced to sign a treaty that handed over Puerto Rico (and several other Spanish colonies) to the United States.

At first the rights of Puerto Ricans were even more restricted than they had been under the Spanish. The Foraker Act of 1900 set up a two-part legislature. It gave Puerto Ricans the right to elect their own people to the less-important part of the regional legislature (the group that creates laws), but the higher-ranking members of the legislature, as well as Puerto Rico's governor, were selected by the president of the United States. A non-voting representative of Puerto Rico (called a delegate) was allowed to represent Puerto Rico in the United States Congress.

Eventually reforms were made. In 1917 the Jones Act made Puerto Ricans United States citizens and gave them the right to

control the upper part of Puerto Rico's legislature. But, by becoming U.S. citizens, Puerto Rican men also became eligible for the U.S. military draft. Just one month after the Jones Act was established the United States joined the many other countries who were battling in World War I, a war in Europe that had begun in 1914. Many Puerto Ricans served in World War I (which ended in 1918), and many others have served in every war that the United States has been involved in since. The 65th U.S. Infantry Regiment, which was made up almost entirely of Puerto Ricans and which was referred to as "the Borinqueneers," fought proudly in World War I, World War II (1939–1945), and the Korean War (1950–1953).

In 1947 Puerto Rico was granted the right to elect its own governor. Two years later, Luis Muñoz Marín became the first Puerto Rican governor. His father, Luis Muñoz Rivera, had been the leader of the independence movement and a representative to the U.S. Congress in Washington many years before.

In 1950 the Puerto Rico Constitution Act enabled the people of Puerto Rico to establish their own government. In 1952 Puerto Rico declared itself to be an "associated free state," or commonwealth, of the United States. By declaring itself an associated free state, Puerto Rico reserved the right to become independent at the time of its choosing. As a result of its status as a commonwealth, Puerto Rico enjoys the advantages of being part of the United States, but it also has a degree of independence from the United States.

Puerto Ricans elect all of their own representatives to government, have their own flag, are citizens of the United States (but cannot vote in U.S. elections unless they are living

A Rich Stew of Culture

In Puerto Rico the native Taino, the Spanish settlers, the African slaves and their descendents intermarried, and a colorful tapestry of cultures evolved.

Puerto Rican people range in skin tone from very light to very dark; they can have Native American, African, or European features, and their eyes range from the lightest blue to the darkest brown.

Puerto Rican food includes the hearty Spanish paella (pay-EH-yah), a stew of rice, seafood, chicken, and vegetables; the African snack *mofongo* (MOH-fohn-goh), which is made of plantains (a banana-like fruit) and pork cracklings; and *frituras de yautía* (free-TOO-rahs day jow-TEE-ah) which combines the Taino-grown taro root (yautia) and the African fritter.

Over the years the Catholic religion of the Spanish has mixed with the religious customs of the African Yoruban tribe, resulting in a religion called Santeria (san-tuh-REE-uh). The Native American Taino religion Espiritismo (es-pee-ree-TEES-moh) also has elements of Catholicism.

Taino, Spanish, and African influences are all found, and are often combined, in Puerto Rican music. The types of music most commonly associated with Puerto Rico are the *bomba* (BOHM-bah) and the *plena* (PLEH-nah), which feature various influences from Spanish and African music.

on the mainland), are eligible for the same services and federal programs available to the 50 states, are protected by the United States military, and do not pay federal income tax. Since 1992 the Puerto Rican delegate to Congress has been allowed to vote (although only in committees), giving a voice to Puerto Rico in the U.S. legislature.

The question of whether Puerto Rico should remain a commonwealth, become a state of the United States, or become an independent country continues to be hotly debated by Puerto Rico's inhabitants. In 1998 more than 50 percent of Puerto Rico's voters opted to remain a commonwealth—at least for the time being.

Make a Guiro: A Popular Musical Instrument

The guiro (WEE-roh) is another example of Puerto Rico's blended culture. Made from a hollowed-out gourd, the percussion instrument was originally used by the Taino, and it was later incorporated as a rhythmic instrument in Afro-Spanish Puerto Rican music.

What You Need

16-ounce water bottle with ridges
Acrylic paint in 3 or 4 colors of your choice
Paintbrush
3–4 paper cups
12-inch-long, ¼-inch-thick dowel
CD of Latino music (salsa, bomba, merengue,
    mariachi, or other)
CD player

What You Do

1. Remove the label, then wash and dry the bottle.
2. Pour a small amount of each color of paint into a paper cup. Using the paintbrush, paint 3 or 4 wide, different-colored horizontal stripes on the bottle. (Clean the paintbrush after painting with each color.) Let dry.
3. Repaint the stripes, cleaning the paintbrush after painting with each color. Let dry.
4. To play your guiro, scrape the dowel up and down the bottle. Notice how different sounds are produced in different places on the bottle.
5. Now put on some music and play along with your guiro!

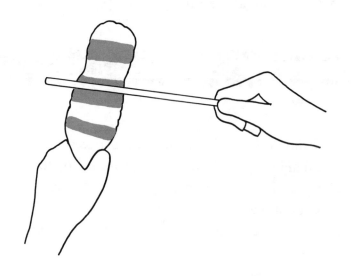

Migration to the Mainland

Although sugarcane had always been an important export for Puerto Rico, it was second to coffee, and farmers had always raised food for their families as well. This changed after the United States took control of Puerto Rico in 1898, and American sugar companies bought up land from Puerto Rican landowners to build large sugarcane farms. Now, instead of raising their own food for their families, Puerto Rican farmers were working on big sugarcane plantations for money. This made the farmers completely dependent on how well the sugar market was doing—when sugar sold for a good price, the farmers did well, but when it sold for little money, they suffered. To make matters worse, the price of sugar changed frequently and was very unpredictable.

During the early years of the 20th century, Puerto Rico experienced a population explosion. This, combined with the unstable sugar-based economy, caused much of the island to fall into poverty.

In 1948 a program called Operation Bootstrap was sponsored by the Puerto Rican and U.S. governments to help alleviate some of the economic problems. The program encouraged people to move from rural areas into the cities to work in new United States–owned factories. There were more jobs available in the cities than on the farms, and many Puerto Ricans were able to support themselves by working in the factories. Although it did not solve every problem, the program was a success.

Eventually, however, the factories hired as many people as they could use, and many Puerto Ricans who moved to the cities to find work were left unemployed. Some of these people decided to look for work in big cities in the United States. At that time, factories in some U.S. cities—especially those in the garment (clothing) industry in New York—were in need of additional workers. As a result, thousands of Puerto Ricans migrated from Puerto Rico to various cities in the United States between 1947 and 1957. The newcomers settled in New York, Chicago, Philadelphia, Florida, California, and other parts of the United States. In New York, many Puerto Ricans made homes in Brooklyn and in an area of New York City known as Spanish Harlem.

Puerto Rican women joined men in the U.S. workforce. In New York, they worked primarily as seamstresses (sewers) in the garment industry. Throughout the country, thousands of Puerto Rican men and women worked in low-level, low-paying manufacturing jobs. They made shoes, clothing, home goods, electrical supplies, and more. They worked in meatpacking plants, laundries, hotels, and restaurants. Some worked as migrant farmworkers; still others worked as servants in private homes.

Prejudice and Discrimination

Like many migrant groups before them, Puerto Ricans have suffered discrimination and prejudice in the United States. Language is a barrier—although Puerto Ricans are U.S. citizens, many are not fluent in English. Dark-skinned Puerto Ricans have encountered many of the same hardships and injustices that African Americans have suffered, and Puerto Ricans of all skin colors have, at times, been denied housing or jobs because of their ethnicity.

In response to many of the hardships that Puerto Ricans on the mainland faced, mutual aid societies sprang up in Puerto Rican communities. These societies offered comfort and insurance against the uncertainties of life in the barrio. They provided financial assistance, medical care, and a place for neighborhood residents to congregate.

Puerto Rican Music

Salsa is a type of Latin music that actually originated in New York. It features African, Cuban, and Latin rhythms, and it is fast paced and spicy, like its name. Salsa means "the sauce that starts the party." After World War II, a popular Puerto Rican musician and bandleader named Tito Puente brought salsa to the forefront of music in New York City through his jazz-influenced big band.

Bomba and *plena* are two styles of music that are commonly associated with Puerto Rico. The *bomba* style of music was brought to Puerto Rico by the African slaves who had been shipped there to work. Played with drums and other percussion instruments, the *bomba* is a kind of duel between the drummer and the dancer in which the drummer attempts to pound out a beat that matches the dancer's gestures and movement. *Plena* is Puerto Rican folk music in which dancing also plays a part. Musical instruments used in the *plena* include the guiro; the *cuatro,* a stringed instrument known as Puerto Rico's national instrument; and the tambourine. Like the Mexican *corrido,* the *plena* is used to tell stories.

There are other styles of Puerto Rican music as well. *Jíbaro* (HEE-vah-roh) music, which features the *cuatro* as well as drums, is simple folk music that originated in the mountains of Puerto Rico. *Reggaetón* (ray-gay-TOHN), the newest type of music from Puerto Rico, combines Jamaican reggae, Latin hip-hop, and rap.

Spanish Harlem (El Barrio)

After World War II, thousands of Puerto Ricans fled the poverty of their island to start a new life in an area of New York City called East Harlem. Soon the area became known as Spanish Harlem. Puerto Ricans called it El Barrio, which means "the neighborhood."

In the 1940s the streets of Spanish Harlem resonated with the beat of Spanish and Latino music. The music of Cuban singer Celia Cruz, Puerto Rican bandleader Tito Puente, and Cuban bandleader Mario Bauza blared from transistor radios that mixed with the horns and sirens of city traffic. Spanish Harlem's walls were decorated with both murals and graffiti. Extended families—mothers, fathers, children, grandparents, cousins, and other relatives—lived together in crowded tenements (high-rise apartments). Puerto Rican, African American, and Italian people all lived in the barrio, and each group lived in its own tight-knit neighborhood within the concrete and asphalt blocks of East Harlem.

In the barrio, there was no need to learn English. All the residents and business owners spoke Spanish. Street and store signs were written in both Spanish and English, and both Spanish- and English-language newspapers, magazines, and books were widely available. Families shopped for beans and rice at the local bodega (small grocery store) and bought healing herbs and incense at the botanica (a shop that sells herbs and religious items). They purchased live chickens at the chicken market and haggled with sidewalk vendors at the *marqueta* (mahr-KEH-tah), or outdoor market. For the most part, the only people who were forced to learn English were the children, who had to attend schools in which the only language that was taught—and the only language that was understood by the teachers and non-Latino schoolchildren—was English.

When they weren't in school, the children filled their days playing games. The families were poor and could not afford to buy many toys or sports equipment, so the children used what was available. In games of stickball, manhole covers served as bases, and broom handles were used as bats. Hours were spent playing ring-a-levio, double-dutch jump roping, hopscotch, and stoop ball. To cool off during the hot summer months, people opened fire hydrants and played in the cold water that gushed out. Neighbors talked and gossiped on front stoops, fire escapes, and apartment hallways and men played domino games on the sidewalks. Clotheslines, sagging under the weight of drying laundry, were strung high in the air between tenement buildings.

Puerto Rican restaurants served mouthwatering foods that reminded the people of their island home. Popular dishes included *bacalaitos* (bah-cah-lah-EE-tohs), or codfish fritters, and fried pork rinds. Pushcart vendors sold *piraguas* (pee-RAH-gwahs), snow cone–like treats of shaved ice flavored with sweet syrup and served in cups. Nightclubs attracted sizzling young dancers in vibrantly colored dresses and suits who showed off the latest dance steps in dances such as the mambo, the meringue (mehr-EN-gay), and the bolero (boh-LEH-roh).

Tenement apartments were usually poorly heated and ventilated, and most had few windows to let in light. Still, they were often filled with music, laughter, and the mouthwatering aroma of Puerto Rican foods being cooked.

Life in the barrio was sometimes difficult, and people were very poor, but, by coming together as a community and working hard to make better lives for themselves, Puerto Ricans made great strides. Each new generation has achieved better educational and job opportunities, and thousands of Puerto Ricans have moved out of El Barrio and into the suburbs of New York and New Jersey. Today Spanish Harlem is still home to a large population of Puerto Ricans, and new immigrants from Mexico, the Caribbean, and Asia have joined them there, bringing their own languages and cultural traditions to the neighborhood.

Play Stickball

For many years, stickball was the most popular sport on the streets of El Barrio. The game is very similar to baseball, with one exception: instead of using actual sports equipment, everyday items on the street are put to use. Manhole covers, parked cars, storm drains, fire hydrants, or street lights become the bases. An old mop handle or broom handle serves as the bat. Actual balls are used, but they are usually made of a pink rubber that is soft enough for a person to catch without wearing a glove.

Stickball was played in neighborhood streets from the 1930s to the mid-1960s, before the streets became clogged with so many cars. If a car did come down the street when a game was being played, everyone ran to the curb and waited for it to pass. Then the game resumed. These days, stickball is usually played in a park or a schoolyard. There are many ways to play the game, and part of the fun is to make up the rules as you go along. Here is one traditional version; once you've mastered it, have fun making up your own game!

What You Need

4 or more people
A large, safe area to play, such as a
   playground or paved schoolyard
Chalk (optional)
4-foot-long stick or broom handle
Tennis ball or rubber ball that bounces

What You Do

1. Divide into 2 teams of at least 2 people each.
2. Choose your foul lines and bases from items that are around you, such as a fence, a basketball hoop, painted lines on asphalt, a sign, or a trash can lid. (If you can't find enough items to use, use the chalk to draw them onto the paved ground.)
3. Play the game as if you were playing baseball, but with the following differences:

   • Instead of throwing the ball, the pitcher bounces it to the hitter.
   • There is no catcher.
   • Each hitter gets only 2 swings to hit the ball.
   • Balls and strikes are not called.
   • Bunting and ground balls are not allowed.
   • A foul is an out. If the ball is caught by a fielder, it's an out.

Join in a Game of Ring-*a*-Levio

Ring-*a*-levio, 1, 2, 3!

Kids growing up in Spanish Harlem enjoyed this rough-and-ready game. It requires no equipment, but the more players there are, the better!

What You Need

4 or more people

What You Do

1. Pick a spot, such as the front steps of a house or an area near a sign, to be the "jail."
2. Divide into 2 teams of at least 2 people each.
3. One team runs away while the other team counts to 100. Then that team tries to catch the runners. Chasers can work alone or in a group. A chaser catches a runner by grabbing hold of him or her and yelling, "Ring-*a*-levio, 1, 2, 3!" Then the chaser puts the runner that's been caught "in jail"—in the designated spot.
4. A runner who has not yet been caught can free his or her teammates from jail by sneaking up to the designated spot and yelling, "Free All!" before he or she is caught.
5. When all of the runners are together in jail, the game is over.

Try Stoop Ball

The typical tenement in East Harlem had a concrete stoop (a series of large steps) that led from the street to the main door. People of all ages gathered on the tenement stoops to talk, eat, drink, and play games. One of these games was called stoop ball. In it, players bounced a ball against a stoop and caught it as it bounced back. There are many variations of the game; here is the traditional version. You can play this by yourself or with other players.

What You Need

Small rubber ball that bounces
Stoop or outdoor set of solid steps

What You Do

1. Throw the ball against the steps and try to catch it as it bounces back. Here is how to keep score.

   - If you catch the ball after it bounces off the step and onto the ground one time, you get 5 points.
   - If you catch the ball in the air as it bounces off the step (before it bounces on the ground), you get 10 points.

   - If you catch a "pointer" (a ball that hits the edge of the step) before it bounces on the ground, you get 100 points.
   - If you miss catching the ball or if the ball bounces off the step and onto the ground more than one time, you get 0 points. If you are playing with another person, your turn is over, and it's your fellow player's turn to bounce the ball and try to score points.
   - The first player to score 500 points wins.

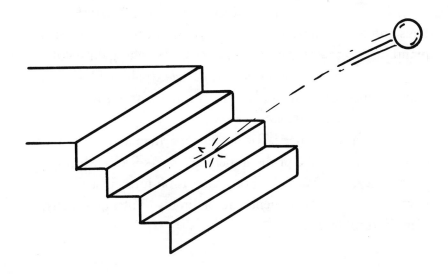

The National Puerto Rican Day Parade

Each year, the second Sunday in June is designated as National Puerto Rican Day in the United States. On this day, Puerto Ricans living in the United States pay tribute to their heritage, culture, and traditions. Nowhere is this more evident than in New York City, home to thousands of Puerto Ricans living on the mainland. Each year the city hosts a huge procession called the National Puerto Rican Day Parade. This annual parade draws more people than any other outdoor event in the entire United States! Close to a million people come from everywhere in the nation to New York City to watch or participate in the parade and to celebrate Puerto Rican culture.

The parade is a moving party of song, dance, and color. There are brightly decorated floats, and marching bands, dancing groups, clown-like characters called *vejigantes* (vay-he-GAHN-tays), show horses, beauty queens, police and firemen, veterans and current members of the military, Latino organizations, religious groups, and more march down the streets to the lively beat of Latino music. Street vendors sell Puerto Rican flags and traditional foods such as *piraguas; bacalaitos*; fried plantains; *arroz con gandules* (ah-RROHS cohn gahn-DOO-les), or rice with pigeon peas; and *pasteles* (pah-STEH-lehs), which consist of mashed plantains stuffed with meat and vegetables wrapped in banana leaves.

Many famous Puerto Ricans have participated in the parade over the years. Some of them include singers Ricky Martin, Jennifer Lopez, and Marc Anthony; television journalist Geraldo Rivera; musician Tito Puente; actor Jimmy Smits; and many New York politicians.

¡Que Bonita Bandera! (My Puerto Rican Flag)

To Puerto Ricans living on the mainland in the United States, the Puerto Rican flag is an important symbol that represents their unique culture and island heritage. Many people incorporate images of the flag in artwork, clothing, murals, masks, bandanas, and more to display pride and respect for their Puerto Rican heritage.

"¡Que Bonita Bandera!" ("What a Pretty Flag!") is a song that is sung in both Puerto Rico and the United States.

Que bonita bandera (keh boh-NEE-tah bahn-DEh-rah),
Que bonita bandera,
Que bonita bandera,
Es la bandera Puertorriqueña (ehs lah bahn-DEh-rah poo-air-toh-ree-KAYN-yah)

What a pretty flag,
What a pretty flag,
What a pretty flag,
Is the flag of Puerto Rico

Make a *Piragua*: An Icy, Sweet Treat

Street vendors are a common sight both at the National Puerto Rican Day Parade and in Spanish Harlem. Many street vendors sell *piraguas*—cups of shaved ice flavored with sweet syrup. Street vendors in Spanish Harlem make *piraguas* the traditional way: they use a special tool to shave ice from a large block of ice, spoon it into a paper cup or cone, and top it with one or more of a wide variety of flavored syrups.

A *piragua* is similar to a snow cone, but the syrup that is used is thicker. Fruit flavors, such as coconut, tamarind, orange, cherry, raspberry, and lemon, are very popular.

4 servings

What You Need

1 small bowl
1 cup cream of coconut (available in the ethnic
 sections of most grocery stores)
1 cup unsweetened pineapple juice
3 cups ice cubes (about 42 ice cubes from a
 standard ice cube tray)
Blender or food processor
1 medium bowl
Mixing spoon
4 8-ounce insulated beverage cups (the foam
 type often used for coffee)
Ice cream scoop or spoon
Ladle or spoon
4 straws

What You Do

1. In the small bowl, mix together the cream of coconut and the pineapple juice. Refrigerate.
2. Place ⅓ of the ice cubes in the blender or food processor and chop fine until the ice resembles snow (if necessary, add a tiny amount of water while chopping). Place the chopped ice in the medium bowl. Repeat twice.
3. Using the ice cream scoop or a spoon, scoop equal amounts of chopped ice into each cup.
4. Remove the coconut-pineapple mixture from the refrigerator. Using the ladle or a spoon, pour about ½ cup of the mixture over the top of each cup of ice.
5. Pop in the straws and enjoy!

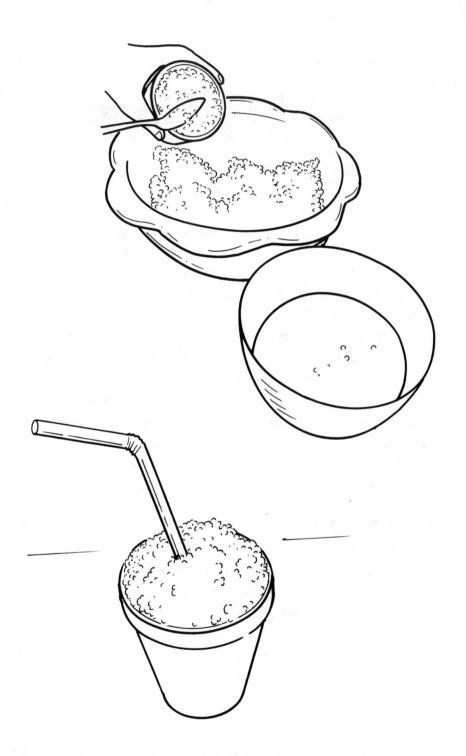

Create a *Vejigante Mask*

Vejigantes are mystical creatures that are friendly but scary looking (in the same way that the Chinese dragon is both friendly and scary looking). They wear elaborate, colorful masks and lively, clown-like costumes. The *vejigantes* are supposed to chase away evil spirits. On the island of Puerto Rico, *vejigante* masks and costumes are worn during Carnival, a celebration that occurs before the Christian observance of Lent. Today you can see *vejigantes* march in Puerto Rican parades and celebrations in the United States.

The making of *vejigante* masks is a traditional folk art in Puerto Rico. They are usually made of papier-mâché (in some parts of Puerto Rico they are made with coconut shells or gourds) and are traditionally painted in red, yellow, black, and blue. Most of the masks feature spots, pointed teeth, bulging eyes, a big snout, and lots of horns!

What You Need

Adult Supervision Required

Several layers newspaper (to use as a work surface)
6 paper cups
Warm water
Scissors
1 4-inch-by-180-inch plaster cloth (available at craft
    stores) or homemade papier-mâché
Plain plastic mask (available at craft stores)
Empty egg carton
Masking tape
Pencil or marker (optional)
Glossy acrylic paint in yellow, blue, red, and black
Paintbrush

What You Do

1. Cover your work surface with a few layers of newspapers. Pour enough warm water in one of the paper cups to fill it about half full.
2. Using the scissors, cut a few strips of plaster cloth. Working over the layers of newspaper to avoid getting plaster on anything else, dip each strip in the warm water and place it on the mask. Repeat until the mask is completely covered with 4 or 5 layers of plaster cloth. Let dry for 24 hours. (Do not pour the water that's left in the cup down the drain; the plaster in the water could clog up the pipes. Instead, stuff newspaper into the cup to absorb the water and throw the cup in the trash.) Set aside the layers of newspaper for use the next day.

3. Remove the plaster mask from the plastic mask (the mold) carefully (you may need to loosen it around the edges with your fingernail before you take it off). You can use the plastic mask as a mold for other masks many times.

4. Cut up the egg carton to make a snout and horns. For the snout: use one upside down egg "cup" and tape it to the mask. For the horns: cut up 5 pieces of the leftover carton to make different sizes and shapes of horns. Look to the drawing for ideas. Tape the bottom inch of the first horn to the mask. Flip the rest of the horn up and tape around the bottom so that it sticks out. Repeat with the rest of the horns. Set aside the remaining pieces of egg carton to help prop up the mask as it dries.

5. Fill another paper cup about halfway with warm water. Cut more strips of plaster cloth, a few strips at a time. Working over the newspaper surface, dip each strip into the warm water. Cover the horns and snout with the wet pieces of plaster cloth. You can bend these pieces to stick out. If necessary, prop up these pieces with the remaining pieces of egg carton so that they stay in place. Let the mask dry for 24 hours. (Remember not to pour the leftover plaster water down the drain.)

6. If you'd like, use a pencil or a marker to draw your design on the mask before you paint it.

7. Pour each color of paint into a paper cup. Using the paintbrush, paint your mask. You can paint it any way that you choose—you can make it scary looking, funny looking, or just crazy and colorful.

8. Let dry and display.

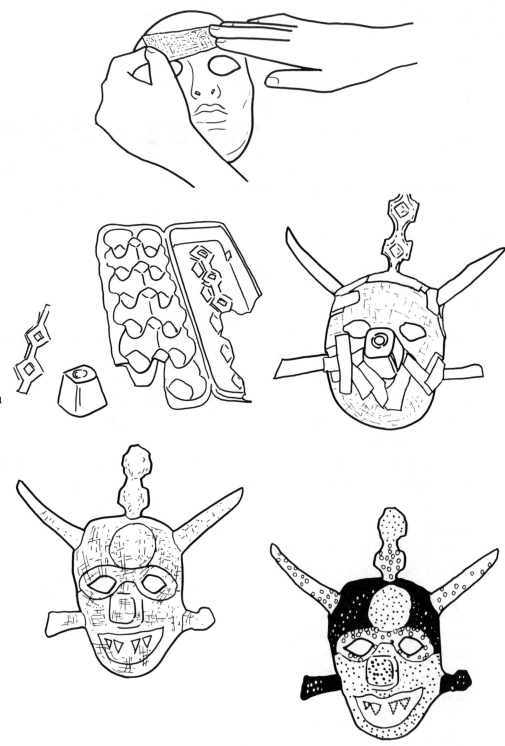

Puerto Rican Holidays

Christmas (Navidad)

In the early years of Puerto Ricans' migration to the United States, Christmas Eve was celebrated with very traditional Puerto Rican customs. These included processions of *parrandas* (pah-RRAHN-dahs), groups of people who—like Christmas carolers—traveled from home to home, playing musical instruments and singing *aguinaldos* (ah-ghee-NAHL-dohs), or Christmas songs. They also recited poetry and told stories about living on their native island. The hosts would good-naturedly feed the *parrandas* and would often accompany them to the next house. It was a night filled with warmth and community.

Today Puerto Ricans who live on the mainland enjoy a combination of old traditions from Puerto Rico and modern customs that are practiced in the United States. On Christmas Eve many Puerto Rican families enjoy a feast of *arroz con gandules*, *pasteles*, a coconut drink called *coquito* (coh-KEE-toh) that is similar to eggnog, and—if the family can arrange for it—a roasted pig. Christmas presents are opened on Christmas Day.

Three Kings Day (Día de los Tres Reyes)

This holiday, which is also known as the Epiphany, celebrates the gifts that the Three Kings brought to the baby Jesus. If you've heard the song "The Twelve Days of Christmas," you might be interested to know that the "first day" in the song is Christmas Day, and that the "twelfth day" in the song is Three Kings Day.

It's customary for children to celebrate Three Kings Day by placing a box of grass (for the Three Kings' camels) under their beds the evening before the holiday. In the morning, the grass is gone and the box is filled with toys from the Three Kings.

In New York City, a museum called El Museo Del Barrio sponsors a Three Kings Day Parade that includes live animals such as donkeys, camels, and sheep, as well as, of course, the Three Kings.

Rites of Passage

Puerto Ricans celebrate baptisms, birthdays, *quinceañeras*, showers, and weddings with great enthusiasm. Family, friends, and neighbors are always encouraged to join in. There is always an abundance of food and Latin music. A symbol of the importance of these occasions is the *capia*, a kind of permanent corsage that is given as a token or gift to the guests.

Craft a *Capia*: A Traditional Keepsake

Capias are decorative keepsakes that resemble corsages (small flower arrangements that are worn as fashion accessories). Instead of being made of flowers, though, *capias* are made of small trinkets and other decorative items. At special occasions, guests are given *capias* to thank them for coming to the celebration. Puerto Rican families often have keepsake collections of the *capias* they've made or have been given over the years. *Capias* usually reflect the theme of the event they are made for. The *capias* shown here were made with three different party themes in mind: "beach party," "baseball party," and "birthday party."

You can make *capias* to give out as party favors at your next birthday party or other celebration. Be sure to make enough *capias* so that you can give one to each guest. Create a design that suits your own event!

What You Need
For Each Capia
2 cupcake liners (available in many different colors and designs at craft stores and party supply stores)
18-inch-long, ½-inch-wide strip ribbon or paper (any color)
Stapler
Fine-point permanent marker (any color)
1-inch square felt (any color)
Medium-sized safety pin
Glue
5 or 6 small trinkets and other items such as small craft foam shapes, small erasers, inexpensive charms, and scrapbook shapes (available at craft stores, or you can make your own items)

What You Do
1. Nest one cupcake liner inside the other one. Flatten the liners slightly.
2. Make a loop in the ribbon (see picture). Staple the loop to the middle of the cupcake liners. (Make sure the staple goes through both of the cupcake liners.)
3. Using the marker, write your name or the name of the occasion, such as "beach party," at one end of the ribbon (see picture). At the other end of the ribbon, write the date of the party or event.
4. Attach the safety pin to the square of felt. Glue the square of felt to the middle of the back of the cupcake liner. Let dry.
5. Glue trinkets or other decorative items to the front of the capia (see picture). Let dry.

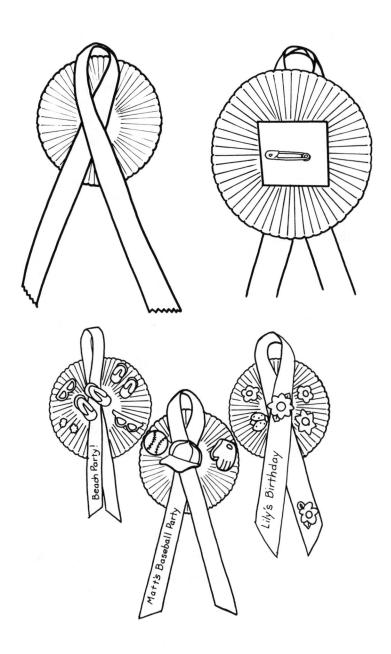

Puerto Rican Food

Puerto Rican food is very flavorful, but, unlike many other Latino cuisines, it isn't spicy hot. Two key ingredients in many Puerto Rican dishes are *sofrito* and *adobo*. *Sofrito* (soh-FREE-toh) is a mixture of cilantro (a type of parsley), peppers, garlic, onions, *culantro* (an herb), olive oil, and tomato paste. It is the base of many Puerto Rican stews and dishes. *Adobo* (ah-DOH-boh) is a mixture of black pepper, salt, garlic, onion powder, oregano, olive oil, and vinegar. The mixture is rubbed onto meats before they are cooked. Another important ingredient in Puerto Rican cooking is achiote (ah-chee-OH-tay), a powder made from cooked, ground annatto seeds. Achiote gives foods, such as Spanish rice, a lovely golden color.

If you were to visit with a Puerto Rican family, you might find a traditional *asopao* (ah-soh-POW), or stew, simmering on the stove. One favorite Puerto Rican stew is *asopao de pollo* (ah-soh-POW day POY-oh), a hearty mixture of chicken, rice, ham, vegetables, and chorizo. Other favorite dishes include *pernil* (pehr-NEEL), or roast pork shoulder; *arroz con habichuelas* (ah-RROHS cohn ah-bee-CHWAY-lahs), or rice and beans; and plantains.

Typical "American" foods such as spaghetti, hot dogs, pizza, and burgers are also part of Puerto Ricans' everyday diet, both on the mainland and in Puerto Rico. In addition to colas and other popular American beverages, Puerto Ricans enjoy their own tropical drinks. These include guava, tamarind, and passion fruit nectars; pineapple- and coconut-flavored sodas; and *malta*, a carbonated beverage made from malt (processed barley or other grain).

At breakfast, many Puerto Ricans (even children) drink *café con leche*, a strong mixture of coffee and lots of milk and sugar. Flan (a type of custard), coconut kisses (a type of cookie), and rice pudding are all popular Puerto Rican desserts.

Puerto Ricans Today

Beginning in the 1970s, many of the manufacturing companies that had employed thousands of Puerto Ricans in New York relocated to the southern part of the United States or overseas, leaving many Puerto Ricans in the Northeast without jobs. In part because of this, there has been an increase in unemployment and poverty in the Puerto Rican community.

Despite their hardships, however, many Puerto Ricans have succeeded in business, entertainment, medicine, law, academia, politics, technology, and more. Today more and more Puerto Ricans are getting college educations and finding good jobs in careers that offer opportunities for advancement. This is especially true of second-generation Puerto Ricans, who were born and brought up in the United States by parents (first generation) who were born on the island.

Notable Puerto Ricans

Puerto Ricans have enriched and contributed to the United States in a myriad of ways. As performers, legislators, writers, athletes, and more, they continue to add their unique island heritage to the mainland. Here are just a few notable Puerto Ricans.

Athletes

Angel Cordero Jr. (1942–)	A jockey who has won many important horse races and who is in the National Horse Racing Hall of Fame
Roberto Clemente (1934–1972)	The first Puerto Rican to be voted into the National Baseball Hall of Fame
Chi Chi Rodriguez (1935–)	The first Puerto Rican to be voted into the World Golf Hall of Fame

Authors

Martín Espada (1957–)	An author and poet whose books include *Imagine the Angels of Bread*
Nicholasa Mohr (1938–)	An author whose books include *Nilda*
Esmeralda Santiago (1948–)	An author whose books include *When I Was Puerto Rican*
Piri Thomas (1928–)	An author whose books include *Down These Mean Streets*

Entertainers

Marc Anthony (1968–)	A singer who has been called "the king of Latin music"
Benicio Del Toro (1967–)	A film actor who won an Academy Award for his role in *Traffic*
José Feliciano (1945–)	A singer whose hit songs include "Feliz Navidad"
José Ferrer (1912–1992)	An actor whose films include *Cyrano de Bergerac*
Raul Julia (1940–1994)	An actor whose films include *The Addams Family*
Jennifer Lopez (1969–)	An actress and singer whose films include *Antz, The Wedding Planner,* and *Selena*
Ricky Martin (1971–)	A popular singer whose hit songs include "Livin' la Vida Loca"
Rita Moreno (1932–)	An actress who has won an Emmy Award, a Grammy Award, a Tony Award, and an Academy Award and whose films include the movie version of *West Side Story*
Tito Puente (1923–2000)	A bandleader and a founder of salsa music

Chita Rivera (1933–)	An actress whose Broadway shows include the stage version of *West Side Story*
Jimmy Smits (1955–)	A film and television actor who was in *Star Wars: Episode II* and *Star Wars: Episode III*

Politicians

Herman Badillo (1929–)	The first Puerto Rican to serve in the U.S. Congress
Nydia Velázquez (1953–)	The first Puerto Rican woman to be elected to the U.S. House of Representatives

Other Notable Puerto Ricans

Joseph Acaba (1967–)	The first Puerto Rican astronaut
Antonia Novella (1944–)	The first Latina—and the first female—surgeon general of the United States
Geraldo Rivera (1943–)	A well-known investigative reporter and TV journalist
Horacio Rivero (1910–2000)	The first Puerto Rican four-star admiral in the United States Navy

From Sea to Shining Sea— in Spanish!

Some animals in the United States have names that come from Spanish words. Here are a few of them.

Burro. This is the Spanish word for donkey.

Alligator. The name of this animal comes from the Spanish term for "the lizard"—*el lagarto*.

Barracuda. This ferocious fish's name comes from the Spanish word *barraco*, which means "overlapping tooth."

Chihuahua: The smallest dog breed in the world, it is named after the Mexican city and state of Chihuahua.

Armadillo: With its powerful claws and strong, bony plates that protect its skin, it's no wonder that this animal gets its name from the Spanish word *armado*, which means armored.

❖ **6** ❖
Cuban Americans

The island of Cuba lies only 90 miles away from the coast of Florida. It was discovered by Christopher Columbus in 1492. In 1511 Spain appointed Spanish conquistador Diego Velázquez de Cuéllar to be governor of Cuba, and the island's harbor became an important port for other Spanish explorers to stop at, rest, and replenish their ships' food and supplies on their way from Spain to the Americas.

Living on the island at the time of the Spanish conquest were Ciboney and Taino Indians who lived as peaceful farmers. The Spanish under Velázquez de Cuéllar established settlements on the island with the purpose of mining gold. They enslaved the natives, as they had on the other islands, to work in the mines, as well as on sugar, coffee, and tobacco plantations. Within 50 years of their enslavement, nearly all the natives were dead from overwork, disease, and brutal treatment. To replace the labor force, the Spanish imported slaves from Africa.

From 1756 to 1763, France and Great Britain were at war with each other. This was called the "Seven Years War." Spain got involved when it decided to take sides with France against Great Britain. The British stormed the city of Havana in retaliation, and took over Cuba in 1762. They threw out Spanish laws that only allowed trading with Spain and opened trade to merchants all over the world. As a result the island became a major trade center with a large-scale sugarcane industry and an international slave trade market for the Americas. In 1763 Spain again regained control of the island after signing a treaty that gave Great Britain Florida in exchange for Spain retaking Cuba.

Sugarcane continued to be an enormous enterprise on the island; by the early 1800s, Cuba had become the world's largest exporter of sugar. In order to keep up with the demand, thousands and thousands of African slaves were captured and forced to work on Cuban plantations. By 1850 there were more Africans on the island than there were Europeans.

Santeria

Santeria is a faith that developed in the New World, specifically in Cuba. It is a combination of the Yoruban religion of the West African slaves and the saints of Spanish Catholicism. It has aspects of both religions. Santeria was created because during the years of slavery, Christian slave owners did not allow their slaves to practice their native African religions. The slaves devised a way to secretly worship their African gods and goddesses, called orishas (oh-REE-shahs): instead of calling to their orishas by name, they used the names of Catholic saints. For example, they used the name of the Catholic Saint Barbara when they prayed to Shango, their god of war and thunder; the name of the Christian Saint Francis when they prayed to Orunmila, their god of wisdom; and Our Lady of Charity, the name of the patron saint of Cuba, when they prayed to Oshun, their god of rivers and streams. The slaves all knew what they really meant when they said those Christian names, and the slave owners never suspected that the Africans had found a way to keep their own religious practices intact.

The religion of Santeria includes not only worship of the orishas, but also divination (a type of fortune telling) and the controversial practice of animal sacrifice, which is still practiced today in some areas.

Botanicas which carry religious items used in Santeria can be found in many Latino neighborhoods today. A *santero* or *santera*, which means priest or priestess in the religion of Santeria, is available in the botanica to consult with. Botanicas sell incense, potions, religious medals, and more, as well as advice for how to solve everyday problems from illness to love problems.

The slaves in Cuba were treated poorly, but they were treated better than slaves in other parts of the Americas. Children who had one Spanish parent and one slave parent were generally given their freedom, slaves were given the right to buy their freedom, and intermarriage between free Africans and Spanish people was accepted and commonplace. Finally, in 1886, slavery was abolished in Cuba.

Early Immigration to the United States

Cubans began to immigrate to the United States in the 1820s. Although some of them included political refugees (people who come to live in a new country in order to escape their home country's political practices), most of the Cubans who came to the United States in those years were wealthy, educated people who wanted to establish businesses and increase their fortunes in a new country. With them came skilled workers, such as cigar makers, to work in the factories they built. Most of these immigrants settled in Florida, but many others moved to New York, New Jersey, and other areas in the United States.

In 1869 a Cuban cigar maker named Vicente Martínez Ybor opened a cigar factory in Key West, Florida. Other cigar makers followed, and workers came from Cuba to work at the factories. Workers were allowed to go back and forth on ferries between Cuba and the United States whenever they chose.

In 1885 Ybor and a partner bought 40 acres of swampland north of Miami, Florida, near the town of Tampa. There the two men developed a planned community of cigar factories and neighborhoods for workers to live in. The area became known as Ybor City.

Grill a Cuban Sandwich

Cuban sandwiches first became popular among the workers in Ybor City. Now they are enjoyed by Cuban Americans and many other ethnic groups in the United States as well. The sandwiches are filled with layers of meat, cheese, and pickles, then pressed and grilled. A Cuban sandwich makes for a very satisfying and delicious meal.

4 servings

What You Need

Adult Supervision Required

Sharp knife

About 8 ounces fully cooked, slow-simmered pork roast *au jus* (which means "in its own juice"; available in the refrigerated prepared meat section of most grocery stores)

Paper towels

12-inch-long loaf Cuban bread (available in Latino bakeries) or crusty Italian bread (available at most grocery stores)

Mustard

4 slices ham

6 dill pickle sandwich slices *or* about 18 dill pickle chips

4 slices Swiss cheese

4 tablespoons butter

Medium-sized nonstick frying pan

Heavy, flat-bottomed pan (to use as a press)

Spatula

What You Do

1. Using the knife, cut the pork roast into thin slices. Place on paper towels to blot juice. Set aside.
2. Cut the loaf of bread in half. Cut each half lengthwise, to make four slices of sandwich bread, total.
3. Spread mustard on each slice of bread. Set 2 pieces of bread aside.
4. On each of the other two bread slices place: 2 slices of ham, half of the pork slices, half of the pickle slices or chips, and 2 slices Swiss cheese. Now top each sandwich with the slices of bread you set aside.
5. Place 1 tablespoon of the butter in the frying pan and melt over low heat.

6. Put one sandwich in the frying pan. Place the heavy, flat-bottomed pan on top of it. Gently press the pan to make the sandwich flatter.

7. Cook over low heat for 3 to 4 minutes. While it is cooking, continue to gently press the sandwich flatter. Using the spatula, flip over the sandwich and add another tablespoon of butter to the pan. Cook, gently pressing the sandwich, for 3 to 4 more minutes, or until the cheese is melted and the bread is browned. The cooked sandwich should be about half as thick as it was before you began to cook it.

8. Transfer the cooked sandwich to a plate and cut in half diagonally. Cover to keep warm, and repeat with other sandwich. Enjoy!

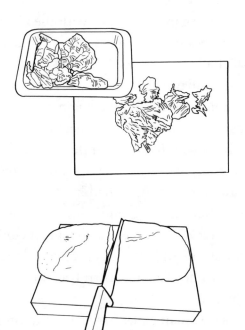

Cuba's Struggle for Independence

The Cuban people became unhappy about living under the rule of a country that was so far away. In 1868, after many years of struggle to break free from Spain, Cuba's plantation owners took matters into their own hands and declared Cuba an independent country. Spain responded by waging a war on Cuba that would last a decade. From 1868 to 1878, the Ten Years' War, as it would later be called, claimed the lives of 250,000 Cubans, and the country was unable to break free of Spain's rule.

José Martí, a Cuban poet, had been a leader in the struggle for Cuba's independence. When Spain regained control of the country, Martí fled to New York to avoid being imprisoned or killed. In 1895, though, Martí decided to fight for Cuba's independence once again, and he led a revolution against the Spanish colonizers. Although Martí died in battle, the renewed struggle he had sparked continued. Finally, with the help of the United States during the Spanish-American War, Cuba became independent from Spain in 1899.

But Cuba was still not a truly independent country. The U.S. military occupied the country, and Cubans lived uneasily under the country's protection. In 1901 the United States enacted the Platt Amendment, which declared that the United States was allowed to intervene, if necessary, in Cuban affairs of state. To the relief of many Cubans, U.S. military occupation of Cuba ended in 1902 and, in 1934, the Platt Amendment was overturned. Cuba was finally a truly independent country. But its citizens found themselves ruled by a series of corrupt and dictatorial governments, and they continued to struggle for freedom—this time, from their own leaders. In 1959 a Cuban revolutionary promised to give power back to the people, and he took over the government. His name was Fidel Castro.

Cuba and the Regime of Fidel Castro

At first Castro was hailed as a hero, but within months of taking over the country he, too, became a dictator who ruled with an iron fist. All property—from people's homes, privately owned land, and farms to stores, restaurants, and factories—was taken away by the government and redistributed to Cubans in whatever way their new leader saw fit. Newspapers were not allowed to print anything negative about Castro. The Catholic and private schools were closed, organized religion was forbidden, and Cuba became a Communist country. Anyone who spoke out against Castro or his government was jailed.

In 1960 the cold war (see page 111) between the United States and the Soviet Union was in full force. Under its dictator, Fidel Castro, Cuba began an alliance with the Communist Soviet Union. As a result, the United States broke off its relationship with Cuba.

Thousands of Cubans fled their home country to escape Castro's Communist regime and the harsh conditions under which the Cuban government forced them to live. But, unlike the wealthy Cubans who had immigrated to the United States before Castro's reign, the Cubans under Communist rule were forced to give up everything they had in order to leave the country. These Cubans left behind their money, homes, cars, jewelry—almost everything except a change of clothes—to find a new home in the United States. As the years progressed and people continued to flee Cuba, Castro began to prevent Cubans from leaving the country at all.

About 200,000 Cuban exiles arrived in the United States by airplane between 1959 and 1962. Most of them settled in or near Miami, Florida, a city that had fallen into economic dis-

What Is Communism?

Communism is a type of government in which the state owns everything; there is no such thing as personal property. People who live under Communist rule are usually not allowed to speak out against or disagree with the government. The government makes all decisions in the lives of its people—from where they can live, work, and worship to what they can read, discuss—even what they can buy. The theory is that everyone should be treated in exactly the same way and that the government knows what is best for the people.

After World War II, two world superpowers, the United States and the Soviet Union, became fierce enemies. The Soviet Union promoted and supported countries that embraced (or wanted to participate in) Communism, while the United States promoted and supported countries that were anti-Communist. For almost 50 years, relations between the two countries were very tense and hostile. Although the United States and the Soviet Union never actually went to war, the possibility of an enormous battle was always present. This period of unease and conflict is known as the cold war. It finally ended in 1991, when the Soviet Union collapsed.

tress. Although many of the exiles were doctors, lawyers, businesspeople, teachers, and other professionals, they were not able to practice their professions in the United States because they did not have the certifications that the United States required for people to perform those jobs. Many of the exiles did not speak English, which made life in their new country even more difficult. But the exiles were a hardworking and industrious group that made the most of their circumstances. Many had to take low-level jobs as janitors, maids, and dish-washers in the hotel and service industries, but they saved money, educated their children, and started small businesses. Due in large part to the contributions of these Cuban refugees, Miami once again became a bustling, prosperous city.

Operation Pedro Pan

An American priest named Bryan Walsh became concerned about Cuban children growing up in such a repressive country. Fidel Castro had imposed harsh restrictions on Cuban citizens

Refugee Status

Cubans were given a special rank among U.S. immigrants. Because they came to the United States to seek refuge, or safety, from the oppression of Fidel Castro and the Cuban government, they were classified as refugees, or exiles, and they were allowed to come into the United States without obtaining the U.S. documents that were required of immigrants from other countries. In addition, the U.S. government provided them with housing, medical, and financial assistance.

In 1966 Congress passed the Cuban American Adjustment Act, which granted "permanent resident" status to Cuban refugees who had lived in the United States for at least one year. This gave the Cubans an enormous advantage over other immigrant groups, who often had to struggle to obtain legal permission to live in the United States.

who wished to leave the country, and the families were not allowed to emigrate. In 1960 Walsh organized Operation Pedro Pan (Pedro is Spanish for Peter) as a way to bring the children to the United States. Operation Pedro Pan was a cooperative effort by the priest, the families of children in Cuba, and the U.S. government to bring Cuban children to the United States. About 14,000 children—some as young as three years old—left their families behind in Cuba to travel alone to the United States. In the United States they were placed with foster families until they could be reunited with family members fleeing Cuba or with those who were already living in the United States.

The Bay of Pigs

The U.S. government, as well as the exiles who had been able to escape Cuba, believed that Castro and his Communist government were dangerous to the United States. They organized a plan whereby Cuban exiles would be trained by the U.S. Central Intelligence Agency (CIA) to overturn Castro's government. On April 17, 1961, 1,500 Cuban American fighters landed at the Bahía de Cochinos (which was incorrectly translated as the Bay of Pigs) in Cuba. The invasion turned out to be a disaster. Castro had been told by his spies that the invasion was going to take place, and he was prepared for them when they arrived. In addition, the exiles were poorly trained, the pro–United States forces in Cuba did not give the exiles the support they had been counting on, and the U.S. government changed its mind about providing air support, fearing that it would lead to a world war.

Castro's army easily defeated the exiles who invaded Cuba. One hundred soldiers were killed, more than 1,000 others were captured, and thousands of Cubans were jailed as possible accomplices to the plan.

Unsuccessful in its attempt to overthrow Castro's government, the United States imposed a trade embargo on Cuba. The trade embargo prohibits U.S. citizens from buying products from and selling products to Cuba and from traveling to Cuba. This trade embargo is still enforced today.

Cuban Missile Crisis of 1962

The United States discovered that the Communist Soviet Union was building nuclear missile sites in Cuba. The U.S. president, John F. Kennedy, demanded that the missiles be dismantled, and he forbade ships from leaving or traveling to Cuba by establishing a military blockade. A blockade is an act of war that is enforced by air or by sea. Two weeks later, the Soviets took down the Cuban missiles. In exchange, the United States had to agree that it would never invade Cuba again.

Freedom Flights: 1965–1973

After several years of ruling as a dictator, Castro grew tired of being portrayed as a bad man in the news reports of exiles who continued to escape Cuba. In September 1965 he decided to "open the doors" and let disgruntled Cubans leave the country. He said that relatives of these people, who had already relocated to Miami, could pick up the Cubans by boat in Camarioca, Cuba. Within the first two months, 5,000 Cubans had been brought to Florida! It was a dangerous mass exodus, and many Cubans were transported from Cuba in hastily prepared boats that were sometimes lost at sea.

Concerned about the safety of the exiles, the U.S. president, Lyndon Johnson, called for them to travel to the United States by airline. Castro allowed two flights per day from Varadero,

Cuba, to Miami, Florida. More than 300,000 Cuban refugees left Cuba between 1965 and 1973.

Many Cubans settled in Miami and other areas in Florida, but others went to New York City, Chicago, Boston, Washington, DC, Los Angeles, and other areas.

The Mariel Refugees

In 1980 a small group of Cubans who were desperate to leave the country crashed their bus into the Peruvian Embassy in

Cuban Jewish Exiles

At the time that Castro took over, there were about 15,000 Sephardic Jews living in Cuba. Sephardic Jews are Jewish people whose ancestors lived in one of the Jewish communities of Spain, Portugal, North Africa, or the Middle East. After the Communists gained power, 10,000 Cuban Sephardic Jews left Cuba for the United States, and most of them settled in the Miami area. Sephardic Jews speak Ladino, a combination of Hebrew and Spanish.

Elián González: Alone at Sea

The most widely publicized *balsero* was a five-year-old boy named Elián González. In 1988 he was found floating on a car tire in the middle of the ocean off the Florida coast. He was all by himself. Two fishermen found him and brought him to safety. His mother had perished at sea along with others who had made the trip.

The case of Elián González captured the attention of the world. Some people thought he should be allowed to stay with relatives in Miami and enjoy freedom; others thought he should go back to Cuba to live with his father. Eventually the U.S. government decided to send Elián back to his father in Cuba.

Cuba. (An embassy represents a foreign country and is there to offer help and assistance in the country where it is assigned.) Castro's soldiers shot at them, but they survived. They and 30 other Cubans begged for refuge in the Peruvian and Venezuelan embassies. Within days, thousands of other Cubans showed up at the embassies seeking help in leaving the country.

Wanting to avoid more bad publicity, Castro again decided to let Cubans leave the country, this time through Cuba's port of Mariel.

Over the next six months, 125,000 Cuban refugees left for Florida in what was called the Mariel Boatlift. Once again, relatives who had already relocated to the United States were told to come by boat to pick up the Cubans who wanted to leave. But critics said that Cuban officials forced people who had come to get relatives to also take criminals and other undesirable people that Castro wanted to get rid of. Many of these "undesirable" people were very poor, and some did not have any relatives in the United States to take them in. Most of them were male, and two thousand of them were prisoners who had been released in order to get them out of the country. Some of these men were placed in prisons in the United States, and many of the refugees who did not have relatives to take them in were placed in temporary shelters.

Although at the time the arrival of thousands of refugees overwhelmed the city of Miami and the state of Florida's social services, some now credit the "Marielitos" with eventually revitalizing the city of Miami.

The Balseros (1990s)

After the fall of the Soviet Union in 1991, life in Cuba became desperate. The Soviet Union had been Cuba's number one ally and supporter, and it was the main provider of money and weapons to Cuba. When the Soviet Union collapsed and Russia gave up Communism, Cuba was left as one of the last Communist countries in the world. The country fell into an economic decline, and Castro became even more dictatorial and repressive. As time passed, Cubans experienced shortages of everything, including food. People on the island began to protest. Once again, Castro agreed to allow Cubans to leave the country.

Instead of having relatives from the United States come to get them, however, these people had to make it to their new country on their own. Many left in makeshift rafts that were very poorly constructed; some of these rafts were nothing but empty oil drums tied together. Others attempted to cross the ocean on inner tubes. The distance between Cuba and Florida is only 90 miles, but the seas are fierce and the waters are shark-infested. Thousands of *balseros* (which means rafters) made it to freedom, but many others did not survive the voyage.

Little Havana

Although they were happy to be free of the dictator Fidel Castro and his government's harsh policies, Cuban exiles longed for the island country they'd left behind. The large bulk of Cubans settled in Miami, Florida. Miami's tropical weather, palm trees, and beaches closely resembled those of Cuba. They miraculously transformed what was, in 1959, a run-down tourist area into a vibrant, economically sound, productive community. The center of this revitalization was, and still is, a section of Miami called Little Havana.

In Little Havana, Cubans felt at home. There they could shop in bodegas that sold Cuban foods, read Cuban newspapers and magazines, and play a game of dominoes in the park, just as they had in Cuba. If they were sick, they could

see a Cuban doctor; if they wanted their car fixed, they could go to a Cuban auto repair shop; and if they needed to borrow money, they could ask for a loan from a Cuban-owned bank. Eventually the area offered Spanish-speaking radio and television programs, movie theaters that showed Spanish films, and plays that were performed in Spanish.

Little Havana continues to be a thriving, bustling section of Miami. There you can buy tropical fruits at *fruterías* (fruit stores); *café Cubano* (Cuban coffee) on every street corner; fresh sugarcane juice, which is called *guarapo* (goo-ah-RAH-poh); *coco frío* (the water of a fresh-cut coconut, which is sipped through a straw directly from the coconut); and *batidos* (bah-TEE-dohs), or tropical milkshakes. Stores sell guayaberas (a popular type of men's shirt), hand-rolled cigars, Spanish music CDs, DVDs of Spanish-language movies, and piñatas; botanicas sell herbal medicines, incense, candles, and spiritual goods for the practice of Santeria. The constant sounds of salsa and other forms of Latin music spill from storefronts and cars, giving Little Havana a vibrant and lively atmosphere.

Restaurants in Little Havana sell a traditional stew of thick meat and vegetables called *ajiaco* (ah-HEAH-coh); *fritas* (FREE-tahs), or Cuban hamburgers; Cuban black beans; and pizza topped with Caribbean ingredients such as plantains, pineapple, and spicy beef.

Little Havana is home to immigrants from other countries as well. Part of Little Havana is now called Little Managua (after Managua, the capital of Nicaragua) because it contains many small businesses owned by Nicaraguan, Honduran, Salvadoran, and other Central and South American immigrants.

Make a *Batido*: A Tropical Milkshake

A *batido* is something to be savored on a hot day in Little Havana. It's milky, fruity, and very Cubano! *Batidos* are sold in open-air markets, in restaurants, and at all celebrations and fiestas in Little Havana. Here's a simple *batido* that you can make at home.

4 servings

What You Need

2 cups milk
Blender
1 cup peeled, seeded, and diced papaya, mango, guava, passion fruit, or tamarind *or* about 7 ounces tropical *fruta*, or fruit pulp (available in the frozen-foods section of Latino and many other grocery stores)
1 cup (about 14) ice cubes
½ cup sugar
4 8-ounce glasses
4 straws (optional)

What You Do

1. Pour the milk in the blender. Add the diced fruit or the *fruta*. (If the *fruta* is frozen, break it into small chunks before placing it in the blender.) Add the ice cubes and the sugar.
2. Place the lid on the blender and blend at low speed until the ice cubes are crushed and the liquid is creamy (about 3 minutes).
3. Pour equal amounts of the beverage into each glass. Place a straw in each glass, if desired. Enjoy!

Roosters

In Cuban American communities, the rooster is an important symbol of male strength, procreation (the act of creating new life), and the past. Cuban Americans often have pet roosters. In Little Havana you can see roosters running around in backyards, as well as figurines of roosters made of various materials such as clay, wood, feathers, papier-mâché, and plastic. There are even "talking" rooster toys! Roosters are often seen in Cuban American paintings.

Street Party! Carnaval Miami

Carnaval Miami is often called the "world's largest street party." It is a celebration of Cuban and Latino culture. Every year before Easter, 23 blocks of Little Havana's Eighth Street, which is also called Calle Ocho (KA-yeh O-choh), is blocked off to traffic. Stages are set up to feature all types of Latino music and performances. Food stalls sell ceviche (say-VEE-chay), a dish that is made with marinated fish; Venezuelan arepas (ah-REH-pahs), which are cornmeal pancakes stuffed with cheese; paella; and *ropa vieja* (ROH-pah vee-AY-ha), a traditional dish of shredded beef, vegetables, and sauce (*ropa vieja* means "old clothes"). Kids enjoy face painting, stilt walking, and carnival rides.

In recent years, Carnaval Miami and Calle Ocho have hosted more than a million people each year. In 1988 the festival made the *Guinness Book of World Records* when more than 119,000 people created the world's longest conga line!

Cuban Music and Dance

Some of the greatest gifts that Cubans have brought to the United States are their music and dance forms, which blend the rhythms and beats of African drums with traditional Spanish music.

The conga is a dance that is named after the tall, narrow African drum. The rumba is a ballroom dance that was very popular in the United States from the 1930s through the 1950s. It is danced to percussion-based music that has a syncopated (irregular) rhythm.

Latin jazz combines Afro-Cuban music with American jazz. Salsa is both a dance and a type of music that fuses together Latin Jazz, Afro-Cuban, and American pop music. It became very popular during the 1960s. The mambo is similar to the rumba, and it has an infectious quality that makes you want to move to its quick beat.

The *cha cha cha* is also both a dance and a type of music. It's similar to a fast waltz, and the dance is characterized by the shuffling, "cha-cha-cha" sound of the dancers' feet as they glide across the floor.

Start a Conga Line

A conga line is more like a moving party than a dance. People form a line, one behind the other, with each person's hands placed on the waist of the person in front of him or her. As each person moves to the beat of the music, the line winds its way through a street, home, or party area. Conga lines usually keep up the dance for no more than 5 or 6 minutes.

What You Need

CD of lively Latin music
6 or more people (the more, the better!)

What You Do

1. Put on the music.
2. Select a person to lead the conga line. Have the other people line up behind the leader, with each person's hands on the waist of the person in front of him or her.
3. Follow the leader while you snake around a room, using your feet to dance to the beat of the music. People in conga lines often perform the same steps together, with an emphasis on every fourth beat of the music. One common dance move is to step, step, step, and kick. The leader,

whose hands are free, can move his or her arms and hands to the music as well. Conga lines are all about having fun, so enjoy yourself!

Build Afro-Cuban Bongos

What You Need

2 empty, circular ("drum-shaped") containers
   of different sizes (such as oatmeal or bread
   crumb containers, or you can buy papier-
   mâché containers from a craft store)
1½-inch cube lightweight wood block
   (available at craft stores)
8 thumbtacks
Black and red acrylic paints
2 paper cups
Paintbrush

What You Do

1. Lay one container on its side. Place the wood block on top
   of the side of the container about an inch up from the
   bottom. Working from the inside of the container, push
   4 thumbtacks through the container and the wood block so
   that the wood block is attached to the container.
2. Set the container upright on the floor or on a table. Place
   the other container next to it, also upright, on the floor or
   table. Working from the inside of the container, push

4 thumbtacks through that container and the wood block.
Make sure that both containers are level with the floor or
table so that one "drum" is shorter than the other.

3. Squirt each color of paint into a paper cup. Using the
   paintbrush, paint the sides of the containers and the wood
   block any way that you like. Do not paint the top of the
   containers. Let dry.
4. Use your hands to play your bongos!

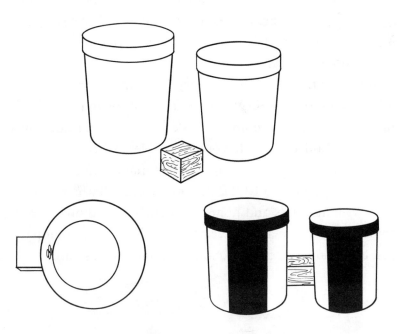

Cuban American Celebrations

Like most families, Cuban Americans mix their native foods, traditions, and celebrations with an American twist. Families are at the center of Cuban American celebrations, and kids are always included. Parties start late and go on for hours! Many Cuban families have returned to religious traditions that were banned in Cuba under Castro.

Christmas Eve (Nochebuena)

In a traditional Cuban American home, the family gathers for a large feast on Christmas Eve, or Nochebuena, which means "Good Night." At the center of the family dinner is a roasted pig. It's tradition for the men in the family to dig a hole in the ground and make a charcoal pit to roast the pig in. It usually takes the whole day for the pig to cook, and family and friends gather together to talk, share stories, munch on snacks, and play as the delectable smells of the pig and other foods fill the air. These days, many families are too busy to spend a whole day roasting a pig themselves. Instead, they either have a baker roast it for them or they roast a smaller piece of meat, such as a pork shoulder, in the oven.

When its time for dinner, everyone gathers for a feast of *lechón asado* (lay-CHOWN ah-SAH-doh), or roast pork; rice and beans; *yuca con mojo* (YOO-kah cohn MOH-hoh), which consists of boiled yucca (a root vegetable) served with garlic sauce; fried plantains; and, for dessert, flan, guava-filled pastries, and *turron* (too-ROHN), a rich candy that is usually made with almonds and honey. Christmas Eve dinner is a big family party where all are welcome, and parents, grandparents, aunts, uncles, cousins, children, and friends gather together to enjoy the holiday. After dinner, some families attend midnight mass.

In some Cuban American families, gifts are exchanged on Christmas Day. In other families, the children receive their gifts on Three Kings Day.

Three Kings Day (Día de los Tres Reyes)

It's tradition, on the night before Three Kings Day, for Cuban American children to put grass in their shoes and tuck them under the bed for the camels that accompany the Three Kings. In the morning the children wake up to find presents in their shoes. Miami hosts an annual Three Kings Day Parade, at which people can see the Three Kings riding on camels and enjoy floats, music, and more.

New Year's Eve

Cuban Americans have a tradition of drinking cider and eating 12 grapes—one for each month of the year—at midnight on New Year's Eve. The tradition may have been started as a way to wish for enough food during the 12 months of the new year.

Just before midnight on New Year's Eve, some Cuban Americans participate in a fun tradition of dumping a bucket of water onto the street as a symbol of getting rid of all the negative or bad things that happened in the past year and welcoming new, good things to come.

Cuban American Food

The first Cuban refugees in the United States had little money to buy food. Their first meals in their new country were made

Chinese Cubans

In the mid-1800s the Spanish plantation owners in Cuba needed many people to work in the sugarcane fields. They turned to the Chinese, bringing thousands of them to Cuba to work as contract laborers. Contract laborers signed an agreement that they would work for a period of years in return for their fare to Cuba and living arrangements. They worked long hours under harsh conditions. Many of the Chinese laborers stayed in Cuba after their contracts were fulfilled, and they opened businesses that catered to both the Chinese and the Cuban communities on the island. When Fidel Castro became Cuba's leader, his government took over the Chinese businesses. As a result, most of the Chinese chose to leave Cuba. They settled in the United States, where they were free to own their own businesses. Many of the Chinese people from Cuba established restaurants and other businesses in southern Florida. Today, visitors can still find restaurants that offer interesting combinations of Chinese and Cuban foods!

from products given to them by the U.S. government. Cubans look back at what they ate during those times and call it "refugee food." Refugee food included cheese, powdered milk, powdered eggs, powdered mashed potatoes, and peanut butter. Cubans were not familiar with most of these items, and they tasted odd to the exiles, who were used to eating fresh seafood, fruits and vegetables, and other foods found in the Caribbean. After settling in the Miami area, Cubans opened their own stores, butcher shops, and bakeries that catered to Cuban tastes.

Cuban food has native Indian, Spanish, African, and even Chinese roots, thanks to the thousands of Chinese who came to work in Cuba in the mid-1800s. It is hearty, filling, and not very spicy. The base of many Cuban dishes is a *sofrito* (a mixture of onion, mild peppers, tomato, and garlic). Foods found on the Cuban table include salads, stews, rice and beans, fried plantains, roast pork, beef, and various root vegetables such as potato, yucca, and malanga (taro).

Cuban sandwiches are popular lunch items, and empanadas (meat-filled pastries) and fried stuffed potatoes, which are called *papas rellenas* (PAH-pahs reh-YEH-nahs), are enjoyed as snacks. Yerba mate soda, which tastes like a soft drink made of tea and cream, is a popular Cuban beverage, as is *cafecito*, a sweetened espresso beverage that is enjoyed at any time of day by both adults and children. Popular desserts include flan, rice pudding, and fruit-filled pastries called *pastelitos* (pah-steh-LEE-tohs).

Play *Cubilete*: A Traditional Cuban Dice Game

Cubilete (khu-bee-leh-TEH) is a popular Cuban dice game that is played by both children and adults. *Cubilete* means "tumbler" in Spanish. The traditional game uses special dice, but we will use standard dice in this activity.

Each number on the dice has a name (see below). The object of the game is to throw 5 of the same dice: 5 "aces"; 5 "kings"; 5 "queens"; 5 "jacks"; 5 "10s"; or 5 "9s." Aces are wild, which means that they can be used as kings, queens, jacks, 10s, or 9s, depending on what the player needs.

Names of Dice

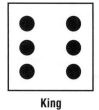

King

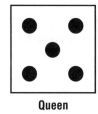

Queen

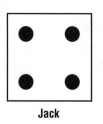

Jack

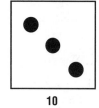

10

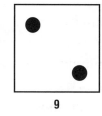

9

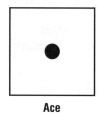

Ace

The first player to get 10 points wins the game. Here is how *cubilete* is scored:

5 aces: 10 points
5 kings (with no wild aces): 5 points
5 kings (with one or more wild aces): 2 points
5 queens (with or without any wild aces): 1 point
5 jacks (with or without any wild aces): 1 point
5 10s (with or without any wild aces): 1 point
5 9s (with or without any wild aces): 1 point

What You Need

2 or more players
5 dice
Cup to use as a tumbler in which to shake up the dice

What You Do

1. Each player rolls one die. The player who rolls the highest number goes first. The player to that person's left goes next, and so on.

2. On each turn, a player gets to roll the dice 3 times. Each time the dice are rolled, the player may hold, or set aside, any number of dice that he or she chooses in the hope that, on the next roll, more of that number will come up. For instance, if a player rolls all 5 dice and gets 3 jacks, a 10, and a 9, he or she would probably hold (set aside) the 3 jacks, throw the 10 and the 9 dice back into the tumbler, and roll them again. If the player got another jack on the second roll, he or she would hold that one as well and roll the single remaining die on his or her third try. Players may use all 3 of their turns to roll or they may choose to roll the dice only once or twice.

3. After everybody has rolled the dice, points are scored. If nobody has rolled 5 of a kind, nobody gets any points. If two or more players have rolled 5 of a kind, the player who rolled the highest rank gets the points associated with his or her roll. (For example, 5 aces beats 5 kings with no wild aces; 5 kings with no wild aces beats 5 kings with one or more wild ace; 5 queens beats 5 10s; and so on.)

4. Players continue rounds of rolling the dice until one person gets 10 points.

Cuba Today

More than 1 million Cubans have immigrated to the United States since the dictator Fidel Castro took over Cuba's government in 1959. Many Cuban exiles left the island thinking they would return to Cuba once Castro was no longer the country's leader. No one could have imagined that his reign would last close to a half century.

On February 19, 2008, after 49 years in power, a frail, sick, and elderly Castro finally resigned as Cuba's president. Less than a week later, Castro's brother Raúl was chosen by Fidel to succeed him. Little change in Cuba's Communist policies is expected under Raúl Castro.

Almost all of Cuba's exiles have given up the dream of returning to their homeland. Most of them have established new lives in the United States, and Cuba is likely to remain a very poor country that has few basic amenities. Many of the newest generation of Cuban Americans were born in the United States and have never even been to Cuba. This generation has always called the United States "home," and they have little desire to live in a foreign country.

Notable Cuban Americans

There are many Cuban Americans who have contributed to the United States in significant ways. Cuban Americans have influenced the country's music, and they have enlightened and entertained us through writing, acting, and other artistic endeavors. Cuban Americans have included powerful members of U.S. government, awe-inspiring athletes, and more. Here are just a few of the Cuban Americans who have made a difference.

Athletes

Orlando Hernandez (1969–) — A Major League Baseball pitcher for the New York Mets whose nickname is "El Duque"

Pablo Morales (1964–) — A swimmer who won the gold medal in the 1984 Summer Olympics

Tony Oliva (1941–) — A former Major League Baseball player who won the American League batting title three times

Jennifer Rodriguez (1976–) — A speed skater who won two bronze medals in the 2002 Winter Olympics

Authors

Nilo Cruz (1960–) — A playwright and the first Latino to win the Pulitzer Prize for Drama (for his play *Anna in the Tropics*)

Oscar Hijuelos (1951–) — The first Latino author to win a Pulitzer Prize for Fiction (for his book *The Mambo Kings Play Songs of Love*)

Entertainers

Desi Arnaz (1917–1986) — An actor, producer, and director who created and co-starred in the TV show *I Love Lucy* (which also starred his real-life wife, Lucille Ball)

Fernando Bujones (1955–2005) — A ballet dancer who was considered one of the finest male dancers of the 20th century and who was the first U.S. citizen to win a gold medal at the International Ballet Competition

Cameron Diaz (1972–) — An actress whose films include *Shrek* and *Charlie's Angels*

Gloria Estefan (1958–) — A Grammy Award–winning singer, songwriter, and member of the musical group Miami Sound Machine whose hits include "Rhythm Is Gonna Get You" and "Conga"

Emilio Estefan (1952–) — The creator of the musical group Miami Sound Machine

Andy Garcia (1956–) — An actor whose films include *Beverly Hills Chihuahua* and *The Godfather Part III*

Cesar Romero (1907–1994) — A dancer and actor who played the Joker in the 1960s TV show *Batman* and the grandson of Cuban patriot José Martí

Cristina Saralegui (1948–) — The host of the Emmy Award–winning talk show *The Christina Show* and the creator of her own magazine

Politicians

Mel Martinez (1946–) — A U.S. Senator from Florida

Robert Menendez (1954–) — A U.S. Senator from New Jersey

Ileana Ros-Lehtinen (1952–) — The first Cuban American to be elected to the U.S. Congress

Other Notable Cuban Americans

Aristides Agramonte y Simoni (1868–1931) — A physician, scientist, and member of the Reed Yellow Fever Board (U.S. Army) that helped to discover the way in which mosquitoes transmit yellow fever

Carlos Finlay
(1833–1915)   A physician and scientist whose early studies helped to discover the way in which mosquitoes transmit yellow fever

Roberto Goizueta
(1931–1997)   A businessman who, as chief executive officer of the Coca-Cola Company, led that organization to become one of the top companies in the world

Soledad O'Brien (1966–)   A TV news reporter, anchor, and producer

Pedro Sanchez (1940–)   A scientist who has worked for years to improve agriculture in tropical areas while protecting the environment and the winner of the 2002 World Food Prize

From Sea to Shining Sea— in Spanish!

Here are some Spanish and Taino words that could be used when talking about a day at the beach.

Hammock. This word comes from the word *hamaca*, which means "hanging bed" in the Taino language.

Cabana. This comes from the Spanish word *cabaña*, which means cabin or hut.

Barbecue. This word comes from the Taino word *barbacoa*, which means a four-legged stand made of sticks, used to roast meat

Canoe. This is the English version of the Spanish word *canoa*.

Breeze. This comes from the Spanish word *brisa*.

◇ 7 ◇

Central Americans

entral America includes the countries between Mexico (which is in North America) and South America: Costa Rica, El Salvador, Guatemala, Honduras, Nicaragua, Panama, and Belize. This chapter concentrates on El Salvador, Guatemala, Honduras, and Nicaragua, the countries from which the greatest number of Central Americans immigrated to the United States.

Only a small number of Central Americans immigrated to the United States before the second half of the 20th century. During the 1980s and 1990s, however, Central Americans fled their countries by the thousands to escape brutal military dictatorships, civil wars, earthquakes, drought, and poverty. Many of them relocated to the United States, where they hoped life would be safer, more predictable, and less harsh.

The United States was slow to react to the plight of the Central Americans and only reluctantly allowed them into the country as refugees. Part of the reason was that the United States government had involved itself in the problems of Central America. In several Central American countries there were two opposing forces: military dictatorships and Communist revolutionaries. The United States at that time was in fear of Communism. The U.S. government believed that, if one country in Central America became Communist, Communism would sweep through Central America and Mexico and eventually reach the United States.

To prevent the Communist revolutionaries from taking over governments in Central America, the United States helped the military dictatorships stay in control. Unfortunately, both the revolutionary organizations and the military dictatorships waged violence against not only each other, but on the citizens of Central America as well.

When thousands of Central Americans tried to enter the United States in order to escape the violence and harsh conditions under which they lived, the United States took the position that the refugees were not in danger in their home countries. They labeled them "economic" refugees who simply wanted to come to the United States to escape poverty. Only a small percentage of Salvadorans, Guatemalans, and Hondurans were given asylum, which granted them legal permission to

Central America

Mexico

Belize

Guatemala

Honduras

El Salvador

Nicaragua

Pacific Ocean

Costa Rica

Panama

Atlantic Ocean

SOUTH AMERICA

stay in the country. Nicaraguans were granted asylum in greater numbers because they came from a Communist country, which the United States believed was more dangerous. Central American immigrants who were not granted asylum had to come into the United States illegally or wait months or years to go through the regular channels of immigration.

Jim Corbett and the Sanctuary Movement

Individual citizens and community organizations throughout the United States were the first to respond to the troubles of the Central Americans who had been denied asylum, most of whom were Salvadorans and Guatemalans. The American people could clearly see that, whether their home countries were led by Communists or by military dictatorships, these people were in danger and running for their lives.

More than 300 churches of all faiths banded together to form a network of safe havens to shelter Central Americans from the eye—and the legal action—of the U.S. government as they made their way into the United States. The action of these churches and their members is known as the sanctuary movement.

A retired rancher in Arizona named Jim Corbett inspired the movement in 1981 after hearing about Salvadorans and Guatemalans who were in detention centers (where immigrants who were caught entering the United States illegally were sent before being deported). He went to one of these detention centers and heard heart-wrenching stories about immigrants dying of thirst or drowning trying to cross the border into the United States. Over the years, Corbett helped hundreds of desperate Central American refugees secretly make their way across the Mexican border and into Arizona. His example spurred religious organizations to take up the challenge. In 1982 Reverend John Fife's Southside Presbyterian Church in Tucson, Arizona, became the first church to shelter Central American refugees.

Immigration Act of 1986

The U.S. Immigration Act of 1986 provided a measure of relief to the many Central Americans who had taken illegal refuge in the United States and who lived in constant fear of being discovered and deported (sent back to their home countries). The act declared that any and all immigrants who had been in the United States illegally for the past four or more years could receive visas and live in the United States legally. Having legal visas also made them eligible to apply for United States citizenship. In addition, the act declared that farmworkers who had worked in the United States for at least 90 days from 1985 through 1986 were eligible to become U.S. resident aliens, and therefore could legally live and work in the country even though they were not U.S. citizens.

◈ El Salvador

The Mayan people created a sophisticated culture in what is now El Salvador, Guatemala, Honduras, Belize, and Mexico in the years between 2000 B.C.E. and C.E. 900. They had a written language, religion, mathematics, astronomy, a calendar, and magnificent temples and pyramids. Mayan descendents still live in these areas. Amazing remnants of Mayan culture were found in 1976

Temporary Protection Status

A devastating hurricane called Hurricane Mitch hit Honduras and Nicaragua in 1998, killing 9,000 Hondurans and ripping out most of the country's crops and infrastructure (roads and bridges). During that time, the United States granted temporary protective status to tens of thousands of Hondurans as well as Nicaraguans, which allowed them to live and work in the United States until it was safe to return to their home countries.

In 2001 Salvadorans were awarded the same protections after two destructive earthquakes occurred in El Salvador.

when a bulldozer clearing some land hit the side of an adobe home. Archeologists were called in and discovered an entire village that had been buried in volcanic ash for hundreds of years. A 30-year archaeological dig has uncovered ancient tools, half eaten food (1,400 years old!), furniture, and a farm where manioc, a starchy plant similar to the potato, had been planted.

Spanish conquistadors first came to El Salvador in 1522, when it was called Cuscatlán by the native Pipil Indians. Two years later a Spanish conquistador named Pedro de Alvarado led the first effort to claim the land for Spain. The Pipil Indians and other natives who lived there fiercely resisted the Spaniards' attempts to take over the land but, after several years, they were defeated. El Salvador would remain under Spanish control for 300 years.

In 1821 El Salvador, along with the other Central American colonies that were under Spanish rule at the time, declared their independence from Spain. Two years later, what are present-day El Salvador, Costa Rica, Guatemala, Honduras, and Nicaragua banded together and established the United Provinces of Central America. The union, which was modeled after the union of the states in the United States, lasted for 15 years, then was disbanded. In 1840 El Salvador became an independent country.

During Spain's 300-year-long rule of El Salvador, the Spanish had established an unfair system in which most of the land was given to a small number of wealthy Spanish families. Because they had no other way to support themselves, the poor mestizo peasants were forced to work as farmers on plantations owned by these wealthy families, and they often endured harsh treatment and poor living conditions. In the mid-1800s the

Bloodless Independence

Although El Salvador and other regions of Central America had been under Spanish rule for 300 years, the Spaniards did not put up much of a fight when they declared their independence from Spain in 1821. At that time, the Spanish were already fighting revolts in Spanish-ruled Mexico and South America, and they did not have enough soldiers to wage war in yet another area. As a result, the colonies of Central America were able to gain independence from Spain without war or bloodshed.

plantation owners began to grow coffee beans to export to markets around the world. Thanks to the labor of the poor farmers who worked on the plantations, coffee became a major source of income for the Spanish families. The nation has been largely dependent upon this crop ever since.

Even after El Salvador declared independence from Spain, the unfair distribution of wealth and land there remained. This led to many uprisings and revolts against El Salvador's government. In 1932 a Communist revolutionary named Augustín Farabundo Martí led a peasant rebellion against the govern-

ment of Maximiliano Hernández Martínez. To put an end to the revolt, the government massacred more than 15,000 people. This horrific event is known as *La Matanza*, which means "the Slaughter."

Civil unrest and violence continued in El Salvador for many years. In 1980, a popular Catholic archbishop named Oscar Romero, who spoke out on human rights and was a public critic of the government, was assassinated. This outraged the Salvadoran people, who believed that the military government was behind his death. The assassination led to civil war between the military government and a pro-Communist group of guerillas (fighters who are not associated with a country's government and who frequently engage in surprise attacks) who wanted to topple the government. During the 12 years of war that followed, 75,000 civilians (people who are not soldiers) were killed by

Catholic Missionaries

Wherever the Spanish explorers went, Catholic missionaries soon followed. Just as they had in the Spanish-ruled Southwest of the United States, the missionaries established Catholic churches in Central America, and they converted the native people (sometimes against their will) to Catholicism.

both the guerillas and the military government's death squads, which were organized to crush opposition.

In 1992 a peace accord between the two groups was finally reached. The military was no longer allowed to be in control of the country, and the guerillas were given a voice in the government. Today, El Salvador is still working to rebuild the country. In March 2009, Mauricio Funes, the first leftist leader (from the pro-Communist side), was democratically elected.

Salvadoran Americans

Salvadorans in the United States are very poor. Many find it very difficult to learn to read and write in English because they had never been taught to read and write at all, even in their native Spanish language. Most Salvadorans who immigrated to the United States had been farmworkers in their home country, and they have had a hard time finding employment in the U.S. cities they settled in. Salvadoran Americans compensate for their lack of skills and education by being hardworking, dependable workers. Many Salvadoran Americans work as laborers (unskilled workers) in restaurants, hotels, private homes, and other businesses in the service industry. There are 1.3 million Salvadoran Americans living in the United States. Half of all Salvadoran Americans live in the Los Angeles, California, area. Others settled in New York City, Houston, Texas, Washington, DC, and other cities.

Salvadoran American Day

August 6 has officially been named Salvadoran American Day by the U.S. Congress. This celebration honors Salvadoran customs and contributions to the United States. The day is celebrated in Salvadoran American communities with parades, singing, soccer matches, beauty pageants, and performances of the *cumbia* (COOM-bee-ah), a traditional dance. In the air are the delicious aromas of Salvadoran foods such as *pupusas* (poo-POO-suhs), thick corn tortillas that are filled with a variety of ingredients, including fresh cheese, pork, and refried beans.

Although they do not earn much money, many Salvadoran Americans continue to send part of their earnings to relatives who are still in El Salvador. Because most people in El Salvador are extremely poor, this money is an important source of income to them. It is estimated that Salvadoran citizens receive about 3.3 billion dollars per year from relatives who have immigrated to the United States.

Create Corn Husk Flowers

Corn is a major staple of Central Americans' diets. In poor countries such as El Salvador, nothing goes to waste, and Salvadorans use the husks from corn to make a variety of crafts. One popular Salvadoran craft uses corn husks to make pretty "flowers," which are often sold at festivals and street fairs. Try your hand at making some corn husk flowers!

What You Need

24 dried corn husks (available at craft stores and in the ethnic section of some grocery stores)

Large bowl filled with warm water

Paper towels

Light brown acrylic paint

Paper cup

Paintbrush

6 1-inch-diameter Styrofoam dome shapes (or have an adult cut three 1-inch diameter balls in half)

Scissors

Glue

2 paper plates

Thumbtack or pushpin

7 12-inch-long brown chenille stems, also called pipe cleaners (available at craft stores)

Container: Recycle a container such as an empty, clean frozen juice container or bottle

What You Do

1. Place the corn husks in the bowl of warm water. Let soak for 20 minutes.
2. Transfer the corn husks to paper towels. Cover them with more paper towels and set them aside.
3. Pour paint into the paper cup. Using the paintbrush, paint the rounded "top" of each Styrofoam dome (leave the flat side unpainted).
   Let dry.
4. Using the scissors, cut the corn husks into 48 2-inch-long "petals." The corn husks should be wet enough to work with, but not dripping wet.

5. Glue 8 petals, in the pattern of a flower (see drawing), to the unpainted side of each Styrofoam dome. Place the flowers, dome side down, on paper plates. Set aside to allow glue to dry (at least 1 hour).

6. Push a thumbtack or pushpin into the center of the unpainted side of each Styrofoam dome to make a small hole. Remove the thumbtack or pushpin. Push a chenille stem into each hole and into the Styrofoam. If any of the petals come loose, cut a ½-inch piece of the extra chenille stem and use it like a pin to attach the petal to the Styrofoam.

7. Arrange the flowers in the container. If you want to make the flowers shorter, bend each chenille stem at the bottom to achieve the height you want.

Try a Salvadoran Street Food

Street vendors in El Salvador and in Salvadoran American neighborhoods sell green mango slices seasoned with lime, salt, and ground pumpkin seeds. It's a tropical treat!

3 servings

What You Need

Adult Supervision Required

Vegetable peeler

1 green mango

Sharp knife

Serving plate

1 lime

2 ounces whole roasted, salted pumpkin seeds (or ground pumpkin seeds) often called *pepitas*, available at most grocery stores

Salt in shaker (optional)

What You Do

1. Using the vegetable peeler, peel the mango.
2. Using the knife, cut the mango into small slices of various sizes. (Do not cut into the pit in the middle of the mango.) Place the slices on a serving plate.
3. Using the knife, cut the lime in half.
4. Squeeze a bit of lime juice over each slice. Sprinkle the *pepitas* over the mango slices. If desired, sprinkle a bit of salt over the slices. Enjoy!

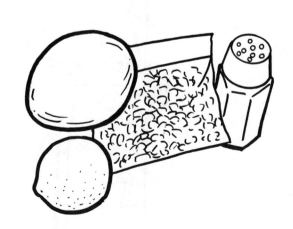
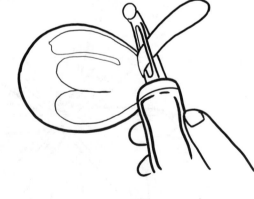

◈ Guatemala

For hundreds of years before the Spanish arrived in Guatemala, the Mayan culture thrived. The remains of a spectacular Mayan city called Tikal give us some clues about the complexities and accomplishments of Mayan culture. The Mayans started as hunters and gatherers, then progressed to farming and the building of city-states. Tikal is one of the city-states that have been preserved in the jungles of a National Park in Guatemala.

Tikal has the remains of Mayan temples, palaces, and plazas, some of which are 3,000 years old! It is surrounded by more ruins, including the homes of peasants. Tikal was once home to tens of thousands of Mayans but was mysteriously abandoned by the end of the 10th century.

When Pedro de Alvarado and the Spanish conquistadors arrived in Central America in 1522, the descendents of the Mayans were living in scattered agricultural villages. Alvarado and his men took over the Mayan city-states as Spanish colonies.

Spain controlled present day Guatemala for 300 years until it declared its independence in 1821. In 1824 Guatemala briefly joined the United Provinces of Central America until it was dismantled in 1838.

Guatemalans of pure Spanish or of Spanish and native Guatemalan heritage held all the wealth and power in the country. They owned the tobacco and sugarcane plantations, as well as the coffee bean plantations that became a very important part of Guatemala's economy in the 19th century. The native people were not allowed to own land; as a result, they had no choice but to work as plantation laborers for the wealthy landowners in order to survive.

Coffee was not the only major product grown in Guatemala. In the 20th century, bananas became another important source of income. The largest banana operation in Guatemala was actually owned by a U.S. company called the United Fruit Company. This company contributed in both good and bad ways to Guatemala and other Central American countries. The company built roads and established a port to support its business, and it exported huge shipments of bananas from Guatemala to areas all over the world. Unfortunately, the company interfered in the country's government by paying off government officials and giving support to military dictatorships that would favor United Fruit. It took over land that should have belonged to the Guatemalan people and encouraged the government to squash uprisings among the people.

The government of Guatemala was in a state of constant turmoil between left-wing and right-wing groups. In 1954, the United States was directly involved in toppling the left-wing

Left-Wing Versus Right-Wing Governments

When we refer to governments as being "left-wing" it means that the members believe that there are inequalities between the citizens and that action must be taken (even revolution) in order to offer the same opportunities to all. Right-wing governments generally support the current government or a return to an earlier form of government. Either type can be good or bad.

Guatemalan government and putting in a right-wing leader that favored United Fruit and other American companies. The United States believed that because the left-wing government was Communist, it would encourage the spread of Communism throughout the region and prevent American companies from being able to profit there. A terrible civil war broke out in 1960 and continued for 36 years between the left-wing (mostly) Mayan rebels and the right-wing government. Atrocities (cruel acts) were committed by both sides, but most violently by government "death squads" who hunted down rebels in the jungles.

As news about the civil war traveled to the United States and the rest of the world, the United States made the decision to dissolve its ties to the Guatemalan government. In 1977, President Jimmy Carter cut off military assistance and credit (lending money). In 1983 President Ronald Reagan reestablished military aid in the mistaken belief that the violence and human rights abuses were at an end.

Finally, in 1996 Guatemalan government leaders signed peace accords with leftist guerrillas, or rebels. The accords included calling for an end to the hostilities and a commitment to recognizing the rights of the Mayans, to human rights in general, and to establishing social programs to help the poor.

In September 2007 Álvaro Colom, a leftist candidate, was elected president of Guatemala. He has vowed to fight poverty and to crack down on illegal drug trafficking (selling), which has become a major problem in Guatemala. It is hoped that Guatemalans will continue to enjoy more reforms and changes in the future.

Guatemalan Americans

The majority of the 896,000 Guatemalans in the United States are Mayan and other native peoples. Each native Guatemalan group has its own language, and a Guatemalan American may speak one or more of any of the 20 native languages of these groups. Most speak Spanish and English as well. Many Guatemalan Americans live in Houston, Los Angeles, Phoenix, and Indiantown, Florida, which is about 100 miles north of Miami.

Farmwork is the most common occupation of Guatemalan Americans. Others work as gardeners and landscapers, construction workers, factory workers, roofers, restaurant workers, and hotel workers. Guatemalan American women often work as house cleaners, babysitters, and cooks for other U.S. families.

Create Guatemalan Worry Dolls

Guatemalans are known for their magnificent, colorful weavings, which are collected all over the world. Guatemalan women weave traditional clothing and goods, both for their families to use and as products to sell. Instead of throwing away scraps of material, they sometimes use them to create small dolls, called "worry dolls," for children. The dolls are usually made in small groups of six. According to a Guatemalan legend, if a person talks to each doll and shares a concern, or worry, with it, then puts the dolls under his or her pillow before going to sleep, the dolls will take away that person's worries during the night.

You can find Guatemalan worry dolls in U.S. stores that sell goods from Guatemala and Central America—or you can make your own! You can use one color or several colors of yarn to make your doll—it's your choice. There is no right or wrong way to wrap the yarn around the clothespins to make the dolls. You can follow the directions provided below or wrap the yarn in any way that seems easiest to you.

What You Need (to make 6 dolls and a carrying bag)

Scissors

3 12-inch-long chenille stems (pipe cleaners), available at craft stores

6 clothespins (straight wooden clothespins, not the type with a metal spring; see drawings)

18 (approximately) 3-foot lengths yarn, in 2–6 colors (for dolls)

Glue

Fine-point black and red markers

1 adult-sized sock

4 (approximately) 12-inch lengths of yarn (colors of your choice) to tie bag

14 (approximately) 8-inch lengths of yarn (colors of your choice) to decorate bag

What You Do

1. Cut each chenille stem in half.
2. Tie 1 piece of chenille stem around the "neck" of 1 clothespin to make arms for 1 doll.
3. Tie one end of the yarn to the clothespin, underneath the chenille stem (see drawing). Wrap the yarn around the doll's arms and behind the clothespin several times, until you have what look like sleeves.
4. You can make either a dress or a shirt and pants for your doll. To make a dress, wrap the yarn several times around

the clothespin, beginning at the neck and working your way down to the bottom of the clothespin. To make a multicolored dress, use lengths of different-colored yarn, tying one length to the next as you wrap. When you get to the bottom of the clothespin, cut the yarn and glue its end to the clothespin.

5. To make a shirt and pants, wrap the yarn around the clothespin as if you were making a multicolored dress, using one color for the shirt and switching to another color for the pants. Twist around about 4 times to make the seat of the pants, then come around the back (to the left of the clothespin) and twist the yarn over the "left leg," through the center space, around the back of the "right leg," over the "right leg," through the center space, around the back of the "left leg," over the "left leg" and repeat until the yarn has covered both "legs." Trim off any unused yarn, and glue the end of the yarn to the bottom of the clothespin.

6. Using the markers, draw a face on the doll.

7. Make hair for the doll, either by drawing it on with a marker or by gluing short lengths of yarn to the doll's head.

8. To make a headdress, place glue on the top area of the clothespin. Press one end of yarn onto the glue and coil the yarn around in a circle, pressing it into the glue. To make a two-color headdress, glue another coil of yarn onto the first coil.

9. Repeat 5 times, until you have 6 dolls.

10. Now make a bag to hold your dolls. Cut the sock about 3 inches up from the heel part of the sock. Glue lengths of different colors of yarn to the sock to form multicolored lines, zigzags, and geometric shapes. Put the dolls in the bag. Tie the bag with 3 or 4 different-colored 12-inch-long lengths of yarn.

For dresses

For pants

Make a Guatemalan Weaving

Guatemalans are well known for their beautiful and intricate weavings. To get a sense of what it is like to weave, you can make a simple loom out of cardboard and use yarn to weave a bookmark. Guatemalans use bright shades of yellow, turquoise, red, green, blue, purple, and black in their weavings. You can use 4 or 5 colors of your choice to make your bookmark.

What You Need

Ruler

Pencil

3-inch-by-8-inch piece sturdy
    cardboard

Scissors

Tape

14-foot length yarn, any
    color

4 2-foot lengths yarn,
    each a different color

What You Do

1. Using the ruler to measure, mark 11 ¼-inch segments from left to right across the top and bottom of the cardboard.
2. Cut a ½-inch-deep notch for each mark.
3. Make the warp (the material that runs from top to bottom). Tape one end of the 14-foot length of yarn to the top right corner of the cardboard (see drawing). Flip the cardboard over and pull the yarn through the top left notch and into the bottom left notch. Go behind the cardboard and then back down the front to the second left top notch to the second left bottom notch, until all the notches have yarn from top to bottom. When you get to the end, flip the cardboard over and secure by the tying the end of the yarn piece to the last warp. Trim off the excess yarn.
4. Flip the cardboard back over so that the front is facing you. Beginning at the bottom left corner of the cardboard, weave the first 2-foot length of yarn into the yarn that has been strung: leave a couple of inches of yarn loose (see drawing) and, working from left to right, thread the yarn over one length of strung yarn, then under the next, then over the next, and so on. When you get to the end of the row, go up to the next row on the right side of the cardboard and continue to weave, working from right to left. Continue until about 2 inches of the yarn length remains. Tie another 2-foot length of yarn to that piece. Trim off the excess length of the first piece of yarn. Continue to weave.

5. When you have filled up the cardboard piece, tie your yarn to the last warp. Now tie the yarn you left loose (bottom left) to a warp.

6. Flip the cardboard over and cut the back warps in half. Pull off the tape and remove the cardboard.

7. Now tie the fringe pieces together across the top. Make 3 groups of 3 and tie each group together. Do the same at the bottom. Cut the fringe to the length you would like.

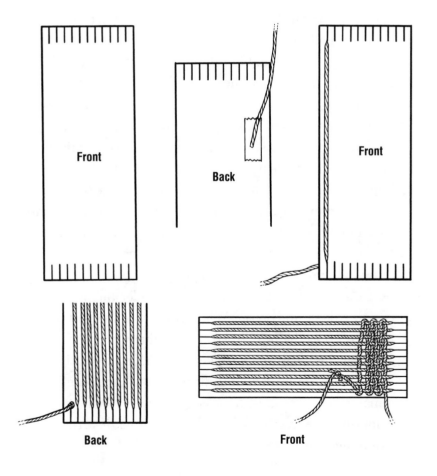

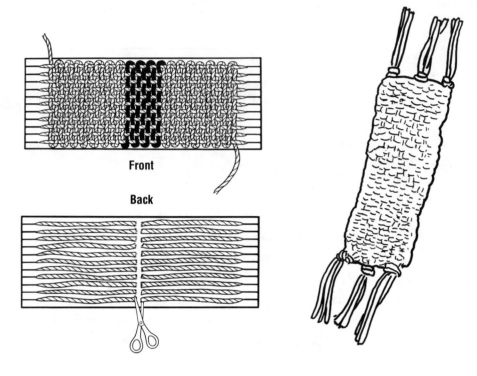

◈ Honduras

Honduras is Guatemala's southeast neighbor. When Christopher Columbus first set foot here during his fourth and final trip to the Americas in 1502, he named the country Honduras, which means "depths," in reference to the deep waters off its coast. Like Guatemala, Honduras is home to many magnificent remains of the Mayan culture.

In 1524 Pedro de Alvarado established Spanish settlements and mining towns along Honduras's coast. Several native tribes lived on the land at the time, and many of them resisted the Spanish settlers' attempts to take over the area. One tribe, called the Lenca, executed a well-planned attack on the Spanish in 1537. After more than a year of fighting, the Spanish killed the Lenca's leader and defeated the native warriors.

The Spanish developed Honduras in order to mine for gold and silver, and they enslaved the natives to work on the mines. Soon, most of the native populations died because of their exposure to European diseases.

After Honduras obtained its independence from Spain in 1821, it did not settle into a democratic country. One military leader after another took control, and this turbulence allowed more powerful countries such as the United States to intervene in their governments.

The United States and other foreign countries have played a large role in shaping both the government and the industry of Honduras. In particular, United States fruit companies that export bananas and other fruit have had a lot of power and influence in Honduras. The involvement of the United States in Honduran affairs has not always been welcome, nor has it always benefited Hondurans.

Honduras has also been negatively affected by wars in neighboring El Salvador and Nicaragua. In the 1960s thousands of Salvadorans crossed the border into Honduras seeking refuge. Many were forced to return to El Salvador. In 1969, tensions between the Hondurans and the Salvadoran refugees erupted into a five-day-long conflict in which 2,000 people were killed. (The conflict is sometimes called the Soccer War because the two countries' teams were in a soccer series at the time.) There was no clear winner.

Today, Honduras is among the poorest countries in the world, with most of the wealth owned by only a few families. Income is largely from the export of bananas and coffee. There is a very high rate of unemployment and crime.

Honduran Americans

Today there are about 486,000 Honduran Americans in the United States. After World War II some Hondurans immigrated to the United States in order to find better job opportunities. Many of these people had been employed in Honduras by the United Fruit Company, a U.S. corporation that exported fruit from Central America to areas all over the world. When they arrived in the United States, some of these Hondurans looked for jobs in the fruit import industry, and they settled in the port areas, such as New York City, New Jersey, New Orleans, and Boston, where there was a booming import industry. Hondurans also came to the United States—in much larger numbers—in the 1970s and 1980s in order to escape problems caused by guerilla warfare in the neighboring nations of Nicaragua and El Salvador. Refugees from the war sought safety in Honduras, which did not have enough money, jobs, and resources to help.

In 1998, Hondurans came to the United States seeking refuge from the devastation of Hurricane Mitch that killed thousands and ruined a large part of the country.

Today, many Honduran Americans work as migrant farmworkers in the United States. Others have settled in New York City, Los Angeles, Houston, and New Orleans. Honduran Americans work hard to support their families in the United States and to help family members who still live in their home country. Each year, they send about 1.8 billion dollars to their relatives in Honduras.

Spin a *Ronron*: A Traditional Honduran Toy

Most Hondurans live in rural mountain communities, and the country is very poor. Honduran children play games that require little or no equipment, and they create toys out of everyday items that are easily found. Here is a traditional Honduran toy that is enjoyed in the United States as well.

What You Need

1 18-inch length sturdy string
Large button that has at least 1 hole

What You Do

1. Thread the string through the hole in the button.
2. Hold the string at both ends. Twirl the string very quickly in front of you, like a mini-jumprope, allowing the button to spin in the middle. Now pull both ends tight. It will make a buzzing sound as the button stops spinning.

Play Button in the Hole

This game is similar to a game of marbles—but, instead of actual marbles, buttons are used. Get some friends together and try this fun game!

What You Need

2 or more players

Spade or spoon

Area of hard dirt on which to play

Stick

1 large and 10 small buttons per person. Each player should keep their buttons in a small pile in front of them.

What You Do

1. Using the spade or the spoon, dig a hole in the dirt that is wide and deep enough for the buttons to fall into.

2. Use the stick to draw a shooting line about 5 feet from the hole.

3. Each player stands behind the shooting line and, using a larger button as a "shooter" to hit a smaller button, tries to shoot the small button into the hole.

4. The first person to get his or her small button in the hole wins 1 point. The first person to score 10 points wins.

Try Your Hand at a Honduran Game of Jacks with Seeds

This is another game that is played with found materials: just seeds and a stone. It's free and fun!

What You Need

This game can be played alone or with others.

10 large seeds, such as pumpkin or sunflower seeds (dried beans or small, uncooked pasta shells may be used instead)

Small stone

What You Do

1. Sit on the ground. Hold the seeds in one hand and drop them on the ground in front of you.

2. With one hand, toss the small stone up into the air. Using the same hand, pick up one seed, then catch the stone as it falls. You must catch the stone before it hits the ground! Repeat until each of the 10 seeds has been picked up. If the stone hits the ground before a seed is picked up, the player's turn is over, and the next player tries.

3. Place all the seeds back on the ground. Repeat the game, this time picking up 2 seeds at a time.

4. Repeat the game picking up 3 seeds, then 4, then 5, then 6, then 7, then 8, then 9, then 10.

5. The player who makes it the farthest in the game without letting the stone hit the ground is the winner.

6. You can practice some Spanish when you play this game by calling out the numbers of seeds you've picked up. Here are the Spanish words for the numbers 1 through 10:

1: uno (OOH-no)
2: dos (dohs)
3: tres (trays)
4: cuatro (CWAH-trow)
5: cinco (SEEN-coh)
6: seis (says)
7: siete (see-AY-tay)
8: ocho (OH-choh)
9: nueve (noo-WAY-vay)
10: diez (dee-AYS)

◈ Nicaragua

Spain's first attempt to conquer Nicaragua was not as successful as it had been with other Central American countries. In 1522 the Spanish conquistador Gil González Dávila tried to take the land from the native peoples who lived there, but he was defeated by their chief, Nicarao (for whom the country is named). Two years later, however, the Spanish conquistador Francisco Hernández de Córdoba and his men did successfully claim the land for Spain and establish settlements there. Spanish rule continued in Nicaragua for 300 years, until the country declared its independence in 1821. In 1823 it joined the United Provinces of Central America and, in 1838, Nicaragua became an independent country.

Over the course of Nicaragua's history, the United States (as well as Great Britain) often meddled in the country's affairs. Among other activities, the United States worked to build a canal through Nicaragua that would provide an easily traveled waterway between the Pacific and Atlantic oceans. Eventually the project was abandoned, and in 1914 the United States opened a waterway—the Panama Canal—in Panama instead. Nevertheless, the United States Marines were stationed in Nicaragua almost continually from 1912 to 1933. They arrived in 1912 to support the leader in power at the time, Adolfo Día, when the country was embroiled in a civil war. The United States and Nicaragua signed a treaty that gave special rights to the United States, which allowed them to stay. In 1927 a Nicaraguan revolutionary named Augusto César Sandino led a rebellion against U.S. occupation of the land. Eventually the Marines did leave Nicaragua. A short time later, a Nicaraguan general named Anastasio Somoza García had Sandino executed and established a military dictatorship of the country. The Somoza family ruled Nicaragua for 40 years.

In 1979 a group of rebels called the Sandinistas (in honor of their slain hero, Sandino) overthrew the government and put their own Communist government in place with a five-member revolutionary council. In 1984, Sandinista leader Daniel Ortega was elected President of Nicaragua. Backed with support from the United States, an anti-Communist rebel group called the Contras worked to overturn the Sandinista government. This resulted in civil war.

Finally, in 1989, the war ended. An agreement between the Sandinistas and the Contras led to free elections in Nicaragua, and in 1990 a democratic government was installed. Ten years later the Sandinistas came back into power when Nicaragua's former president, Daniel Ortega, was again elected president, this time in a democratic election. Ortega was elected again in 2006, and remains Nicaragua's president today.

Nicaraguan Americans

Nicaraguans entered the United States in large numbers between 1982 and 1992 to escape their country's turbulent political environment. Because they were fleeing a Communist regime, the United States was more lenient about granting Nicaraguans asylum than it had been with other Central American groups. Today there are estimated to be about 298,000 Nicaraguan Americans who are primarily mestizos—their heritage includes both Spanish and native peoples. They work hard to succeed in the United States. Many Nicaraguan Americans hold jobs in professional and managerial positions or own their own businesses. Others hold lower-level service jobs. Many Nicaraguans settled in Miami, Los Angeles, and New York City. Nicaraguan Americans call themselves Nicas.

"Little Managua" is a nickname that is sometimes used to describe an area, usually within a community or city, in which there is a large Nicaraguan population. The name refers to Managua, the capital city of Nicaragua. You can find a Little Managua in the city of Sweetwater, Florida, and in the community of Little Havana in Miami. In each Little Managua, residents and visitors alike can enjoy Nicaraguan restaurants and purchase Nicaraguan foods, baked goods, clothing, and household items. Almost everyone who lives in the Little Managua communities speaks Spanish, and the residents' language is reflected everywhere, from the Spanish-language newspapers and magazines that are sold there to the neighborhood signs and restaurant menus.

Bake a *Tres Leches* Cake: A Traditional Nicaraguan Dessert

This is a simple version of a very popular cake in Nicaragua. *Tres Leches* (trehs LAY-chays) literally means three milks. Nicaraguans who immigrated to the United States introduced this dessert to other populations in the country, and it is now enjoyed by people of all nationalities throughout the United States.

What You Need

Adult Supervision Required

13-inch-by-9-inch baking pan
Cooking spray
1 box yellow cake mix
3 eggs (or what cake mix calls for)
1 cup water (or what cake mix calls for)
⅓ cup vegetable oil (or what cake mix calls for)
Large mixing bowl
2 wooden mixing spoons

Toothpick
2 oven mitts or pot holders
Fork
¾ cup heavy whipping cream
1¼ cups canned sweetened condensed milk
1 cup canned evaporated milk
Medium mixing bowl
1 can whipped cream
Rubber spatula

What You Do

1. Preheat the oven according to the package directions.
2. Spray the bottom of the baking pan with cooking spray.
3. Place the cake mix, eggs, water, and oil in a large mixing bowl. Using a wooden spoon, stir until the mixture is well blended (3 to 4 minutes). Pour into pan.
4. Follow package directions for baking.
5. Using oven mitts or pot holders to protect your hands, carefully remove the pan from the oven. Let cool for 30 minutes.
6. Using the fork, gently poke the cake to make small holes all over its surface.
7. Place the heavy whipping cream, sweetened condensed milk, and evaporated milk (the "tres leches") in a medium-sized mixing bowl. Using a clean mixing spoon, stir the liquids until they are well blended.
8. Pour the milk mixture, a little bit at a time, over the entire cake until all of the mixture has been poured onto the cake. (You may wonder if there is too much of the milk mixture, but there isn't—the cake will absorb it!)

9. Spray whipped cream onto the cake. Using a rubber spatula, spread the whipped cream until it forms an even layer over the top of the cake.

10. Refrigerate the cake for at least 1 hour. Serve and enjoy!

La Purisima

La Purisima (lah poo-REE-see-mah) is a celebration of the conception (beginning of life) of the patron saint of Nicaragua, the Virgin Mary. The holiday is observed both in Nicaragua and in U.S. Nicaraguan American communities, especially Miami. From November 26 to December 7 each year, parties are held inside and outside of people's homes. There, family and friends are invited to say the rosary and sing *villancicos* (vee-yan-SEE-kose), songs of praise to the Virgin, at a simple altar. Guests are given small gifts, sugarcane stalks, fruits, and sweets by the hosts of the parties.

The public part of the holiday, when crowds gather in the community, is called the *Gritería* (gree-teh-REE-ah), which means "the shouting." It is held on the first Sunday closest to December 7. Altars are elaborate in the public areas, and each features a statue of the Virgin Mary surrounded by such items as flowers, candles, palm leaves, sugarcane, bananas, oranges, and traditional sweets. People move from altar to altar like carolers, singing and receiving small gifts and treats from the organization or homeowner. The holiday is particularly enjoyed by children. They yell in Spanish, "What causes so much happiness?" and, in response, "The conception of Mary!"

Nicaraguan Americans say that, in their home country, the sound of firecrackers and fireworks during the holiday is deafening. Because many U.S. communities do not allow private citizens to set off fireworks, some Nicaraguan Americans pop rows of balloons during the holiday instead.

Wrap Sugarcane Treats for *Purisima*

Most of us eat sugar every day without thinking about where it comes from. But, in many countries in Central America, sugarcane is a major source of income, and people grow up with sugarcane crops all around them. It is used for cooking, baking, and making sugarcane juice. Many people in Nicaragua and other Central American countries chew pieces of sugarcane as a treat. Although sugarcane does have a sweet flavor, it isn't as sweet as pure sugar. (Note: Sugarcane stalks are chewed, but not swallowed. Once the sugarcane juice is gone from a stalk, discard it.)

Wrap up pieces of sugar cane for party favors to get a "taste" of Nicaraguan *Purisima* and island life.

Makes 10 individual favors

What You Need

1 20-ounce can sugarcane stalks (available at
    Latino and Asian grocery stores)
Paper towels
Plastic wrap
10 12-inch-by-12-inch sheets of green tissue paper
Scissors
Raffia ribbon (available at craft stores)
Clean, decorative container, such as a flower pot

What You Do

1. Drain the can and place the sugarcane stalks on paper towels. Let dry about 20 minutes.
2. Wrap each dry piece in plastic wrap, then in a piece of tissue paper.
3. Tie raffia ribbon around each stalk.
4. Place the wrapped stalks upright in the container. Place the container in the refrigerator until the stalks are given to guests.
5. Offer a sugarcane stalk to each guest, and explain to everyone that the stalk should be chewed for its juice, but not swallowed. The sugarcane stalks should be refrigerated until they are enjoyed.

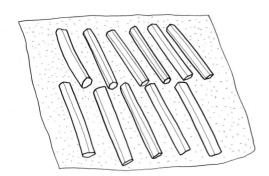

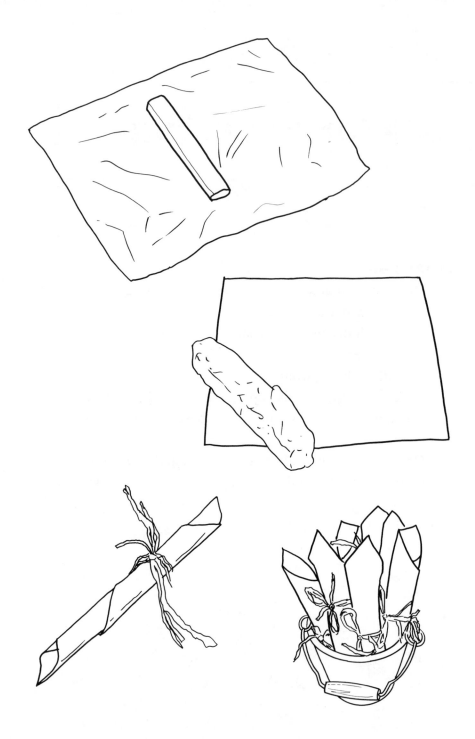

Central American Food

Central American food has been influenced by the many peoples who have lived in Central America over time, including the pre-Columbian native peoples as well as Spanish, African, and Caribbean people. The main components of Central American food are thick corn tortillas, rice, beans, plantains, yucca and other root vegetables, grilled meats, fresh fish, and tropical fruits such papayas, mangos, guavas, and coconuts. Fruit drinks and fruity milk shakes are popular beverages.

In Salvadoran American communities, *pupusas* (stuffed corn tortillas) are very popular. There are even restaurants, called *pupuserías* (poo-poo-seh-REE-uhs), that specialize in *pupusas*. These delicious treats are often topped with a vinegary cabbage salad called *curtido* (coor-TEE-do). Salvadorans also eat a traditional soup called *sopa de pata* (SOH-pah day PAH-tah), which is made from cows' feet, and *yuca frita* (YOO-kah FREE-tah), which is fried yucca root.

Nicaraguan Americans enjoy a rice and bean dish called *gallopinto* (gah-yo-PEEN-toh); *bajo* (BAH-hoh), a dish made of beef, plantains, and cassava (a root vegetable); and *nacatamales* (nah-cah-tah-MAL-ays), large tamales made of corn dough stuffed with meat and vegetables, wrapped in banana leaves, and steamed. A Nicaraguan snack that is particularly popular in Miami is *vigorón* (vee-goh-RHON), or fried pork rinds on top of shredded cabbage and yucca.

Guatemalan Americans enjoy black bean soup; *paches* (PAH-chays), which are pork and potatoes or mashed rice wrapped in banana leaves; *pepián* (PAY-pe-ahn), a hearty meat and vegetable stew; and *chiles rellenos* (CHEE-lays ray-YAH-nohs), which are chili peppers stuffed with meat, cheese, and vegetables. Some of the best coffee in the world comes from beans grown in Guatemala, and Guatemalan Americans drink it sweetened with plenty of sugar.

Traditional dishes enjoyed by Honduran Americans include *plato tipico* (PLAH-toh TEE-pee-coh), which means "typical plate." This dish features a combination of fried plantains, rice, beans, meat, and vegetables and is served with tortillas to scoop up the mixture. Other traditional dishes include *sopa de caracol*, a soup made of coconut milk, conch or clams, and plantains; and *baleadas*, which are flour tortillas filled with different combinations of meat, cheese, avocados, and beans.

Notable Central Americans

In the short period of time that Central Americans have been in the United States, they have contributed greatly to U.S. life and culture. Here are just a few notable Central Americans.

Athletes

Rosemary Casals (1948–)	A Salvadoran American tennis player and a member of the International Tennis Hall of Fame
Dennis Martinez (1955–)	A successful baseball pitcher who became the first Nicaraguan American to play in Major League Baseball

Authors

Francisco Goldman (1954–)	An award-winning Guatemalan American novelist whose first novel, *The Long Night of the White Chickens*, delves into the turbulence of Guatemala in the 1980s

Central American Independence Day

Central Americans celebrate their independence from Spain on September 15 each year. Many cities in the United States hold festivals, parades, and musical events to honor the day and to celebrate Latino and Central American culture.

One of the biggest U.S. celebrations is the annual Central American Independence Day Parade and Festival that is held in Los Angeles. The event features a big parade, folk dances, music, food, and traditional costumes of Central America.

Arturo Arias (1950–)	A novelist and critic who cowrote the screenplay of the movie *El Norte*, an Oscar-nominated film that tells the story of two Guatemalan refugees escaping to the United States

Entertainers

Barbara Carrera (1945–) A Nicaraguan American actress whose films include the 1983 James Bond movie *Never Say Never Again*

America Ferrera (1984–) A Honduran American actress who is best known for the movie *The Sisterhood of the Traveling Pants* and the TV show *Ugly Betty*, for which she has won an Emmy Award and a Golden Globe Award.

Oscar Isaac (1980–) A Guatemalan American actor whose films include *The Nativity Story* and *Body of Lies*

Other Notable Central Americans

Dagoberto Reyes (1945–) A Salvadoran American sculptor and painter whose compelling sculpture about the Salvadoran American experience, *Porque Emigramos* (Why We Emigrate), is installed in Los Angeles's MacArthur Park

Neida Sandoval (1961–) A Honduran American journalist and TV news presenter on the morning TV show *Despierta America*

Christy Turlington (1969–) A Salvadoran American supermodel who is best known for her Calvin Klein fragrance advertisements

From Sea to Shining Sea—in Spanish!

Here are some Spanish words related to song and dance.

Guitar. It's the same word in English and in Spanish!

Mambo. The English word for this dance and type of music comes from the Spanish word *mamboo*, which means percussion instrument.

Flamenco. This is the name of a traditional Spanish dance.

Mariachi. It's the same word in English and in Spanish!

Rumba. The English word for this dance and type of music comes from the Spanish word *rumbo*, which means a spree or a party.

◆ 8 ◆

Dominican Americans

The Dominican Republic is a country that is located on the Caribbean island of Hispaniola, which is also home to another country called Haiti. Christopher Columbus discovered the island, which he called La Isla Española, in 1492. His brother Bartolomeo Columbus established Santo Domingo, the oldest city in the new world, in the country now known as the Dominican Republic in 1496. When the Spanish explorers arrived on the island they were greeted warmly by the Taino people who lived there. But the Spanish plundered the island for gold and riches, and they forced the native peoples to work as laborers in the mines.

The gold and silver mines were quickly depleted, and the Spanish looked for other ways to make money off the land they'd taken from the Taino. They used the native people to build and labor on sugarcane farms. The Taino were forced to endure very difficult working conditions, and they were exposed to European diseases for which they had no immunity. As a result, they died

by the thousands. Depleted of their workforce, the Spanish imported African slaves to work on their farms in 1503. Within only 30 years of the Spanish discovery, most of the Taino were dead and the labor force in Santo Domingo was made up of African slaves.

The Spanish focused on developing the eastern part of the island. The country of France saw an opportunity to claim the western part of the island as its own, and French explorers began to settle there and build their own sugarcane plantations. Unable to maintain control of that part of the island, the Spanish ceded (officially gave) the western area of Hispaniola to the French in 1697, which they named Saint Domingue. In 1795 they gave the entire island to France under an agreement resulting from the wars between France and Spain in Europe. The Spanish took back the western section (what is now the Dominican Republic) 13 years later, in 1808, when the country was in chaos and Spain, France, Haiti, and Great Britain were all fighting for control. By that time the eastern part of the island (what is now

153

Dominican Republic and Haiti and Neighboring Islands

Florida

Bahamas

Cuba

Atlantic Ocean

Hispaniola

Puerto Rico

Jamaica   Haiti

Dominican Republic

N

Haiti) had already declared its independence from France, and the Africans who had lived there as slaves had gained control of the country and its government.

The colonists declared independence from Spain in 1821, calling this part of the island "Spanish Haiti." They were soon taken over by Haiti in 1822. True independence from foreign control finally occurred on February 27, 1844, through a Dominican independence movement under the guidance of freedom fighter Juan Pablo Duarte. The Dominicans declared independence from Haiti, and the Dominican Republic was established.

It has been a rough road for the Dominican Republic since it declared itself an independent country. For a brief period—from 1861 to 1865—the Dominican Republic once again became a colony of Spain in order to protect itself from a Haitian takeover. Over the course of the following decades,

Dominicans suffered through brutal dictatorships, bankruptcy, and even intervention by the United States Marines, who were stationed there from 1916 to 1924 to prevent European countries from invading the country.

From 1930 until 1961, the Dominican Republic suffered under one of the worst dictators in history: Rafael Leónidas Trujillo Molina, or "El Jefe" ("the Chief"), as he was commonly known.

Under his regime, free speech was prohibited, schools were tightly controlled, newspapers could only print news that Trujillo approved of, no one could leave the country, and anyone who disagreed with the government was severely punished. In addition, Trujillo made himself rich with the country's money. He was finally shot to death by his own army in 1961.

The end of Trujillo's reign did not mean that the Dominican Republic's troubles were over, however. Four years after Trujillo was killed, the United States again intervened in the Dominican Republic's government in order to prevent what it feared would be a Communist takeover of the country by rebels. The United States finally left the Dominican Republic after the country held free elections and established a new, more democratic government.

Dominican Americans

After Trujillo was assassinated in 1961, Dominicans were finally free to leave the country. From 1961 to 1970 thousands of Dominicans immigrated to the United States, primarily to escape the economic chaos of their home country.

Washington Heights

New York City is home to an area in which many Dominican Americans live. It is called Washington Heights, but it goes by many other names as well. Its residents usually refer to it as "the Heights," and it's also known as Quisqueya Heights (Quisqueya is the Taino name for Hispaniola) and Little Dominican Republic. The neighborhood is full of the sights, sounds, and aromas of the island on which the Dominican Republic is found. Dominican and American flags fly side by side, and Spanish is spoken everywhere.

In Washington Heights you can buy pastries from Dominican bakeries, grab a quick lunch of red beans and rice from a Dominican restaurant, and see storefront sidewalks overflowing with tropical fruits and vegetables such as papayas, plantains, and cassava.

The sounds of merengue, a moody type of music called *bachata* (bah-CHAH-tah), and *reggaetón* pulse from stores, open apartment windows, and cars passing by. During warm weather, men play dominos on card tables outside. Dominican food trucks line up on busy streets late into the night and sell delicious, inexpensive meals and treats. The aromas of sizzling empanadas, *chimichurris* (Dominican hamburgers), *tostones* (fried green plantains), tripe soup, rice and pigeon peas, and pork *chicharrón*, waft through the air.

In Washington Heights you can purchase Spanish-language newspapers and magazines, send money or a package "home" to the island, have your hair cut by a Dominican American hairdresser or barber, and buy airline tickets to the Dominican Republic from a Dominican American travel agency.

Like most areas of New York City, Washington Heights has become more and more expensive to live in. In recent years, some Dominican Americans have begun relocating from Washington Heights to the Bronx, a less expensive area of the city.

A stream of immigration continued through the 1970s. The 1980s saw a serious economic depression in the Dominican Republic and an explosion in the number of Dominican immigrants to the United States. Immigration continued to rise in the 1990s and into the 2000s. Today, Dominicans are the fifth largest Latino group in the United States. Most Dominicans have settled in the Northeast, primarily in New York, New Jersey, Massachusetts, and Rhode Island; others have settled in Florida.

Over the years, some Dominicans who immigrated to the United States have returned to their home country with money and other resources to help build businesses and communities in the Dominican Republic. Dominican American immigrants who continue to live in the United States frequently assist relatives in their home country by sending money to them.

Dominicans who immigrated to the United States often found jobs in manufacturing and in the hotel and restaurant industries. Many Dominican American women worked in the garment industry or as domestic employees. Today Dominican Americans often own their own small businesses within the Latino community. These include travel agencies, taxi services, and family-owned bodegas that sell ingredients used in Latino cooking.

The children of Dominican American parents who immigrated in the 1960s are usually college educated and work in fields such as business, medicine, and education. Others hold jobs in various trades.

Crossing the Mona Passage: A Desperate Route to the United States

Many Dominicans attempt to make their way to the United States mainland by traveling first to Puerto Rico. To get there,

Dominican Heritage Month

In 2004 New York's Governor George Pataki designated February as Dominican Heritage Month in that state. Each year politicians and organizations honor distinguished Dominican Americans during that month. Among those who have been honored are Tony Sanchez, host of the morning radio show *La Mega*; the leaders of Rocking the Boat, a youth organization that teaches boat-building skills and water safety; and Juan Guillé, the publisher of *Dominican Times Magazine*.

they must cross the Mona Passage, a shark-infested waterway that lies between the island of Hispaniola and Puerto Rico. Often people attempt the voyage in small, poorly made boats, and many have perished at sea trying to complete the dangerous journey. Some of the Dominicans who do make it to Puerto Rico decide to stay there, but most continue on to travel by airplane to the mainland of the United States. By pretending to be Puerto Rican, they can enter the United States without a passport because Puerto Ricans are American citizens and don't need one.

Dance the Merengue

The merengue is the national dance of the Dominican Republic. It is easy and fun! It is important to remember to keep your head and shoulders fairly steady; don't dip them from side to side. It is the lower half of your body that does the moves.

Throughout the dance, the leader initiates each movement and the follower "mirrors" that movement. For example, if the leader steps to the left, the follower steps to the right, so that both people move together in the same direction. It's important for both dancers to lift their feet completely off the ground when they move!

What You Need

2 people

CD of merengue music

CD player

Open space to dance

What You Do

1. Designate one person as "the leader" and the other as "the follower."
2. Play the CD of merengue music as you follow the directions below.
3. Take your positions! Begin by facing each other. The leader puts his right hand on the follower, slightly above the follower's waist, and grasps the follower's right hand with his left hand. The follower puts her left hand on the leader's right shoulder. Each person stands with his or her feet a few inches apart and with knees slightly bent.
4. Begin the dance! The leader places his weight on the right leg, then takes a small step to the left, shifting his weight to the left as this is done. The follower mirrors the movement. Then the leader drags his right foot in toward the left foot. The follower mirrors this as well. Repeat 3 times.
5. Next, the leader takes a step forward with his left leg, shifting his weight from the right leg to the left as this is done. Then he drags the right leg up to meet the left leg. The follower mirrors these movements, taking a step backward with the right foot and dragging the left leg back to close. Repeat 3 times.
6. Finally, the leader takes a step backward with his left leg, shifting his weight from the right leg to the left as this is done. Then he drags the right leg back to meet the left leg. The follower mirrors these movements, taking a step forward with the right foot and dragging the left leg up to close. Repeat 3 times.
7. Keep performing these three moves until the music is finished.

Dominican American Baseball Players

Baseball is the Dominican Republic's favorite sport, and there are a great many Dominican American professional baseball players in the United States. Here are some of the Dominican Americans who have played in Major League Baseball over the years.

Moisés Alou (1966–), the oldest player to have a 30-game hitting streak

Armando Benitez (1972–), a relief pitcher who led the National League in saves in 2004

Tony Fernandez (1962–), a five-time winner of the Rawlings Gold Glove Award and a member of the 1993 World Series champion Toronto Blue Jays

Julio Franco (1958–), the oldest player to participate in more than 100 games in one season

Rafael Furcal (1977–), the 2000 National League Rookie of the Year

Vladimir Guerrero (1976–), the 2004 winner of the American League Most Valuable Player Award

Juan Marichal (1937–), an all-star pitcher who, in 1983, became the first Dominican inducted into the Baseball Hall of Fame

Pedro Martinez (1971–), a three-time winner of the Cy Young Award

David Ortiz (1975–), who holds the Boston Red Sox record of 54 home runs in a single season

Timoniel ("Timo") Pérez (1975–), an outfielder and a member of both the 2005 World Series champion Chicago White Sox and the 2006 World Series champion St. Louis Cardinals

Albert Pujols (1980–), who was voted the 2001 National League Rookie of the Year and the 2005 National League Most Valuable Player of the Year

Aramis Ramirez (1978–), an All-Star third baseman who, by the end of the 2007 season, had batted in 222 career home runs

Manny Ramirez (1972–), who was voted Most Valuable Player in the 2004 World Series and who ranks second (behind Lou Gehrig) in career grand slams

Alex ("A-Rod") Rodriguez (1975–), the winner of two Most Valuable Player Awards

Alfonso Soriano (1976–), a four-time Silver Slugger Award winner who led the American League in runs, hits, and stolen bases in 2002

Sammy Sosa (1968–), one of only three Major League Baseball players to hit 50 home runs in each of three different seasons

Miguel Tejada (1976–), the 2002 winner of the American League Most Valuable Player Award

Put Together a Dominican American Baseball Hall of Fame Exhibit

Use the wall of your room or classroom, a bulletin board, a table, or a poster to display pictures and information about Dominican American baseball players. The Internet is a great source of information on baseball players; check out the following Web sites:

www.latinosportslegends.com
www.latinobaseball.com
www.baseballhalloffame.org
www.mlb.com

If you really want to get creative (and you have the necessary equipment), you can add sound or video clips of baseball games, interviews of baseball players, or other baseball-related media to your exhibit. Use your imagination!

What You Need

Materials such as baseball cards, programs, pictures of players and baseball equipment, and articles and other information cut from magazines and newspapers or printed from Web sites
Tape (optional)
Poster board (optional)

What You Do

1. Use your materials to put together a display of Dominican American baseball players.
2. Invite your friends, family, or fellow students to enjoy the exhibit.

Dominican American Music

Music is an important part of Dominican American culture. Dominican Americans enjoy a wide variety of musical styles, including merengue, salsa, and *bachata*, romantic (and sometimes sad) music from the Dominican countryside. Hip hop and *reggaetón* are also popular among young Dominican Americans.

Holidays and Celebrations

Dominican American celebrations are a lively mix of traditional Latino observances and Caribbean culture that include everything from Caribbean-flavored carnival parades to Noche Buena (Christmas Eve) and Three Kings Day.

The Dominican Republic's Independence Day

The Dominican Republic's Independence Day of February 27 celebrates that country's independence from Haiti. Parades and festivals are organized by community groups in various parts of the country to celebrate the many facets of Dominican culture, from dance to music to folk art and more.

Dominican Day Parade

Each summer, New York City hosts the Dominican Day Parade, one of the largest U.S. parades and festivals to celebrate Dominican culture and the 1863 restoration of the Dominican Republic's independence from Spain. People yell, "Republica Dominicana," bands on floats play merengue music, and thousands of people wave the red, white, and blue flag of the Dominican Republic.

Dominican American parades always include the colorful, vibrant aspects of Carnival, which is a unique celebration that occurs in many Latin countries. It combines Catholic rituals and African ceremonies and traditions. Carnival takes place in the days that lead up to Ash Wednesday, the Catholic holiday that marks the beginning of Lent.

Groups of parade participants wear Carnival-inspired costumes and elaborately painted devil, or *diablo* (dee-AHB-loh), masks made of papier-mâché and wire. Cars go by riding on three wheels (quite a trick!), beautiful pageant queens wave from floats, and local politicians, Latino police officers and firemen, and members of various other Latino organizations march. Gaily decorated floats carry singers, dancers, and performers. Marching bands and other participants wearing regional costumes from the Dominican Republic join in the celebration.

The people who line up to watch the parade have just as much fun as the marchers. They dance in the streets, blow whistles, wave flags, get their faces painted, enjoy Dominican street food, and clap as the procession passes.

Craft a Dominican Carnival Mask

You can make your own Carnival mask to celebrate Dominican Independence Day. In this activity, we will create a mask of a character that is described as "a bat-winged, horned, three-eyed monster." All of the materials required are available at craft stores.

What You Need

Scissors
2 8- to 10-inch-long red feathers
24 3- to 4-inch-long red feathers
12 3- to 4-inch-long small yellow
   feathers
12 6-inch-long black feathers
Glue
Black half mask
3-inch-by-3-inch piece white felt
Black marker
Gold or red glitter

What You Do

1. Clip the bottom stem (if needed) from each feather so that there is no more than ½ inch of bare stem showing.
2. Glue the 2 long red feathers to either side of the mask to make "horns" (see drawing).
3. Glue yellow feathers to the tips of the long red feathers. To get a really full look, glue layers of 2 or 3 yellow feathers to each tip.
4. Glue the remaining yellow feathers and the shorter red feathers all the way across the top of the mask, alternating colors as you go.
5. Glue the black feathers to each side of the mask so that they look like wings.
6. Make a "third eye" for the mask by cutting a small circle out of the white felt. Use the marker to draw an eye in the middle of the circle. Outline the eye with glue and shake glitter on top of it. Do the same to the eyes on the mask. Shake excess glitter into a wastebasket and let the glue dry.
7. Glue the eye to the top middle of the mask. Don't worry if excess glitter gets on the feathers; it will make the mask look more festive! Let dry.

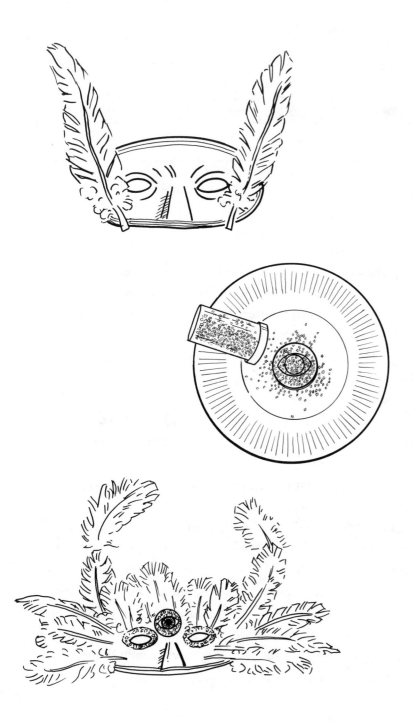

Christmas (Navidad) and Three Kings Day (El Dia de Los Reyes)

The celebration of Christmas starts in early December and goes through Three Kings Day on January 6. Christmas Eve (Noche Buena) dinner is the biggest part of the celebration. A typical Dominican American Christmas Eve dinner might include roasted pork, rice with pigeon peas in coconut milk, plantain patties called *pasteles en hojas* (pah-STEHL-ehs ehn OH-hahs), stuffed banana leaves, a sweet dessert such as flan, and plates of fruits and nuts. Drinks may include eggnog and cider.

After dinner, many families attend a midnight mass. Some families exchange gifts on Christmas, others wait until Three Kings Day, and some families do both! Usually children receive gifts from relatives on Three Kings Day. Before they go to sleep the night before the holiday, they put water and grass under their beds for the camels of the Three Kings to eat. When they wake in the morning, they find presents where the water and grass had been.

Families decorate their homes with lighted Christmas trees or a painted white branch called a *charamico* (chah-rah-MEE-coh), under which is placed a nativity scene. Many Dominican Americans also decorate with poinsettia plants, which grow outside in the Dominican Republic.

Make a *Charamico*: A White Christmas Branch

Dominican Americans sometimes make a nostalgic reminder of Christmas celebrations in the Dominican Republic. Traditional Christmas trees don't grow in the Caribbean, so people there make their own. They take a dry branch or branches, paint them snow white, and decorate them with ornaments and lights. *Charamicos* are also made in the shapes of animals, wreaths, pots, and angels.

What You Need

Adult Supervision Required

4-quart metal pail (painted or unpainted)

Small bag (about 5 pounds) clean kitty
     litter or sand

6 bare tree branches 2 to 4 feet wide and 4 to
     5 feet high (these may be cut from bigger
     pieces with help from an adult)

White acrylic paint

Paper cup

Sponge paintbrush

Glue

About 12 1-inch red pom-poms

About 12 1-inch green pom-poms

What You Do

1. Fill the pail with kitty litter.
2. If needed, ask an adult to help you break big branches into smaller pieces. (The adult may choose to cut them using small garden clippers.)
3. Push the branches into the kitty litter, arranging them into a tree shape.
4. Pour the paint into the paper cup. Using the sponge paintbrush, paint the branches. (It is not necessary to cover the branches completely; you want them to look like they are frosted with snow.) Let dry.
5. Glue the pom-poms to the branches to make decorative tree ornaments.

Make *Arroz con Leche*: Creamy Rice Pudding

Arroz con leche (creamy rice pudding) is one of the most popular desserts in Latino communities. It is not difficult to make, but it takes more than an hour of watching and stirring.

8 servings

What You Need

Adult Supervision Required

½ cup arborio rice

2 cups water

2 tablespoons butter

1 cinnamon stick

3-quart saucepan (nonstick preferred)

Stirring spoon

4 cups evaporated milk

½ cup sugar

1 teaspoon vanilla extract

Medium-sized serving bowl *or*
    8 individual dessert bowls

Ground cinnamon (to shake
    over cooked pudding)

What You Do

1. Place the rice, water, butter, and cinnamon stick in the saucepan. Bring to a boil over medium heat. Reduce the heat to low and simmer for 15 minutes, until the mixture is very thick.

2. Stir in the evaporated milk and sugar. Simmer for about 1 hour, stirring frequently, until it is thick and creamy. (The mixture may form a "skin" between stirrings; just stir it back into the mixture.)

3. Remove the saucepan from heat. Spoon out and discard the cinnamon stick. Stir in the vanilla extract.

4. Let sit about 5 minutes, until the excess liquid has been absorbed into the mixture.

5. Spoon the mixture into a medium-sized serving bowl or individual dessert bowls. Sprinkle with ground cinnamon and serve.

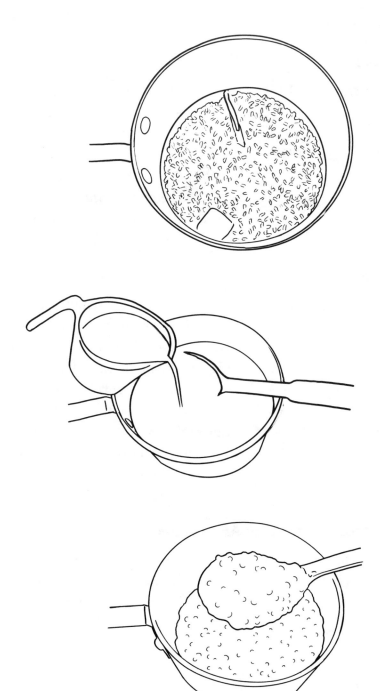

Dominican Food

A favorite dish in the Dominican Republic is *sancocho* (sahn-KOH-choh), a hearty stew of meat, potatoes, plantains, peppers, corn, and tomatoes. Enjoyed by Dominican Americans as well, it is usually made on holidays and special occasions. *La Bandera* (lah bahn-DEH-rah), which means "the flag," is a staple dish that consists of red beans, rice, and fried plantains; it is served with meat or chicken. Other favorite foods include *pastelitos* (fish- or meat-filled pastries), roasted pig, and *arroz con leche* (ah-RROHS cohn LEH-cheh), a creamy rice pudding.

Notable Dominican Americans

Dominicans Americans are one of the newest immigrant groups to come to the United States. They have contributed new forms of Latin music, dance, and food. Dominicans are authors, politicians, athletes, writers, entertainers, and more.

Athletes

(See also page 158, for a list of famous Dominican American baseball players)

Luis Castillo (1983–)	A professional football player and a member of the San Diego Chargers
Mary Joe Fernandez (1971–)	A professional tennis player and two-time Olympic Gold Medal winner
Tutan Reyes (1977–)	A professional football player and a member of the Jacksonville Jaguars

Authors

| Julia Alvarez (1950–) | An author who has written many books for adults and children, including *How the Garcia Girls Lost Their Accents*, *¡Yo!*, and *A Gift of Gracias* |
| Junot Díaz (1968–) | The Pulitzer Prize–winning author of *Drown* and *The Brief Wondrous Life of Oscar Wao* |

Celebrities

| Maria Montez (1912–1951) | A 1940s actress whose films include *Arabian Nights* and *Cobra Woman* |
| Michelle Rodriguez (1978–) | An actress who is best known for her roles in the TV show *Lost* and the movies *Blue Crush*, *Resident Evil*, and *The Fast and the Furious* |

Politicians

Adriano Espaillat (1954–)	A New York State assemblyman who was the first Dominican Republican to be elected to any state legislature in the United States
William Lantigua (1955–)	A state representative in the Massachusetts legislature
Guillermo Linares (1951–)	Currently holds the position of Commissioner of the Mayor's Office of Immigrant Affairs of the City of New York

Other Notable Dominican Americans

| Oscar de la Renta (1932–) | A world-renowned fashion designer |
| José Reyes Jr. (1955–) | A nuclear engineer and a professor at Oregon State University |

From Sea to Shining Sea—in Spanish!

These Spanish words for fruit came from Africa and from the native people of Central America.

Banana. This word comes from West Africa.

Guava. This comes from the Taino word *guayabo*.

Papaya. This is a Taino word.

Avocado. This comes from the Aztec word *ahuacatl*.

Tomato. This comes from the Aztec word *tomatl*.

◆ 9 ◆

South Americans

Below North America and Central America lies the continent of South America. Twelve countries and two dependencies (areas controlled by other countries) are found in South America. Nine of those countries—Argentina, Bolivia, Chile, Colombia, Ecuador, Paraguay, Peru, Uruguay, and Venezuela—were settled by Spain. The remaining countries and dependencies were settled by other European countries. These countries include Brazil, which was settled by the Portuguese; the Falkland Islands, a territory of the United Kingdom; French Guiana, which was settled by France; and Guyana and Suriname, which were settled by the Dutch.

The first wave of South American immigrants came to the United States in the 1960s. The next wave began in the 1980s, and the third wave started in 2000 and continues. South Americans left their home countries to escape repressive or corrupt governments, overpopulation, crumbling economies, unemployment, crime, and violence stemming from poverty.

In recent years, Colombians in particular have emigrated because of the rampant crime, corruption, and violence that have erupted in that country due to Colombia's illegal drug markets. Currently most of the countries in South America have democratic governments and are in various stages of stabilization.

Because the countries of South America are a great distance away from the United States, many South Americans have faced even greater hardships in making their way to their new country than have immigrants from Mexico or Central America. This was especially true before affordable air travel became available in the early 1960s.

Due in part to the distance between South America and the United States, there are far fewer U.S. South American immigrants than there are Puerto Ricans, Mexican Americans, Cuban Americans, Dominican Americans, or immigrants from Central America. This chapter focuses on the three countries settled by Spain, from which most South American immigrants have come: Colombia, Ecuador, and Peru.

South America

N

Atlantic Ocean

Guyana
Suriname
French Guiana

Venezuela

Colombia

Ecuador

Peru

Brazil

Bolivia

Paraguay

Pacific Ocean

Chile

Argentina

Uruguay

◈ Colombia

Colombia lies on the northwestern coast of South America. Before the Spanish arrived to claim it as their own in the 16th century, this land was home to several native tribes. By far the largest of these tribes was the Chibcha. The Chibcha people lived in villages, farmed the land, had an organized religion, and made copper, gold, and pottery crafts.

In 1525 this way of life ended for the natives when the Spanish explorer Rodrigo de Bastidas made his way to the area, claimed the land for Spain, and founded Santa Marta, the first Spanish settlement in what is now Colombia. In 1536 the Spanish conquistador Gonzalo Jiménez de Quesada and 900 men went deep into Chibcha territory in the Andes Mountains and completed the Spanish conquest of the land in 1538. They named the new colony New Granada, and in 1543 it became part of a Spanish viceroyalty called the Viceroyalty of Peru (similar to New Spain). It included all the colonies in South America under Spanish rule with the exception of the coast (present-day Venezuela).

The natives were forced to dig for gold and, as Spanish tobacco plantations were established, to work as laborers on the farms. After great numbers of the native peoples had died from overwork and European diseases, the Spanish imported African slaves to replace the workforce.

In 1717 New Granada (Colombia) became part of the newly organized Spanish Viceroyalty of New Grenada, which would eventually include the present-day countries of Colombia, Ecuador, Panama, and Venezuela. The Spanish created viceroyalties to centralize power (keep it in one area), rather than having several small regions with their own leaders. They felt that this gave Spain more power and control of the profits from the New World.

Independence from Spain

By the end of the 1700s, after centuries of living under Spanish rule, the descendents of the original Spanish conquerors, indigenous (native) people, and Africans felt as though they were more South American than Spanish. They were tired of paying taxes to and following laws made by Spain, a country that was on the other side of the world. After the United States won the Revolutionary War against Great Britain in 1783, independence movements sprang up throughout the Spanish colonies.

In 1819 the territories that are now the countries of Colombia, Venezuela, and Panama declared independence from Spain. The leaders in this fight for independence were a general named Francisco de Paula Santander and a revolutionary named Simón Bolívar, who is known in South America as El Libertador ("the Liberator"). In 1819, after the territories finally achieved independence from Spain, Simón Bolívar became the first president of the newly independent, democratic republic, which was named the "Republic of Colombia." Historians looking back now refer to that region as the "Republic of Gran Colombia" so that it is not confused with present-day Colombia, whose official name is also the "Republic of Colombia." Francisco de Paula Santander became its first vice president. The republic included present-day Colombia, Venezuela, Ecuador, and Panama.

The newly formed Republic of Gran Colombia lasted only until 1830. At that point, the republic dissolved and the land was divided into the separate countries of Venezuela, Ecuador, and the State of New Granada, which encompassed what are now the countries of Colombia and Panama. In 1855 New Granada (present-day Colombia and Panama) was renamed the Republic of Colombia. Panama eventually separated from the Republic of Colombia in 1903.

Colombia After Independence

In 1886 two political parties emerged in the Republic of Colombia: the conservatives, who wanted a strong central government and a church that was involved in government issues; and the liberals, who wanted more power at the local level and a church that was less influential. Power and control of the land has transferred back and forth between these two parties ever since.

The struggle for power between the two parties has sometimes been violent. From 1899 to 1902 they fought each other in a devastating civil war called the "War of a Thousand Days" that resulted in 100,000 deaths. Another civil war, which took place from 1948 to 1958 and led to between 200,000 and 300,000 deaths, was called La Violencia (lah vee-oh-LEN-see-uh). Finally, at the end of the second civil war, the two parties came together in order to restore peace. They removed the dictator who was in power at the time and agreed to share control of the land. This arrangement lasted several years.

During the 1980s a huge illegal drug trade spread throughout Colombia, devastating its citizens and its economy. Many citizens fled the countryside to escape unemployment, poverty, and violence related to the drug trade, and the already over-crowded cities were flooded with people looking for jobs. A great gap existed between the rich and the poor, and violence often erupted. Many times this violence included kidnappings, bombings, and the murders of judges, police officers, newspaper reporters, and other Colombians who tried to stop illegal drug traffickers. In addition, opposing political groups—each struggling to gain control and power—once again contributed to upheaval and devastation in the country.

Colombian Americans

Many hardworking Colombians fled to the United States to escape the violence and unemployment that was rampant in their own country. In the 1960s and 1970s Colombians came by the thousands to the United States to look for jobs.

The Immigration Act of 1965 made legal immigration to the United States more difficult by limiting the number of visas given to immigrants from the Western hemisphere to only 120,000 per year. Prior to the act, there were no limits on immigration from the Western Hemisphere. This was a pitifully small number, which forced many desperate Colombians to enter the United States illegally or to come temporarily to make enough money to return home.

Despite these barriers, Colombian Americans have become professionals, business owners, factory workers, textile workers, domestic workers, and more in the United States. Many send a portion of their paychecks back to relatives in Colombia.

Today, Colombian Americans make up the largest South American immigrant group in the United States. Many of them have settled in northern New Jersey, Florida, Chicago, and areas of New York, including the Little Colombia section of Jackson Heights in New York City. Since the 1990s, increasing numbers of Colombian Americans have been moving out of large cities and into the suburbs.

Colombian Independence Day Festival and Colombian Day Parade

Each summer the New York City borough of Queens holds a vibrant festival of Colombian music, dance, and food. There, people enjoy Colombian food such as arepas, empanadas, and chorizo; watch folk dancers perform; and listen to *vallenato* (vah-yeh-NAH-toh), a type of folk music that features African, European, and Colombian influences.

The festival is followed by the Colombian Independence Day Parade. The parade features colorful floats, pageant winners, folk dancers, marching bands, clowns, and people wearing traditional Colombian costumes.

Create a *Primitivo*: Colombian Folk Art

*P*rimitivos (pree-mee-TEE-vohs) are appliquéd tapestries. Appliqué is a form of art in which one piece of fabric is applied over another. The term *primitivo*, or "primitive," is used to describe tapestries that are created by ordinary people, not professional artists. It also refers to the simple, rural scenes that are created out of bits of cloth. This activity shows you how to make a tote bag that features a decorative *primitivo* scene. If you prefer, you can make a *primitivo* scene on a plain placemat or pot holder instead.

What You Need

Pencil

Paper

Fine-point black marker

6 or more 9-inch-by-12-inch
   pieces felt in different colors

Scissors

Plain canvas tote bag
   (available at craft
   stores)

Glue

What You Do

1. Using the pencil and paper, draw a simple sketch of a *primitivo* scene. You might draw any combination of people, simple homes, the sun, palm trees, the ocean, clouds, butterflies, tropical birds, chickens, or mountains, or you can think of your own simple designs that depict rural life. Each item should be about the same size, even if one is smaller than the other in the real world. For example, you would draw a house and a goat to be the same size, about 3 to 4 inches, top to bottom and side to side.

2. Once you have drawn a sketch that you like, choose one piece of felt to be the background. Refer to your sketch, and use the marker to draw each figure onto a different-colored piece of felt.

3. Using the scissors, cut out each design.

4. Glue your "base" or backdrop piece down.

5. Arrange the cutouts to create a scene on the bag. When you have come up with an arrangement that you like, glue each cutout to the base piece. Let dry.

Gabriel García Márquez and Magical Realism

Gabriel García Márquez, who was born in 1928, is one of Colombia's best-known writers. He writes in his native language of Spanish, but his books have been translated into several different languages, and his work is loved by people all over the world. His most famous books are *One Hundred Years of Solitude* and *Love in the Time of Cholera*.

Márquez left Colombia and has lived in many places all over the world, but he often returns to his homeland of Colombia. Although his writing was once considered "too liberal" (because he supports Communism)—both by his own country's leaders and by people in other countries— he has gone on to achieve worldwide acclaim, and he won the Nobel Prize in literature in 1982.

Márquez is famous for writing in a style called magical realism. It combines the reality of everyday life, with all of its mundane details, and fantasy. Some examples of magical realism that are featured in books by Márquez include an old man with enormous wings who falls from the sky into a village, a young woman flying up to heaven because she is too beautiful for Earth, and yellow butterflies preceding a man's entrance into any room. In Márquez's stories, none of these events seems odd or fantastic to the other characters— they are just accepted as being part of life.

Write a Short Story Using Magical Realism

Write your own short story using elements of magical realism. Try to focus on something odd that has actually happened in your life. For instance, Gabriel García Márquez said that, when he was five years old, he watched a meter repairman come to his grandparents' house on several occasions. One day when the workman came, Márquez noticed that his grandmother was swatting a yellow butterfly with a duster. She told Márquez that every time that man came to the house, a yellow butterfly followed him.

The Panama Canal

For years, sailors dreamed of a shortcut that would allow them to sail through the Americas to get from the Atlantic Ocean to the Pacific Ocean. In 1903 U.S. President Theodore Roosevelt persuaded Panama, which was part of Colombia, to become an independent country and to allow the United States to build a canal there to provide a direct route from one ocean to the other. The United States paid Panama $10 million dollars, plus an additional $250,000 a year, in exchange for Panama's agreement to let the United States build and maintain the canal in its country.

In 1904 the United States began construction on the Panama Canal. The canal, which cost the United States $350 million to build, was an engineering marvel. Instead of digging through miles of rock to create the waterway, U.S. Army engineers created a system of locks that could be opened and closed individually. Each lock could be filled or drained of water, allowing ships to float from one lock to the next and, eventually, to the open sea.

Ten years after construction had begun, the Panama Canal opened on August 15, 1914. It continues to be used today. Ships that are traveling from the Atlantic to the Pacific Ocean use the Panama Canal to cut through Central America instead of traveling all the way around the continent. Using the Panama Canal, a ship sailing from New York to San Francisco saves about 7,800 miles!

The Panama Canal was given back to the country of Panama to own and manage on December 31, 1999.

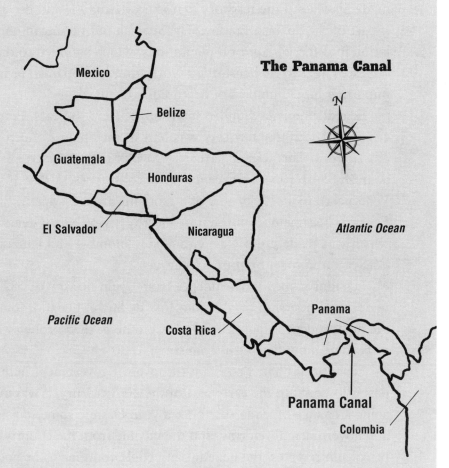

The Panama Canal

◈ Ecuador

Ecuador is a small country in South America that lies southwest of Colombia. Before the Spanish arrived to claim it, the land was home to several groups of native peoples ruled by the Incas. In 1532 the Spanish conquistador Francisco Pizarro, who had already staked claims in other areas of South America, made his way to the territory that is now Ecuador and declared it part of the Spanish Empire. The Spanish put the Incan population into forced labor on plantations, which soon led to their demise. Eager to replenish their work force, the Spanish began importing large numbers of captured Africans.

Ecuador remained under Spanish rule for 300 years. From 1563 until 1720 the territory was part of the Spanish Viceroyalty of Peru. This was an early Viceroyalty that included all of Spanish South America except for the coast (present-day Venezuela). In 1720, as part of a reorganization by Spain, Ecuador became part of the new Viceroyalty of New Grenada, which was made up of New Granada (Colombia and Panama), Ecuador, and for a brief time Venezuela.

Ecuador gained independence from Spain in May of 1822 under the leadership of Antonio José de Sucre. Ecuador joined the independent Republic of Gran Colombia, then broke away to become an independent country in 1830.

Ecuador has had a constant turnover of government in the past 100 years. In the early part of the 20th century, it was averaging a change of leadership once a year. Despite some social and governmental reforms, and the income from the country's petroleum reserves, the Ecuadorian people continue to be poor, with most of the wealth belonging to a small proportion of the population.

Ecuadorian Americans

Ecuadorians have not had to deal with the turbulent political situations that have caused unrest in their neighboring countries, but severe financial problems and natural disasters, including floods and earthquakes, plunged much of Ecuador's population into poverty. As a result, Ecuadorians have been immigrating to the United States since the 1960s to seek employment and better opportunities for their families.

Although many Ecuadorian immigrants eventually made their way to Los Angeles, Chicago, Miami, Orlando, and other cities across the country, the majority of them began life in the United States in New York City. Many Ecuadorian immigrants, especially women, found employment in New York City's garment industry. Others found work in factories, restaurants, hotels, and the construction industry. Some Ecuadorian Americans opened their own businesses, such as restaurants and stores, that cater to their own communities. A large number of Ecuadorian craftspeople have become jewelers.

Ecuadorian doctors, lawyers, and other professionals who have years of education and experience in their home country often find that their degrees and qualifications do not meet the requirements needed to work in their chosen fields in the United States. Sometimes these professionals must work in low-level service jobs until they learn adequate English and fulfill American licensing requirements. This process can take years and cost thousands of dollars. Many Ecuadorian immigrants resolve the problem by changing professions or opening their own businesses.

Ecuadorian Independence Day

In August of each year, Ecuadorian Americans celebrate Ecuador's independence from Spain. In Queens, New York, an annual parade features folk dancing, traditional music, and colorful floats. The parade is part of a festival that features Ecuadorian food, handicrafts, and traditional performances. In addition to the celebration in Queens, Manhattan sponsors a new event called "Ecuafest" in May that includes a parade and festival celebrating Ecuadorian culture and independence.

Several cities in the United States host celebrations, among them: Los Angeles, Chicago, East Windsor, New Jersey, and Bridgeport, Connecticut.

The Otavaleño Weavers

The native South American peoples known as the Otavaleño are textile weavers and farmers from the Andes Mountains of Ecuador. They have inhabited Ecuador for centuries—the Otavaleño lived on the land even before the Incas populated it.

When the Spanish claimed the region as their own, they forced the Otavaleño to use their traditional skills as weavers to make Spanish-style clothing in Spanish-owned workshops. Today the Otavaleño work and sell their woolen textiles, such as ponchos, blankets, and sweaters, all over the world. These handcrafted items are treasured for their beautiful designs and bright colors. They can often be seen selling their wares on the streets of New York City.

Mold Ecuadorian Bread Figurines

The little town of Calderon in Ecuador is known for the small, handcrafted bread dough figurines that are made by the town's residents. The tradition started in 1535 when a Flemish priest named Fray Jodoco Ricke introduced the first wooden plough to the area. It allowed the villagers to have enough time off from farming to indulge in a craft. They used dough to make simple figures of babies and animals. The figures were placed, as tokens of remembrance, at loved ones' gravesites during Day of the Dead observances.

In workshops that are set up in homes, Calderon children and adults come together to make the small, highly detailed dough figurines. The shapes are molded, baked, and painted, and then they are sold in shops. Ecuadorian Americans have shared this traditional craft with others in the United States through festivals, craft fairs, and Ecuadorian celebrations.

Try your hand at making an Ecuadorian bread figurine.

Makes about 4 figurines

What You Need
Adult Supervision Required
1 cup salt

2¼ cups all-purpose flour, divided
Large mixing bowl
1 cup warm water
Pastry board or cutting board
Rolling pin
1–4 cookie cutters of various shapes
Spatula
Cookie sheet
Pot holder or oven mitt
Paper plate
White acrylic paint
2 paper cups
Paintbrush
Puffy fabric paint in several bright colors, such as purple, yellow, green, blue, red, and black (available at craft stores)
2 ounces nontoxic, water based, polyurethane gloss varnish (this is available in craft stores, sold with the acrylic paints)
Optional: 1 toothpick and 8-inch piece of string or yarn for hanging

What You Do

1. Preheat the oven to 225° F.

2. Place the salt and 2 cups of flour in a large mixing bowl. Adding a little bit of warm water at a time, use your hands to mix the ingredients together.

3. Sprinkle a little bit of flour onto a pastry board or a cutting board. Transfer the dough mixture to the board. Sprinkle a little bit of flour into your hands to keep the dough from sticking to them. Knead the dough (squeeze and turn it) for 10 minutes.

4. Using the rolling pin, roll the dough flat until it is about ½-inch thick. Using 1 or more cookie cutters, cut out shapes in the dough.

5. Using the spatula, carefully pick up each shape and transfer it to the cookie sheet. If you would like to hang your figurine, use a toothpick to poke a hole in the top. Bake for 2 hours.

6. Remove the cooked dough from the oven and let cool. Using the spatula, transfer the dough shapes to a paper plate. (Hint: if you want to decorate on the smoother side of the dough shapes, flip them over.)

7. Squeeze some of the white paint into a paper cup. Using the paintbrush, paint one side of each dough shape with the white paint. Let dry. Paint the other side of each dough shape. Let dry. (Note: you may need to paint each side twice to get full coverage.) Clean the paintbrush and set it aside.

8. Use the puffy fabric paints to add 3-dimensional decorations to each dough shape. Squeeze small balls of paint directly from the tubes; don't try to "paint" with the puffy paint. If you make a mistake, just scrape that paint off, paint the dough piece white again, and start over. Let dry.

9. Pour the varnish into a paper cup. Use the clean paintbrush to paint each dough shape with varnish. This will make it shiny. Let dry.

10. Optional: Pull the string or yarn through the hole and tie. Hang on a wall, doorknob, Christmas tree, or anywhere else you choose.

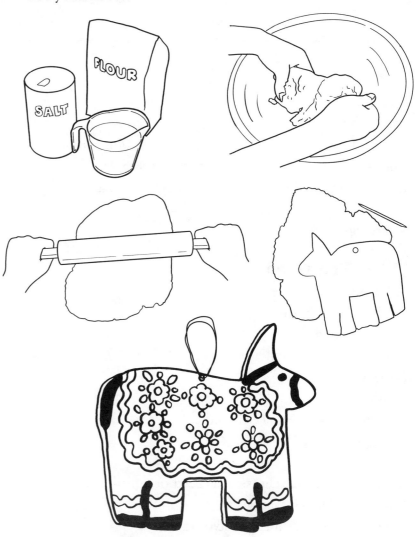

Make *Locro*: Ecuadorian Potato and Cheese Soup

Locro is a traditional hearty soup that comes from the highlands of Ecuador. Potatoes are a staple of Ecuadorian cuisine, and they are grown in many varieties there. Here's a soup that is popular with Ecuadorian American kids and adults alike.

4 servings

What You Need

Adult Supervision Required

2 tablespoons butter

Large cooking pot

½ cup chopped onion

Stirring spoon

4 cups water

4 medium potatoes, peeled and cubed

2 teaspoons salt

1 cup milk

8 ounces Muenster cheese, shredded or cubed

4 individual serving bowls

1 peeled, pitted, and cubed avocado

What You Do

1. Place the butter in the cooking pot and melt over medium heat. Add the onions and cook, stirring constantly, until they are soft (3 to 4 minutes).
2. Place the water, potatoes, and salt in the pot. Bring to a boil over medium heat. Reduce the heat to low and simmer for 25 minutes.
3. Remove the pot from the heat. Using the stirring spoon, mash the potatoes against the side of the pot (the potatoes should still be chunky, though).
4. Return the pot to the heat. Stir in the milk, increase the heat to medium, and bring the mixture to a boil.
5. Reduce the heat to low. Stir in the cheese. Simmer, stirring frequently, until the cheese is melted. Remove the pot from the heat.
6. Pour the soup into individual serving bowls. Top each portion with a handful of avocado cubes. Enjoy!

The Panama Hat Comes from Ecuador!

The famous straw hat that everyone calls a Panama hat is actually a native product of Ecuador. The hats were originally shipped from Ecuador to Panama before being distributed to various parts of the world, and so became known as Panama hats. Traditionally crafted by skilled weavers, the hats are made of thin *toquilla* (toh-KEE-ah) straw that grows on bushes along the Ecuadorian coastline. It may take a weaver weeks to complete just one finely woven Panama hat!

◆ Peru

By the time the Spanish arrived in South America, in the 1530s, the Incas had established a highly advanced civilization with a vast empire in what is now Peru. That empire spread through the Andes Mountains to parts of present-day Ecuador, Bolivia, Chile, and Argentina.

The Incas were ruled by a succession of emperors that they believed to be descendents of their Sun God. Building on the

181

knowledge and skills of smaller tribes they conquered throughout the years, the Incas built roads, rope suspension bridges, magnificent temples and palaces, irrigation canals, and pyramids. An amazing example of Incan civilization that can still be seen today is Machu Picchu, a walled city built between two mountain peaks in the Andes Mountains.

In 1532 the Spanish conquered the Incas in a brutal battle led by the Spanish conquistador Francisco Pizarro. The Spanish ravished the country in search of gold and silver. They put the native peoples to work mining and working on farms. Many Incas died as a result of overwork, harsh living conditions, and exposure to European diseases. As they had done in other areas that they claimed for Spain, the Spanish eventually imported African slaves to Peru in order to replace the native workforce.

The Incas did not give up their land or their freedom easily. They fought with the Spanish to reclaim their land and their own civilization for decades until, in 1572, the last Inca who still held power was executed.

The gold and silver mines produced great riches for the Viceroyalty of Peru. It became the center of power in Spanish South America. The Catholic Archbishop (leader of the church) presided here, and the royal Spanish courts and the University of San Marcos were located in Peru. The port of Callao, near Lima, was a bustling center of trade between South America and Europe.

The 1700s brought many changes to the region. Spain had new rulers who reorganized the area into new viceroyalties, the major source of the wealth—the gold and silver mines—became depleted, and in 1780 there was a major Indian revolt against the Spanish. In spite of the changes, Peru continued to be an international center of culture.

Because Peruvians were more satisfied with their relationship with Spain than other colonies, the country actually became independent through people outside Peru. José de San Martín, an Argentine general, and Simón Bolívar, the revolutionary responsible for freeing the countries that became Bolivia, Colombia, Ecuador, Panana, and Venezuela, also liberated Peru. That liberation was finally realized in 1824, and Bolívar became Peru's first president.

Like many Latin American countries, Peru has suffered from civil war. The ruling party has always been made up of whites and mestizos, and they held power over the natives. These inequalities led to conflict, which eventually reached a boiling point in the 1980s. As part of their attempts to overturn the ruling government, the natives formed two separate political groups. These two groups (which were opposed to each other as well as to the government) were called Sendero Luminoso (which means "Shining Path") and the Tupac Amaru Revolutionary Movement.

Chaos resulted in the clash among these groups and the government as each tried to win the hearts and minds of the Peruvian people. The revolutionary groups tried to enlist the Peruvian people to join their cause, and those who resisted were often kidnapped or slaughtered. People who agreed to support the revolutionaries became targets of the police and the ruling government's military. Thousands of people mysteriously disappeared during the years of conflict among the three groups.

Peruvian Americans

Peruvians began immigrating to what is now the United States in the 1800s, when California was part of Mexico. Because

Peru and Mexico were trading partners, Peruvian sailors sometimes decided to settle in California. Later, when California became part of the United States, still more Peruvians (and other South Americans) were drawn there to seek their fortunes in the California Gold Rush of 1848. From the 1900s on, Peruvians immigrated to the United States to work in the textile industry and other industries after World War II. Many Peruvian doctors, lawyers, and other professionals immigrated to the United States after the passage of the 1965 Immigration Act, which gave preferential status to those immigrants who had professional backgrounds.

Many Peruvian people fled to the United States to escape the civil war in the 1980s, and the problems of unemployment and poverty that accompanied it. Today, even though the war has ended, Peruvians continue to immigrate to the United States in search of better employment opportunities and political stability for the sake of their families.

The Lord of the Miracles (El Señor de los Milagros) Celebration

In 1655 a devastating earthquake hit what is now Peru's capital, the city of Lima. Amid the rubble and destruction, one item survived: a religious mural of Jesus Christ, which had been painted on an adobe wall by an African Peruvian artist. In 1671, the image was moved to its own church. Years later, Lima suffered two more earthquakes—but the mural remained intact. Peruvians consider it a miracle that the mural was never destroyed. In 1687, a three-dimensional copy of the image was made so that it could be carried in a procession. Each year, thousands of Peruvians take to the streets in a celebration of this miracle that is called Señor de los Milagros. Peruvian immigrants brought this celebration to the United States, and each year Señor de los Milagros is celebrated from coast to coast by Catholic parishes that have large Peruvian congregations. There are Peruvian brotherhoods in the United States who are devoted to honoring *Senor de los Milagros*.

During the celebration, a procession of these brothers, garbed in purple gowns, and women as well carry this African image of Jesus Christ (El Señor de los Milagros) through the streets. People pray to the image just as they would to a saint. It is beautifully decorated with flowers, and its journey is accompanied by a marching band. Thousands of believers walk in the procession, singing praises to the Señor. Purple and white balloons float above the crowd, and the scent of incense fills the air.

Make a Collection of *Milagros*: Offerings of Thanks and Prayers

Milagro (mee-LAH-groh) means miracle. *Milagros* (which are also called ex-votos) are tiny silver or gold shapes that are used as offerings, much like candles are used in Catholic churches. They are given symbolically to a saint by someone looking for a miracle. The person in need comes to church with a prayer or a request for assistance, or to give thanks for a prayer fulfilled. The worshipper then places or pins the *milagro* on the image of the saint in the church. *Milagros* are used in Peru, Mexico, and other parts of Latin America, as well as in parts of the United States, to offer prayers and wishes to the saints.

Traditional *milagros* are medals in the shape of body parts, animals, and people, but they can be of almost anything. In this activity we will use *milagros* to symbolize our desire to achieve certain goals.

Heart = love
Hand = sharing or helping
Arm = strength or work
Foot = your journey

Head = wisdom
Fish = plentiful food
Eyes = someone who cares and
    who will watch over you

What You Need

Mechanical pencil
1 12-inch-by-18-inch sheet white craft foam
Scissors
Hole punch
Metallic silver acrylic paint
Paper cup
Paintbrush

What You Do

1. Decide on goals that you would like to achieve during the next year, and think of symbols that can represent those goals. Maybe you'd like to volunteer for a worthy cause; one symbol might be a "helping" hand. Would you like to learn a new sport? You could use an image of a softball or a hockey stick to symbolize the sport you want to pick up. Perhaps you'd like to develop better study habits; a book is a great symbol for that.

2. Using the mechanical pencil (or a very sharp pencil), draw your symbols onto the craft foam. You can use the pencil

to create additional detail for each symbol—you can even use it to dig into the foam to create texture.

3. Using the scissors, cut out each design.

4. Using the hole punch, punch a hole in the top of each design so that you can hang your milagro or pin it to something.

5. Pour the paint into the paper cup. Using the paintbrush, paint the entire surface (all sides) of each shape. Let dry. If necessary, paint again. Let dry.

6. Keep the milagros where you can see them to remind you of your goals.

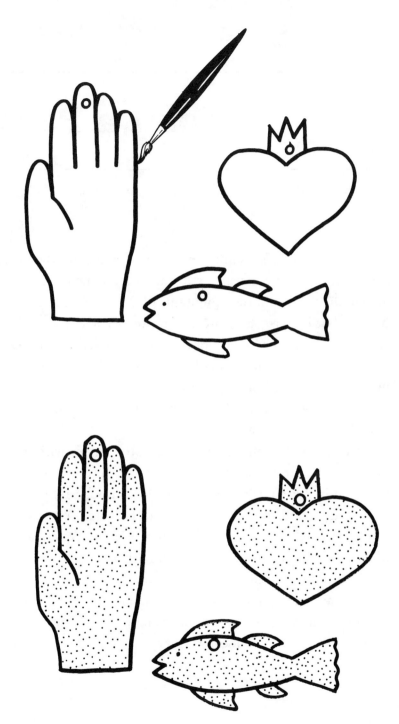

Paint a Peruvian Bird Gourd

Maté (mah-TAY) is another name for a gourd. Maté decoration is an exquisite art form, and the men, women, and children living in the mountains of Peru are famous for their skill at it. Peruvian maté decoration involves a complex process in which the surface of the gourd is dyed or burned to produce different shades of gold and brown. Intricate engravings are then carved into the gourd. These engravings range from scenes of mountain life and work to detailed images of animals to geometric and floral designs.

Peruvian immigrants brought decorative matés with them as they journeyed to the United States. Today, Peruvian matés are displayed in museums and sold to buyers throughout the United States and the rest of the world. Peruvian Americans have even taught the craft of decorative maté to Americans of other heritages. It is the Peruvians, however, who remain the master craftsmen of maté.

You can make your own decorative maté using either a gourd or a butternut squash. Gourds may be difficult to find in some areas; check your local grocery store for them in the fall.

What You Need

1 gourd or butternut squash
Medium-brown acrylic paint
3 paper cups
Paintbrush
Deep red acrylic paint
Medium-point black permanent marker
2 ounces nontoxic, water-based, polyurethane gloss varnish (this is available in craft stores, sold with the acrylic paints)
Quarter
Penny
3-inch square yellow felt
3-inch square black felt
Scissors
Glue

What You Do

1. Wash and dry the surface of the gourd.

2. Pour some brown paint in a paper cup. Using the paintbrush, paint the entire gourd. Use just one coat so that some of the gourd's natural color comes through. Let dry. Clean the paintbrush.

3. Pour some red paint in a paper cup. Using the paintbrush, paint the top part of the gourd. Let dry. If you want a more opaque red, paint again. Let dry. Clean the paintbrush.

4. Draw the "bird's" wings. Using the marker, draw small feather lines on the bottom, round part of the gourd.

5. Pour some varnish in a paper cup. Use the paintbrush to apply a coat of varnish to the entire gourd. Let dry.

6. Make the "bird's" eyes. Using the quarter and the marker, trace two circles on the yellow felt. Cut a 1-inch-by-1½-inch strip from the black felt and set aside. Using the penny and the marker, trace two circles on the remaining piece of black felt. Use the scissors to cut out each of the 4 circles.

7. Glue a yellow felt circle to each side of the top of the gourd. Glue a black circle in the center of each yellow circle.

8. Apply glue and then roll up the strip of black felt you set aside earlier to form a beak. Glue it onto the squash. Let dry.

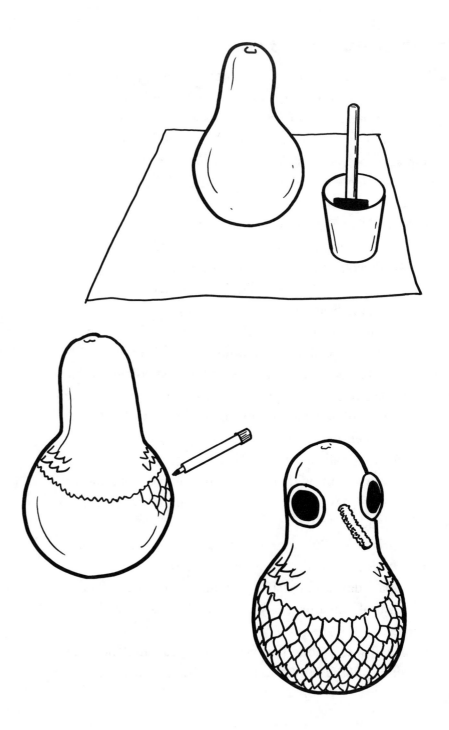

187

South American Food

The South American foods of Colombia, Ecuador, and Peru are influenced by European, African, Caribbean, and native South American cultures. Many of these foods are common throughout much of South America. These foods include rice, potatoes, meats, plantains, soups, seafood, tropical fruits, and very sweet desserts. But each country has its own special dishes and favorite foods as well.

Traditional Colombian foods include *ajiaco*, a stew made with chicken, potatoes, and corn; arepas; marinated steak; *mondongo* (mohn-DOHN-goh), a stew made with tripe; and *bandeja paisa* (ban-DAY-hah paih-sah), a meat dish that is served with cassava, fried plantains, red beans, and rice.

Colombians and Colombian Americans especially enjoy coffee. The country of Colombia is famous for its mountain-grown coffee beans, and it is the second-largest coffee producer in the world. The coffee crops are grown in the shade on small farms, and the coffee beans are picked by hand. Colombians are proud of their national beverage. They enjoy small cups of black coffee they call *tinto* (TEEN-toh); *café con leche*, which is a cup of warm milk with a bit of coffee added to it; and *café perico* (kah-FAY pay-REE-co), which is a cup of hot coffee with a bit of milk added to it.

Ecuadorians and Ecuadorian Americans enjoy corn tamales called *humitas* (oo-MEE-tahs); ceviche and other seafood dishes; empanadas; and roasted pork and other meats. The national dish of Ecuador is *cuy* (kwee), which is roasted guinea pig.

Favorite dishes among Peruvians and Peruvian Americans include *aji de gallina* (ah-hee day gah-YEE-nah), a spicy chicken stew; ceviche; potatoes served in a variety of ways (more than 100 varieties of potatoes are grown in Peru!); *papas rellenas* (PA-pahs ray-YAY-nas), which are potato patties stuffed with meat; and *lomo saltado* (LOH-moh sahl-TAH-doh), a steak, vegetable, and potato stir-fry.

Notable South Americans

South Americans have contributed to the United States in a number of diverse ways. They are athletes, scientists, entertainers, writers, artists, and more.

Athletes

Antonio Cervantes (1945–)	A Colombian American two-time World Boxing Association junior welterweight champion who was inducted into the International Boxing Hall of Fame
Juan Pablo Montoya (1975–)	A Colombian American race car driver who won the Indianapolis 500
Alex Olmedo (1936–)	A Peruvian American tennis player who was inducted into the International Tennis Hall of Fame
Edgar Renteria (1975–)	A Colombian American baseball player who won three Golden Glove awards and who was a member of the 1997 World Series winners, the Florida Marlins

Pancho Segura (1921–) An Ecuadorian American tennis player who won three consecutive U.S. intercollegiate championships and who was inducted into the International Tennis Hall of Fame

Entertainers

Christina Aguilera (1980–) A Grammy Award–winning Ecuadorian American singer whose hits include "Genie in a Bottle" and "Beautiful"

John Leguizamo (1964–) An Emmy Award–winning Colombian American writer, actor, and director whose films include *Moulin Rouge!* and *Ice Age*

Shakira (1977–) A Grammy Award–winning Colombian American singer, songwriter, and record producer whose hits include "Hips Don't Lie"

Other Notable South Americans

Marie Arana (1949–) A Peruvian American editor and author whose books include *American Chica: Two Worlds, One Childhood*

Fernando Botero (1932–) A Colombian American painter and illustrator

Inés Cifuentes (1954–) An Ecuadorian American seismologist (a scientist that studies earthquakes) and science educator

From Sea to Shining Sea— in Spanish!

Here are the English translations of some U.S. city names.

Los Angeles: "The Angels"

San Diego: "Saint James"

El Paso: "The Pass"

San Antonio: "Saint Anthony"

Las Vegas: "The Meadows"

Javier Escobar (1943–) A Colombian American psychiatrist who has studied the effects of drugs on the brain and on human behavior

Carlos Noriega (1959–) A Peruvian American astronaut

George Zamka (1962–) A Colombian American astronaut

189

◆ **10** ◆

Latinos: Past, Present, and Future

Challenges of the Latino Community: Undocumented Immigration

Today the average worker in Mexico makes $7 per day. If you lived in Mexico and you knew that if you traveled only a few miles over the border into the United States you could find work and make $70 a day, would you come here to work even if you did not have the legal permission that is required to come into the country? Would you do it even though you know you could be arrested for breaking the law?

To many poor families in Mexico and other Latin American countries, the idea of making a decent wage in the United States, even illegally, seems worth the risk. And many United States businesses, farms, and individuals have been happy to pay these people to work for them, even though that is also illegal.

Latinos face many challenges in the United States, but by far the greatest challenge is the issue of undocumented immi-

gration. It is believed that there are currently 12 million undocumented immigrants living in the United States, and more cross the border into the country every day. Latinos come to this country—legally or illegally—for the same reasons that other immigrants have and continue to come: to find jobs, freedom, and better opportunities for their families.

It is sometimes difficult for non-Latino U.S. citizens to understand the grinding poverty and scarcity of available jobs in Latin America. Many people have little knowledge of the persecution and violence that Latin Americans faced in their countries before fleeing to the United States. Some non-Latino citizens forget that their ancestors, too, originally came to this country from other lands.

Several U.S. legislators have called for stronger border security to prevent people from entering the country illegally. Others have worked to create legislature that would allow undocumented immigrants to achieve legal status. At present, both issues are hotly debated among both legislators and U.S. citizens.

Some people think that undocumented immigrants are taking away jobs from U.S. citizens, but many of the jobs that Latinos take pay very little and offer working conditions that are harsher than most U.S. citizens are accustomed to. Many Latinos work as laborers on farms and construction sites; as factory workers; as dishwashers, maids, and busboys in hotels and restaurants; and as domestic servants in private homes. Few U.S. citizens want these types of jobs.

The U.S. government allows some immigrants to live and work in the United States for a certain period of time—days, weeks, or years—while maintaining their native citizenship. When that period of time ends, even though they are supposed to leave the United States and go back to their home country, many stay illegally. Others are not able to get permission to come to the United States at all, but they cross the border anyway. This is called illegal immigration.

To cross the border illegally, people wait until nightfall and then run through the dry desert or cross the Rio Grande to make it to U.S. soil. Sometimes they must climb over a fence or a wall, but that is not always the case. They must avoid the U.S. Border Patrol officers that guard the border using radar, spotlights, barbed wire, guns, and trained dogs. The people trying to cross the border must avoid rattlesnakes and other dangerous desert creatures, and they often face a long, hot journey with no water available. Many desperate immigrants pay a helper, called a coyote, to assist them in getting across the border. Coyotes routinely charge hundreds or even thousands of dollars for their assistance, and they are often not trustworthy. Thousands of people have died trying to make it into the United States illegally over the years, and thousands more have been stopped by Border Patrol officers and arrested or returned to their home countries.

Over the last century the U.S. government has made several attempts to better deal with the many issues involved in illegal immigration. The Immigration Reform and Control Act of 1986 offered a fresh start to many illegal immigrants by giving them the opportunity to apply for permission to remain in the country legally, and approximately three million Mexicans were granted *amnesty* (a pardon, or forgiveness, for having been in the country illegally). Still, the issue continues to be a big problem for Latinos, the U.S. government, and many U.S. citizens.

In 2006 the government signed legislation (laws) that allows for a 700-mile-long security fence to be built between the United States and Mexico. More than 600 miles have been completed as of January 2009. It is believed that this fence will help to prevent non–U.S. citizens (Mexicans and others) from illegally coming into the United States from Mexico. Some sections of the fence would be made of metal or other material; other sections would not physically exist at all, but would instead be a "virtual" barrier—a section of land that is monitored by cameras and satellites.

Many U.S. citizens are in favor of the fence, but many others are not. The barrier is expected to cost billions of dollars, and in some places it will harm the environment and the wildlife that live there. In addition, many people do not like the idea of putting up a big fence to keep others out.

Just as there is disagreement about the fence, there is disagreement about whether or not illegal immigrants should be allowed to live and work in the United States. Many people believe that illegal immigrants take advantage of our health care system, low-income housing, schools, and other resources. They think that illegal immigrants take valuable tax dollars away from legal U.S. citizens.

Others side with the plight of the illegal immigrants. Some people even disagree with using the term "illegal immigrant" because they believe that it's misleading and negative to refer to *people* as being illegal. As a result, many reporters and government agencies now use the terms "undocumented worker," "undocumented immigrant," or "undocumented person" instead of "illegal immigrant" or "illegal alien."

Although many Latinos may enter the United States illegally by crossing desert borders in the middle of the night instead of sailing into New York Harbor with hundreds of other immigrants on a ship, their feelings and beliefs about the United States are the same as those that were held by immigrants from Ireland, Germany, Asia, and other countries in years past. Latinos believe that the United States is a country in which anything is possible and all are welcome. They believe it is a place of hope.

Immigration Protests

Immigration is a difficult issue in the United States. Now, as in the past, Americans have greeted immigrants with mixed feelings. Although they are needed for their labor, many native born Americans, most the descendents of immigrants themselves, worry that new immigrants will take away jobs and change the country for the worse. Many citizens believe that additional laws should be passed to limit immigrants' rights. In response, Latinos have adopted the "American way" of using protests as tools for change. They are using marches, rallies, and boycotts to draw attention to their concerns.

Latino March on Washington

On October 12, 1996—Columbus Day—thousands of Latinos and other immigrants gathered together to conduct the first-ever immigrant march on Washington, DC. Latinos from all countries joined the march to protest recent legislation that restricted the rights of immigrants who were not yet citizens and to voice other concerns. The crowd displayed a united group while proudly proclaiming the flags of their native countries.

The march was symbolic of the potential power of Latinos from different countries joining together to solve the mutual concerns of their communities.

"On the Road to Citizenship": The Immigrant Workers Freedom Ride

In 2003, advocates of immigrants' rights organized a nationwide trip to draw attention to the problems and needs of undocumented immigrants. Beginning on September 20, several buses carrying about 1,000 people in total left from 10 different cities: Seattle, Portland, San Francisco, Los Angeles, Las Vegas, Minneapolis, Chicago, Houston, Miami, and Boston. They followed routes across the United States, stopping to meet with legislators in Washington, DC, and visiting hundreds of cities and towns until coming together in New York City for a massive rally on October 4.

The cross-country tour and the rally were meant to bring attention to what participants described as basic rights: the right to live and work in the United States, the right to follow a path to eventual citizenship, the right to bring their families to the United States to live, and the right to basic protections in the workplace.

The New Bedford Immigration Raid

Raids against companies that hire undocumented immigrants strike fear into all immigrant families. One early morning in March 2007, 300 immigration agents raided a leather company in New Bedford, Massachusetts, Michael Bianco, Inc. The agents took 361 of the company's employees into police custody on suspicion that they were in the country illegally. As it turned out, many of them were.

Most of the workers who were rounded up by the agents were from Guatemala, Honduras, and El Salvador. They had found work at the company making products that were sold to the U.S. military. The chaos of the raid terrified many of them. Helicopters flew overhead, and many employees ran from the building in fear. (Later, immigration agents would note that the working conditions inside the factory were deplorable.)

The Department of Homeland Security launched an investigation into the way the raid was handled. It was determined by federal officials that the Bureau of U.S. Immigration and Customs Enforcement (I.C.E.) conducted the raid properly. Advocates for illegal immigrants and their families disagree.

The owners of the company were arrested on charges that they knowingly hired workers who were in the country illegally and that they were exploiting them by making them work under poor conditions for little pay. The workers who were identified as being undocumented were sent to a detention camp in Texas to await deportation to their native countries. As of November 2008, U.S. Immigration had deported 168 of the workers to Central America, 116 cases were waiting to go to court, 26 have orders to deport, and 16 have been allowed to stay in the United States. Many of these people had families in the United States, and their children had never been outside the country. In some families, only one parent was deported, splitting families apart. The remaining parent had to choose between living in the United States alone as a single parent or moving the whole family to what might be a foreign and strange country to the couple's Americanized children.

In November of 2008, the president/owner of the company and two managers pled guilty to charges related to hiring illegal immigrants. The president, Francesco Insolia, was sentenced to 12 to 18 months in jail and fined $30,000.

The company will pay $2 million in fines and $850,000 in overtime money owed to employees.

The company illegally avoided paying overtime to employees. (Overtime is money paid for working over 8 hours on the same day.) Employees were forced to "clock out" (click on a card that stamps the time you leave work) at 5:00 and "clock in" at 5:30. The employee would then receive two checks, but no additional money for overtime. Some employees worked 14 hours a day for 6 days a week.

> "Back in Xicalcal [Guatemala], hardly a day passes without a villager returning. Some headed north again. But most are staying. Victor Garcia, 34, wonders how he will feed his children. At Michael Bianco, he sent home up to $500 a month. Now he is lucky to earn $6 a day. 'I just wanted to work,' he said."

Boston Globe, *Tuesday, December 9, 2008, by Traci Carl, Associated Press "Deported Find Little Back Home."*

A Day Without Immigrants

On May 1, 2006, thousands of immigrants—most of them Latino—took the day off from work or school in a national boycott. They were expressing their frustration that the U.S. government had not yet passed a national immigration bill. Their hope was that the bill would address their concerns and provide a legal way for them to stay in the country. The boycott was also used as a way to draw attention to the importance of the work that undocumented immigrants perform for U.S. businesses.

More than one million immigrants and their supporters marched in "A Day Without Immigrants" rallies that were held in cities across the country from California to Miami. Participants wore the color white to symbolize solidarity. Businesses that rely heavily on immigrant workers were affected most by the boycott, and many were forced to close down for the day.

Bilingual Education

Imagine if you were to suddenly find yourself in a country where everyone spoke a different language than you and your family. Now try to picture learning how to read, do math problems, and learn science, history, writing, and grammar in that language. How much do you think you would be able to learn?

This is the dilemma that Latino students have faced for years in the United States. In 1968 concerned Latinos worked to pass the Bilingual Education Act. This allowed children whose first language was not English to learn other subjects in their native language until they mastered English. The act was reinforced in 1974 by the U.S. Supreme Court.

In the 1990s bilingual education became a hotly contested issue among U.S. citizens. A California resident named Ron Unz started a movement among parents for "English immersion" programs in the schools, citing studies that said children in bilingual programs did poorly in school. The philosophy behind English immersion is that students will pick up the language more rapidly if they hear it and are forced to speak it daily. English immersion advocates believe that bilingual education delays mastery of English.

Voters in California agreed with the advocates, and in June 1998 they passed into law Proposition 227, which called for English immersion in public schools. (Similar initiatives were passed in Arizona in 2000 and in Massachusetts in 2002.) This didn't completely end bilingual education in California, however. A limited number of schools still offer bilingual programs, but only if they are requested by a parent and approved by the school itself.

It is difficult to say whether English immersion has worked because follow-up studies have been mixed. Backers of English immersion say that students have achieved better test results since English immersion was instituted, but advocates for bilingual education say that recent testing changes make it impossible to determine the specific effect that English immersion has had on test scores.

Latinos in the U.S. Military

Latinos have fought alongside non-Latino U.S. citizens in every war in which the United States has participated, from the Revolutionary War in the 18th century to the Iraq War that continues today.

In World War II alone, 12 Latinos received the Congressional Medal of Honor for bravery, the highest honor that the United States military bestows. A total of 39 Latinos have received the Medal of Honor since it was created in 1861.

Puerto Rico's 65th Infantry Regiment, which was made up of almost all Latinos, served in World War I, World War II, and the Korean War. Eighty thousand Latino Americans served in the Vietnam War—among them U.S. Navy Lieutenant Everett Alvarez, the first U.S. citizen to be taken as a POW (prisoner of war) in North Vietnam. He was held as a prisoner of war for eight years—longer than anyone else in U.S. history.

As of 2006, more than 67,000 Latinos were serving in the U.S. military.

Latinos in U.S. Politics

Many Latinos currently represent the citizens of the United States in government positions. Among them is New Mexico's Governor Bill Richardson, 25 Latino members of the United States House of Representatives, and 2 Latino senators: Robert Menendez and Mel Martinez. Other Latinos who hold prominent positions in government include Hilda Solis, Secretary of Labor, and Ken Salazar, Secretary of the Interior, under President Barack Obama; Antonio Villaraigosa, mayor of Los Angeles; and Manny Diaz, mayor of Miami.

Latino Culture in the United States

Although Latinos come from many different ethnic backgrounds, religions, and races, they share many common values and beliefs, especially the importance of family and religion.

La Familia: Latino Family Life

In Latino families, everyone feels a responsibility to each other. This sense of responsibility extends not just to parents, children, and siblings, but also to grandparents, aunts and uncles, cousins, and godparents. Latino heritage includes a long-held tradition of living with extended family. Many children live at home until they are married; grandparents often live with their children and grandchildren; and aunts, uncles, and cousins are frequent visitors.

Children are at the center of Latino families, and everyone in the family contributes to raising them. Latinos bring their children everywhere with them. They don't have to worry about babysitters because children are always welcome at parties and get-togethers. Often the children say they feel as though they have 10 mothers and 10 fathers because they get 10 times the attention, whether it's good or bad.

Godparents, who are called *compadres* (kohm-PAH-drays), have a unique relationship with the family. Godparents are chosen very carefully and are expected to be good role models for their godchildren. They are treated with the utmost respect by the family. Godparents share in the raising of the children and contribute emotionally and financially to the godchild's

upbringing. They often help pay for important celebrations such as the child's baptism, first communion, *quinceañera*, wedding, and more.

When Latinos immigrate to the United States, many send money home to family members who are still living in Mexico, Central and South America, and the Caribbean. The amount of money that is sent to families in these countries is so great that some of the smaller countries actually depend on it as a source of income for their people.

Most Latinos are Catholics, and many Latino Catholic homes feature altars, figures of saints, and other such items. In recent years there has been a growing interest in the Protestant religion within the Latino community. A small percentage of Latinos practice Judaism or Islam. Many Latinos practice the African religion of Santería or follow the Taino spiritual beliefs of Espiritismo or other indigenous religions.

Latino Holidays and Celebrations

These holidays are uniquely Latino and are only celebrated in the "New World."

El Día de la Raza (The Day of Race): Struggling with the Legacy of Columbus

These days many people living in the United States—Latinos and others—commemorate Columbus Day with mixed feelings. After all, Columbus and the other conquistadors plundered land owned by native people, forced them into slave labor, and imported and enslaved African people against their will. Taking all of that into consideration, many people have come to believe that Columbus Day is not really a day to be celebrated. A more optimistic way to think about the holiday is as a celebration of the mix of people who were brought together by Columbus, from the Native Americans and Africans to the Spanish and other immigrants who contributed to the creation of the Latino population.

In most Latino countries and in many Latino American communities in the United States, Columbus Day is celebrated as a day that honors Latinos and the converging of their ancestors' cultures. The holiday is called El Día de la Raza, which means "the Day of Race." Some Latino communities hold festivals and other celebrations that celebrate their particular heritage during that time as well. In New York City, for instance, the Hispanic Day Parade is held on the Sunday of Columbus Day weekend each year.

Día: Day of Children/Day of Books

In 1996 the Latino community established a new holiday to celebrate children, families, and bilingual literacy. Founded by award-winning author Pat Mora, El Día de los Niños/El Día de los Libros ("Day of Children/Day of Books")—which is commonly referred to as "Día"—is celebrated in libraries and schools across the country. Día activities promote not only bilingual literacy, but also the sharing of cultures. In 2008 the Association for Library Service to Children (ALSC) and REFORMA (the National Association to Promote Library and Information Services to Latinos and the Spanish Speaking) celebrated Día with Dora the Explorer bookmarks and posters that encourage children and adults alike to "Celebrate Books!" and "¡Celebremos los libros!"

Have a Día Celebration

You can create your own Día celebration to promote reading and writing and to honor Latino culture. Invite people of all ages to participate in the event, and showcase Spanish- and English-language books that feature Latino characters in the United States. Here are some books you might want to have at your Día party.

I Love Saturdays y Domingos by Alma Flor Ada
Pelitos by Sandra Cisneros
Abuela by Arthur Dorros
Family Pictures by Carmen Lomas Garza
Tomás and the Library Lady by Pat Mora
Chato's Kitchen by Gary Soto
Too Many Tamales by Gary Soto

At your Día celebration, you can also enjoy Latino foods such as tortillas and salsa, tropical drinks, plantain chips, and *chicharrones* (pork rinds); listen to Latino music; and participate in activities to celebrate the day. Here are some ideas for fun activities.

- Create a mural. Use markers to draw scenes from a book onto white paper. Tape your mural to a wall for the day.
- Make paper bag piñatas. Decorate paper lunch bags, and then fill them with tiny toys, candies, and confetti. Use brightly colored ribbon to tie the bags.
- Write and put on a bilingual play based on one of the books featured at your celebration.
- Host a reading circle. Take turns reading aloud from a book that is featured at your celebration.

Spanglish

Many bilingual people hold conversations in a mixture of the English and Spanish languages. This mixture is referred to as Spanglish. For example, a person might say to his or her friend, "My dog es muy gordo porque he eats too much!" ("My dog is very fat because he eats too much!") People sometimes speak in Spanglish because they are thinking in both Spanish and English as they are talking. Some people use Spanglish when they want to say something that they don't want eavesdroppers to understand. Sometimes people combine the two languages to come up with brand new words that are part English and part Spanish!

Hispanic Heritage Month

Hispanic Heritage Month is a celebration of the history and contributions of Hispanic Americans in the United States. It begins each year on September 15, the day that Costa Rica, Honduras, El Salvador, Guatemala, and Nicaragua won independence from Spain. (Mexico won its independence just a day later, on September 16.) The holiday is celebrated in schools, libraries, museums, government agencies, and communities across the country. Parades are held in many cities, and TV and radio programs, newspapers, and magazines offer special shows and stories to celebrate the month.

Each year a particular theme is chosen as a way to highlight specific achievements in the Latino community, and a special poster is created to showcase that theme. Here are a few Hispanic Heritage Month themes from past years.

- 2008: Getting Involved: Our Families, Our Community, Our Nation
- 2007: Hispanic/Latino Americans: Making a Positive Impact on American Society
- 2006: Hispanic Americans: Our Rich Culture Contributing to America's Future
- 2005: Hispanic Americans: Strong and Colorful Threads in the American Fabric

Design a Poster to Celebrate Hispanic Heritage Month

What You Need

Poster board

Markers

Scissors

Materials for a collage, such as felt and yarn

Glue

What You Do

1. Decide on a theme for your poster, such as "Latino Music," "Latinos in our Military," "Latino Leaders," or "Latino Art."

2. Using the markers, write a phrase that captures your theme on the poster board. For example, if your theme is "Latino Music," you might write the phrase "Hispanic Heritage Month: Sharing Our Musical Heritage."

3. Use the markers, scissors, collage materials, and glue to draw pictures and paste cutouts of shapes that represent your theme. You can get ideas of things to include by researching the topic of your theme in books, magazines, and newspapers and on the Internet.

4. Get permission to display your poster at school, at church, or in your community library in order to bring attention to Hispanic Heritage Month.

Latino Quick Facts

- According to the U.S. Census Bureau, as of July 1, 2007, there are 45.5 million Hispanics living in the United States, which is 15 percent of the total population.
- It is predicted that, by the year 2050, Latinos will make up 30 percent of the total population in the United States.
- As of 2006, according to the United States Census' "American Community Survey," the United States was home to 28.3 million residents of Mexican background, 3.9 million Puerto Ricans (living on the mainland), 1.5 million residents of Cuban background, 1.2 million residents of Dominican background, 3.3 million residents of Central American background, and 2.4 million residents of South American background.
- The states with the largest Latino populations are California, Texas, and Florida.

Latinos: The Past and Future of America

It's impossible to look at the history of the United States without seeing its Latino beginnings. Latinos have formed a strong and diverse mix of culture that is the foundation of this country.

The many contributions and accomplishments of Latinos in this country have shaped the ways in which we all live, and Latinos continue to make up a workforce that allows U.S. businesses such as farms and manufacturing industries to prosper. Today, almost every aspect of Latino culture—from music to foods to art and literature—is woven into the fabric of everyday life in the United States.

Latinos have a distinguished past and a bright future in the United States, and the United States continues to be enriched by their contributions to, and presence in, this country.

❖ Bibliography ❖

For Children

Books

Anderson, Joan. *Spanish Pioneers of the Southwest*. New York: E.P. Dutton, 1988.

Atkin, Beth S. *Voices from the Fields: Children of Migrant Farmers Tell Their Stories*. New York: Little, Brown Young Readers, 2000.

Bachelis, Faren. *The Central Americans*. New York: Chelsea House Publishers, 1990.

Ebinger, Virginia Nylander. *Niñez: Spanish Songs, Games, and Stories of Childhood*. Santa Fe, NM: Sunstone Press, 1993.

Freedman, Russell. *In the Days of the Vaqueros: America's First True Cowboys*. New York: Clarion Books, 2001.

Marrin, Albert. *Empires Lost and Won: The Spanish Heritage in the Southwest*. New York: Atheneum Books for Young Readers, 1997.

Media Projects Inc. *Student Almanac of Hispanic American History*. Volume 1. Westport, CT: Greenwood Press, 2004.

Media Projects Inc. *Student Almanac of Hispanic American History*. Volume 2. Westport, CT: Greenwood Press, 2004.

Mohr, Nicholasa. *Growing Up Inside the Sanctuary of My Imagination*. New York: J. Messner, 1994.

Ortiz, Raquel. *The Silk Purse: A Memoir*. Philadelphia: Xlibris Corp., 2004.

Perl, Lila. *North Across the Border: The Story of the Mexican Americans*. New York: Benchmark Books, 2002.

Roberts, Susan A., Calvin A. Roberts. *A History of New Mexico*. Albuquerque, NM: University of New Mexico Press, 1998.

Sandler, Martin W. *Vaqueros: America's First Cowmen*. New York: H. Holt and Co., 2000.

Steele, Christy. *Hispanic Culture*. Rourke: Vero Beach, FL, 2006.

Turck, Mary C. *Mexico and Central America: A Fiesta of Culture, Crafts, and Activities for Ages 8–12*. Chicago: Chicago Review Press, 2004.

For Adults

Books

Acuña, Rodolfo F. *U.S. Latino Issues*. Westport, CT: Greenwood Press, 2003.

Altman, Linda Jacobs. *Migrant Farm Workers: The Temporary People*. New York: Franklin Watts, 1994.

Arnold, Oren. *Irons in the Fire: Cattle Brand Lore*. London; New York: Abeland-Schuman, 1965.

Barnett, Tracy. *Immigration from South America*. Philadelphia: Mason Crest, 2004.

Behnke, Alison. *Mexicans in America*. Minneapolis: Lerner Publications, 2005.

Bloom, Barbara Lee. *The Mexican Americans*. San Diego, CA: Lucent Books, 2004.

Collins, David R. *Cesar Chavez*. Minneapolis: Lerner Publications, 2005.

Crosby, Alfred W. *The Columbian Exchange: Biological and Cultural Consequences of 1492*. Westport, CT: Greenwood Publishing Co., 1972.

De Varona, Frank. *Latino Literacy: The Complete Guide to Our Hispanic History and Culture*. New York: Henry Holt, 1996.

Editors of Time-Life Books. *The Old West: The Spanish West*. Alexandria, VA: Time-Life Books, 1976.

Figueredo, D. H. *The Complete Idiot's Guide to Latino History and Culture*. Indianapolis, IN: Alpha Books, 2002.

Fischkin, Barbara. *Muddy Cup: A Dominican Family Comes of Age in a New America*. New York: Scribner, 1997.

Foster, Lynn V. *A Brief History of Central America*. New York: Facts on File, 2007.

Friedman, Ian C. *Latino Athletes*. New York: Facts on File, 2007.

Gelletly, LeeAnne. *Mexican Immigration*. Philadelphia: Mason Crest Publishers, 2004.

Hart, Elva Treviño. *Barefoot Heart: Stories of a Migrant Child*. Tempe, AZ: Bilingual Press/Editorial Bilingüe, 1999.

Hernández, Roger E. *Cuban Immigration*. Philadelphia: Mason Crest Publishers, 2004.

Hoobler, Dorothy and Thomas Hoobler. *The Cuban American Family Album*. New York: Oxford University Press, 1996.

Hoobler, Dorothy and Thomas Hoobler. *The Mexican American Family Album*. New York: Oxford University Press, 1994.

Houle, Michelle (Book Editor) *Cesar Chavez*. San Diego, CA: Greenhaven Press, 2003.

Márquez, Gabriel García and Mendoza, Plinio Apuleyo. *The Fragrance of Guava*: *Conversations with Gabriel García Márquez*. London: Faber and Faber, 1988.

McCaffrey, Paul, Ed. *Hispanic Americans*. Bronx, NY: H.W. Wilson Co., 2007.

Menard, Valerie. *The Latino Holiday Book: From Cinco de Mayo to Día de los Muertos—The Celebrations and Traditions of Hispanic Americans*. Berkeley, CA: Marlowe and Co., 2004.

Mumford, Jeremy. "Ecuadorian Americans." *Gale Encyclopedia of Multicultural America*. Ed. Jeffrey Lehman. Vol. 1. 2nd ed. Detroit: Gale, 2000.

Newton, David E. *Latinos in Science, Math, and the Professions*. New York: Facts on File, 2007.

Novas, Himilce. *Everything You Need to Know About Latino History*. New York: Plume, 2003, 2008.

Ochoa, George. *Atlas of Hispanic-American History*. New York: Facts on File, 2001.

Otfinoski, Steven. *Latinos in the Arts*. New York: Facts on File, 2007.

Packel, John. "Peruvian Americans." *Gale Encyclopedia of Multicultural America*. Ed. Jeffrey Lehman. Vol. 3. 2nd ed. Detroit: Gale, 2000.

Panyuela, August (General Editor). *Folk Art of the Americas*. New York: Abrams, 1981.

Paredes, Americo. *With His Pistol in His Hand*. Austin, Texas: University of Texas Press, 1958, 1986.

Pearcy, Thomas. *The History of Central America*. Westport, CT: Greenwood Press, 2006.

Rinker, Kimberley A. *Immigration from the Dominican Republic*. Philadelphia: Mason Crest Publishers, 2004.

Rivera, Oswald. *Puerto Rican Cuisine in America: Nuyorican and Bodega Recipes*. New York: Four Walls Eight Windows, 2002.

Santiago, Esmeralda. *When I Was Puerto Rican*. Cambridge, MA: Da Capo Press, 1993, 2006.

Stavans, Ilan. *Latino History and Culture*. New York: Collins, 2007.

Sturner, Pamela. "Colombian Americans." *Gale Encyclopedia of Multicultural America*. Ed. Jeffrey Lehman. Vol. 1. 2nd ed. Detroit: Gale, 2000.

Tausend, Marilyn and Miguel Ravago. *Cocina de la Familia: More than 200 Authentic Recipes from Mexican-American Home Kitchens*. New York: Simon and Schuster, 1997.

Torres-Saillant, Silvio and Ramona Hernández. *The Dominican Americans*. Westport, CT: Greenwood Press, 1998.

Vega, Marta Moreno. *When the Spirits Dance Mambo: Growing Up Nuyorican in El Barrio*. New York: Three Rivers Press, 2004.

Ward, Fay E. *The Cowboy at Work; All About His Job and How He Does It*. New York: Hastings House, 1958.

Ward, Geoffrey C. *The West: An Illustrated History*. Boston: Back Bay Books, 2003.

Webber, Thomas L. *Flying Over 96th Street: Memoir of an East Harlem White Boy*. New York: 2004.

Internet

Adourn, Jorge Enrique. "The Bread Art of Ecuador- and Butter." *Unesco Courier*, July 1984, http://findarticles.com/p/articles/mi_m1310/is_1984_July/ai_3332161.

American Memory. "Immigration . . . Mexican." Library of Congress. http://memory.loc.gov/learn/features/immig/mexican.html.

Borland, Katherine. "Miami's Nicaraguan Communities." Historical Museum of Southern Florida. www.hmsf.org/collections-nicaraguan-communities.htm#Griteria.

Fernandez, Manny. "New Winds at an Island Outpost." *New York Times*, March 4, 2007. www.nytimes.com/2007/03/04/nyregion/thecity/04domi.html?ex=1173844800&en=a6b5e44d3f6f30ec&ei=5070.

Griffin, Wendy. "San Marcos Fair Features Traditional Games and Guancasco." *Honduras This Week* Online edition 16, Monday April 25, 2005. www.marrder.com/htw/2005apr/cultural.htm

Hispanic Online Staff. Did You Know? "Quick Facts on Latinos in the Military." *Hispanic Online*. Hispanic Heritage Plaza 2002. www.hispaniconline.com/hh02/history_did_you_know_sidebar.html

New Jersey Historical Society. "?Que bonita bandera! The Puerto Rican Flag as Folk Art." www.jerseyhistory.org/exhibit_detail.php?recid=36

Newspapers

Ballou, Brian R. "Raided Factory, workers make deal on owed OT." *The Boston Globe*. November 19, 2008.

❖ Resources ❖

Latino Museums

California

The Mexican Heritage Corporation
(A Resident Arts Partner at the Mexican Heritage Plaza)
1700 Alum Rock Avenue
San Jose, CA 95116
(408) 928-5500
E-mail: info@mhcviva.org
www.mhcviva.org/index.html

The Mexican Heritage Corporation is dedicated to preserving the performing arts of Mexico. It presents the San Jose International Mariachi Festival and the Los Lupeños de San Jose ballet folklórico, as well as exhibitions, workshops, concerts, and festivals throughout the year.

Museum of Latin American Art
628 Alamitos Avenue
Long Beach, CA 90802
(562) 437-1689
E-mail: frontdesk@molaa.org
www.molaa.com

The Museum of Latin American Art is exclusively devoted to contemporary (post–World War II) art. Past and present exhibitions include "A Bridge to the Americas: Spiritual and Religious Practices," "Cuban Exhibitions: Unbroken Ties," and "Central American Contemporary Art."

Colorado

Museo de Las Americas
861 Santa Fe Drive
Denver, CO 80204
(303) 571-4401
www.museo.org

The Museo de Americas is devoted to promoting and presenting the arts and culture of Latino people. It features revolving exhibitions as well as educational tours and workshops.

Illinois

National Museum of Mexican Art
1852 West 19th Street
Chicago, IL 60608
(312) 738-1503
www.nationalmuseumofmexicanart.org

This museum preserves and honors the Mexican arts from both sides of the border. Feature exhibitions include "A Celebration of Mexican Masks," "The Barrio Murals," and paintings such as Carmen Lomas Carza's "Quinceañera."

Nebraska

El Museo Latino
4701 South 25 Street
Omaha, NE 68107
(402) 731-1137
www.elmuseolatino.org

El Museo Latino is a "resource and a center for Latino studies in the Midwest." Many celebrations of Latino culture and exhibitions are featured throughout the year. Examples of featured exhibits include "Art and Symbolism of the Huichol," "Holiday Traditions (in Latin America)," and "The History of Latinos in Omaha."

New Mexico

The Museum of Spanish Colonial Art
750 Camino Lejo
Santa Fe, NM
(505) 982-2226
E-mail: museum@spanishcolonial.org
www.spanishcolonial.org

The museum features traditional Hispano arts from 1598. Traditional arts include Santos, straw appliqué, relief carving, and tinwork. The museum organizes and produces the "Spanish Market" held in July and December. The market features exhibitions of traditional Spanish arts by working artists.

El Rancho de Las Golondrinas
334 Los Pinos Road
Santa Fe, NM 87507
(505) 471-2261
E-mail: mail@golondrinas.org
www.golondrinas.org

This is a living history museum that offers visitors a chance to experience what life was like in Spanish colonial New Mexico. A tour of the rancho offers visitors a chance to see people in period costume living and working in areas such as the tin shop, a root cellar, and a wheelwright shop. Festivals and theme weekends allow an in-depth look at Hispano life.

National Hispanic Cultural Center
1701 4th Street SW
Albuquerque, NM 87102
(505) 246-2261
www.nationalhispaniccenter.org
The National Hispanic Cultural Center explores Hispanic culture, arts, and humanities. Exhibitions have included: "Threads of a Different Color: Guatemalan Textiles from the John Shaw Collection"; "Hispanidad," a collection of objects and art from 1930s New Mexico; and "Corridos Sin Fronteras: A New World Ballad Tradition."

New York

El Museo del Barrio
1230 Fifth Avenue
New York, NY 10029
(212) 831-7272
E-mail: info@elmuseo.org
www.elmuseo.org
El Museo del Barrio is committed to preserving the culture of Puerto Ricans, Latin Americans, and Caribbean people in the United States. Exhibitions have included "¡Merengue! Visual Rhythms," "This Skin I'm In: Contemporary Dominican Art," and "Mexico: The Revolution and Beyond: Photographs by Casasola, 1900–1940."

Texas

The Museo Alameda
101 S. Santa Rosa
San Antonio, TX 78207
(210) 299-4300
www.thealameda.org
The Museo Alameda is the first formal affiliate of the Smithsonian Institution. It "tells the story of the Latino experience in America through art, history, and culture." It is the largest Latino museum in the country, with 20,000 feet of exhibition space. The Alameda Theater is a historic Latino theater that was saved from demolition. Supporters of the theater have been raising funds and making plans for a major renovation. The theater will complement the museum by featuring Latino music, dance, film, theater, television productions, and more.

Washington, DC

Art Museum of the Americas
201 18th Street NW
Washington, DC 20006
(202) 458-6016
E-mail: artmus@oas.org
www.museum.oas.org
This museum focuses on art from Latin America and the Caribbean. Recent exhibits include the art of Ecuadorian artist Oswaldo Guayasamin, "Mexico: Festival of Toys," "¡Merengue!," and "Imagining Guatemala: Photographs from the CIRMA collection, 1850–2006."

Suggested Reading List for Kids

Alvarez, Julia. *How Tia Lola Came to Stay*. New York: Knopf, 2001.

    When Miguel and his mother and sister move to Vermont, their lives are turned upside down by the arrival of their flamboyant Dominican aunt, Tia Lola.

Argueta, Jorge. *Xochitl and the Flowers/Xochitl, la Nina de las Flores* (Bilingual Edition). San Francisco: Children's Book Press, 2003.

    Based on a true story. A young Guatemalan girl and her mother brighten their neighborhood when they sell flowers in San Francisco as they had in Guatemala. Their neighbors come to the rescue when their landlord tries to shut down the business.

Garza, Carmen Lomas. *In My Family (En Mi Familia)*. San Francisco, CA: Children's Book Press, 1996.

    This is a bilingual book with 14 beautiful illustrations. Each illustration and its accompanying text celebrates a different aspect of growing up in the Mexican–U.S. border town of Kingsville, Texas.

Jimenez, Francisco. *The Circuit*. New York: Houghton Mifflin, 1997.

    The author describes his childhood struggles as he and family moved from Mexico to the United States to work on the migrant farm labor "circuit."

Mohr, Nicholasa. *El Bronx Remembered*. New York: HarperCollins Children's Books, 1975.

    This is a collection of short stories that describe what is was like to grow up in this Puerto Rican neighborhood of New York City in the 1940s and 1950s.

Mora, Pat. *Tomás and the Library Lady*. New York: Alfred A Knopf, 1997.

    Tomás, a member of a migrant farmworker family, discovers the wonders of the public library one summer in Iowa.

Ryan, Pam Munoz. *Esperanza Rising*. New York: Scholastic, 2000.

    Esperanza's world changes when circumstances transform her from a wealthy girl of leisure in Mexico to a poor, migrant farmworker in California. Her spirit and courage allow her to rise above her circumstances.

Soto, Gary. *Baseball in April*. Orlando, FL: Harcourt, Inc., 1990.

    This is a collection of stories about growing up in California and being Latino.

Latino Movies and Videos

The Ballad of Gregorio Cortez. Embassy Pictures, 1982. Rated PG.

Starring Edward James Olmos and James Gammon and based on a famous *corrido*, the movie tells the story of Cortez, a Mexican ranch hand who was accused of murder and hunted down by hundreds of Texas Rangers in 1901.

The Maldonado Miracle. Hallmark Productions and Showtime, 2002. Not Rated.

Featuring Eddy Martin, Peter Fonda, and Mare Winningham and directed by Salma Hayek, this is the story of a small Mexican boy who accidentally brings back life to a dying town in California.

Selena. Warner Brothers, 1997. Rated PG.

Starring Jennifer Lopez, Jon Seda, and Edward James Olmos, this is the true story of the popular Tejano singer Selena, her Mexican American family, and her rise to fame. The film also deals briefly with her death.

Stand and Deliver. Warner Brothers, 1988. Rated PG.

Starring Edward James Olmos and Lou Diamond Phillips, this is the true story of Jaime Escalante, a math teacher at East Los Angeles's Garfield High School. Escalante pushes and inspires his inner-city students to pass the advanced placement calculus exam.

West Side Story. United Artists, 1961. Not Rated.

Starring Natalie Wood and Richard Beymer, this movie won 10 Academy Awards, including Best Picture. It is the musical story of two rival gangs in New York City. Problems erupt when a Puerto Rican girl whose brother belongs to one gang and an Anglo boy from the other gang fall in love.

Web Sites for Kids

Hispanic Americans in Congress, www.loc.gov/rr/hispanic/congress

Read biographies of Hispanic Americans in Congress, past and present.

The Conquistadors, www.pbs.org/opb/conquistadors/home.htm

Online "learning adventures" of four areas of conquest: Mexico, Peru, Amazonia, and North America.

"Latin America," www.brooklynexpedition.org/latin

This interactive site, created by the Brooklyn Children's Museum, the Brooklyn Museum of Art, and the Brooklyn Public Library, explores themes of Latin America such as: "Discovering the Past," "Time to Celebrate," and "Tales in Cloth."

"Celebrate Hispanic Heritage," http://teacher.scholastic.com/activities/hispanic/index.htm

An interactive site that includes: "Piñata Concentration Game," "Hispanic History in the Americas," and "Latinos in History."

"Latino History and Culture," www.si.edu/Encyclopedia_SI/History_and_Culture/uslatino_history.htm

A treasure chest of all things Latino, this site features (among many other things) "Make the Dirt Fly," an online exhibition of the building of the Panama Canal; "¡Azúcar! The Life and Music of Celia Cruz"; and "Unmasking the Maya."

The Smithsonian Latino Center's Kids Corner, www.latino.si.edu/KidsCorner/index.html

Walk through a virtual portrait gallery in "Latino Virtual Gallery for Kids," explore Latino music through instruments in the "Son Clave Lounge," and go back in time to Mexico in "Meso Time."

Teacher's Guide

A Kid's Guide to Latino History was written with the busy classroom teacher in mind. Most activities can be completed within a short period using inexpensive materials and classroom supplies. The following guide breaks the activities into age levels and suggests how some lessons may be modified for the classroom. Extended learning opportunities are included as well.

Activities by Grade Level

Elementary: K–Third Grade

Design a Straw Art Piece
   Adapt this activity by having the students decorate shapes of black construction paper.

String Chili Peppers
   Substitute chili pepper shapes made out of red felt, paper, or craft foam for dried chili peppers. Punch a hole at the top of each "pepper" and follow directions for stringing.

Create a Ring and Pin Game

Throw a Lariat
   The knot can be tied by an adult instead of by a child.

Design a Cattle Brand
   Simplify this activity by using markers to draw the brands on paper.

Play La Vieja Inez: Buyer of Colored Ribbons

Join in the Game of Ring

Light Christmas Eve *Farolitos*: Candles in Paper Bags

These would be delightful decorations for an outdoor path during a night function at school.

Join in the Mexican Hat Dance

Mold a Day of the Dead Skull
   White construction paper may be substituted for clay. The skull shapes can be precut, and students can decorate them with scraps of colored paper, yarn, stickers, felt, markers, and glue.

Play *Loteria*: Mexican Bingo

Join in a Game of Ring-*a*-Levio

Create a *Vejigante* Mask
   Make a simpler mask using cardboard and markers.

Craft a *Capia*: A Traditional Keepsake

Start a Conga Line

Spin a *Ronron*: A Traditional Honduran Toy

Play Button in the Hole

Try Your Hand at a Honduran Game of Jacks with Seeds

Bake a *Tres Leches* Cake: A Traditional Nicaraguan Dessert
   Substitute a storebought yellow (unfrosted) sheet cake and have the children add the "tres leches." A refrigerator is necessary for chilling.

Wrap Sugarcane Treats for *Purisima*

Paint a Peruvian Bird Gourd
   Students can make the animal of their choice.

Elementary: Fourth and Fifth Grades

Make a Medicine Man's "Gourd" Rattle
   To create the activity in one session, place the popcorn or other "rattling" items inside the water bottle and screw the cap back on. Decorate with markers and yarn. Shake by holding the cap.

Craft a Corn Husk Doll
   Corn husks are very inexpensive. One package of husks should be enough to make a classroom set of dolls, about 20.

Compose a *Corrido*: A Mexican Ballad

Mold a Day of the Dead Skull
   If you do not have access to a stove, substitute white air-dry clay and paint it with bright tempera, acrylic, or watercolor paints.

Make a Guiro: A Popular Musical Instrument

Play Stickball

Try Stoop Ball

Play *Cubilete*: A Traditional Cuban Dice Game

Create Guatemalan Worry Dolls
   You may make clothes from leftover pieces of wrapping paper (to glue on the dolls) instead of yarn.

Make a Guatemalan Weaving

Dance the Merengue

Craft a Dominican Carnival Mask
   For a thriftier version, you may substitute brown grocery bags for the half mask.

Make a *Charamico*: A White Christmas Branch
Instead of making a "tree" with the branches, each student can paint and decorate one branch.

Create a *Primitivo*: Colombian Folk Art
You may substitute white or manila construction paper for the canvas tote and colored paper for the felt.

Write a Short Story Using Magical Realism

Mold Ecuadorian Bread Figurines
You may substitute white, air-dry clay for the bread dough.

Make a Collection of *Milagros*: Offerings of Thanks and Prayers

Have a Día Celebration
Older students can throw a Día celebration for younger schoolmates to attend.

Design a Poster to Celebrate Hispanic Heritage Month
Have a school-wide competition to make the best posters for Hispanic Heritage month. Display them in the community.

Middle School: Sixth–Eighth Grades

Design a Straw Art Piece

Create a *Vejigante* Mask

Build Afro-Cuban Bongos

Create Corn Husk Flowers

Put Together a Dominican American Baseball Hall of Fame Exhibit
This would make a great display for a school entrance, especially during Hispanic Heritage Month.

History Standards and Learning Objectives

A Kid's Guide to Latino History is a resource designed to support history-learning standards in the classroom. Although most states have their own history-learning standards, the following were developed as a national resource by the National Center for History in the Schools at the University of California. They were created under the guidance of the National Council for History Standards.

History Standards for Grades K–4

Topic 1: Living and Working Together in Families and Communities, Now and Long Ago
Standard 1: Family life now and in the recent past; family life in various places long ago.
Standard 1B: The student understands the different ways people of diverse racial, religious, and ethnic groups and of various national origins have transmitted their beliefs and values.
Standard 2: The history of students' own local community and how communities in North America varied long ago.

Topic 3: The History of the United States: Democratic Principles and Values and the Peoples from Many Cultures Who Contributed to Its Cultural, Economic, and Political Heritage
Standard 5: The causes and nature of various movements of large groups of people into and within the United States, now and long ago.
Standard 6: Regional folklore and cultural contributions that helped to form our national heritage.
Topic 4: The History of Peoples of Many Cultures Around the World
Standard 7: Selected attributes and historical developments of various societies in Africa, the Americas, Asia, and Europe.
Standard 7B: The student understands great world movements of people now and long ago.

United States History Standards for Grades 5–12

Era 1: Three Worlds Meet (Beginnings to 1620)
Standard 1: Comparative characteristics of societies in the Americas, Western Europe, and Western Africa that increasingly interacted after 1450.

Standard 2: How early European exploration and colonization resulted in cultural and ecological interactions among previously unconnected peoples.

Standard 2A: The student understands the stages of European oceanic and overland exploration, amid international rivalries, from the 9th to the 17th century.

Standard 2B: The student understands the Spanish and Portuguese conquest of the Americas.

Era 2: Colonization and Settlement (1585–1763)

Standard 1: Why the Americas attracted Europeans, why they brought enslaved Africans to their colonies, and how Europeans struggled for control of North America and the Caribbean.

Standard 1A: The student understands how diverse groups of immigrants affected the formation of European colonies.

Standard 1B: The student understands the European struggle for control of North America.

Era 4: Expansion and Reform (1801–1861)

Standard 1: United States territorial expansion between 1801 and 1861 and how it affected relations with external powers and Native Americans.

Standard 1C: The student understands the ideology of manifest destiny, the nation's expansion to the Northwest, and the Mexican-American War.

Era 6: The development of the Industrial United States (1870–1900)

Standard 2: Massive immigration after 1870 and how new social patterns, conflicts, and ideas of national unity developed amid growing cultural diversity.

Era 10: Contemporary United States (1968–present)

Standard 2: Economic, social, and cultural developments in contemporary United States.

Standard 2B: The student understands the new immigration and demographic shifts.

World History Standards for Grades 5–12

Era 6: The Emergence of the First Global Age, 1450–1770

Standard 1: How the transoceanic interlinking of all major regions of the world from 1450 to 1600 led to global transformations.